Henry Jeffreys was born in London in 1977. After graduating from the University of Leeds, where he studied English and Classical Literature, he spent so much time in Oddbins that they offered him a job. He worked in the wine trade for two years and then moved into publishing. At the same time he worked as a freelance journalist, book reviewer, founder member of the London Review of Breakfasts website and contributor to *The Breakfast Bible* (Bloomsbury, 2013).

In 2010 he started a blog about wine called Henry's World of Booze. Following its success, he was made wine columnist for *The Lady* and in 2014 was shortlisted for Drinks Writer of the Year at the Fortnum & Mason awards. He is now a regular contributor to *The Spectator*, the *Guardian*, *The Economist*, the *Financial Times*, *The Oldie* and *Food & Wine* magazine on booze and other matters. He lives in Blackheath, South London with his wife and daughter. *Empire of Booze* is his first book.

Henry Jeffreys

EMPIRE
of BOOZE

BRITISH HISTORY THROUGH THE BOTTOM OF A GLASS

unbound

This edition first published in 2016

4

Unbound
6th Floor Mutual House, 70 Conduit Street, London W1S 2GF
www.unbound.co.uk

Text Design by PDQ

A CIP record for this book is available from the British Library

ISBN 978-1-78352-224-8 (trade hbk)
ISBN 978-1-78352-225-5 (ebook)
ISBN 978-1-78352-263-7 (limited edition)

Printed in Great Britain by Clays Ltd, St Ives plc

To Marianne & Peter who would, I hope,
have enjoyed this book

Dear Reader,

The book you are holding came about in a rather different way to most others. It was funded directly by readers through a new website: Unbound. Unbound is the creation of three writers. We started the company because we believed there had to be a better deal for both writers and readers. On the Unbound website, authors share the ideas for the books they want to write directly with readers. If enough of you support the book by pledging for it in advance, we produce a beautifully bound special subscribers' edition and distribute a regular edition and e-book wherever books are sold, in shops and online.

This new way of publishing is actually a very old idea (Samuel Johnson funded his dictionary this way). We're just using the internet to build each writer a network of patrons. Here, at the back of this book, you'll find the names of all the people who made it happen.

Publishing in this way means readers are no longer just passive consumers of the books they buy, and authors are free to write the books they really want. They get a much fairer return too – half the profits their books generate, rather than a tiny percentage of the cover price.

If you're not yet a subscriber, we hope that you'll want to join our publishing revolution and have your name listed in one of our books in the future. To get you started, here is a £5 discount on your first pledge. Just visit unbound.com, make your pledge and type **RUBYPORT** in the promo code box when you check out.

Thank you for your support,

Dan, Justin and John
Founders, Unbound

CONTENTS

INTRODUCTION

In the late 1990s I worked for Oddbins, a once mighty and now rather reduced firm of British wine merchants. We were paid little, but instead given a thorough education in wine (so thorough that some employees had to go to rehab). After a long day's work and even longer evening's tasting, a favourite topic of discussion was which wine-producing country could we not do without. The most popular was, if I can remember correctly, France, though seeing this was the late 1990s and the company we worked for had made its reputation pioneering New World wines, some said Australia. Sometimes we even narrowed it down to a specific region that would produce our desert island wines. I always used to say sherry because I thought it made me sound sophisticated.

Later on in life, though, I realised I'd missed a trick because the country with the greatest influence on wine and drink in general wasn't France, Germany or even Australia, it was Britain. Without the British influence, few of our favourite wines would even be in existence. This might sound like patriotic nonsense, that I've had too much port to drink, but think about it. Champagne? The technology for making sparkling wine came from England and the taste for a bone-dry wine also came from these shores. Without Britain, champagne would have been flat and sweet. Port? Well, the names on the bottles are a clue, Taylor's,

1

Churchill's, Smith Woodhouse. Claret? Bordeaux as a wine region was founded under English rule and, as a modern wine, was sold by British merchants. Rum? Beer? Whisky? They all owe something, if not everything, to Britain.

Of course, regions such as Champagne and Bordeaux would have created wine no matter who lay across the channel from them. But would they have become the paradigms of excellence to be admired and imitated the world over? Where the British role was key was in taking a local product, exploiting it and selling it globally. Almost all the world's classic drinks such as gin, whisky, rum, madeira, sherry, claret, champagne and port became known in this way. Their success inspired imitators: there is a direct connection between the bottle of Chilean Cabernet you buy in the supermarket and the traditional English love for claret. The drinks the world enjoys today are, though often in mutated form, the drinks the British loved.

How did this small island exert such an influence on drinking habits across the world? The British do have a special relationship with alcohol. The climate might have something to do with that. It's often cold, damp and grey, but not so cold that all you want from a drink is oblivion like the Russians do with vodka, the Swedes with schnapps and the Mongolians with fermented mare's milk. The British, in contrast, have a whole smorgasbord of drinks to make life's realities a bit more bearable. Even in hot climes, or rather especially in hot climes, the British turn to drink. As Captain Thomas Walduck wrote in 1710: "The first thing the English did was set up a tavern or drinking house ... be it the most remote parts of ye world or amongst the most Barbarous Indians."

Grapes have been grown in England since Roman times particularly by monastic orders. A combination of Henry VIII's dissolution of the monasteries and a change in climate known as the Little Ice Age, which drastically lowered temperatures between the 16th and 19th centuries, meant that large-scale viticulture died out in England. Cereal crops were used to make beer and later whisky and gin, and apples to make cider. In order to drink wine, a drink that was ingrained in the culture of the ruling classes as well as essential for Christian communion, the people of the British Isles had to look abroad. Until England's defeat by France at the Battle of Castillon in 1452, these wines would have come from the English territory of Bordeaux. For over 300 years, much of France was part of England including Bordeaux after the marriage of Eleanor of Aquitaine to Henry II in 1152. Due to its proximity to England and the easily navigable rivers of the Garonne and Dordogne, the south-west of France was planted with vines and the wines they created became a staple export over the Channel. It was the English thirst that drove demand for these wines. When Aquitaine was lost to France there wasn't an immediate problem. The wine trade with Bordeaux continued once it was in French hands, but further wars with France, and the resulting punitive duties on French goods, meant that new sources of wine had to be found. To this end, England's handy geographical positioning combined with a native ingenuity. Sometimes this ingenuity took the form of plain thievery as when Drake stole over 1 million litres of sherry in a raid on Cadiz, but it was merchants in nearby Jerez who pointed the way for how things might be arranged in the future. This small colony of British traders would become the model for communities all over the world making money from alcohol. Trade, rather than piracy, would secure England and later Britain the drink she craved.

Britain was well placed to be wine merchant to the world. With the discovery of America, European trade shifted west. Furthermore by the 17th century Western nations were able to trade directly with the East without having to go through intermediaries. Prominent trading nations such as Venice, which had controlled the spice trade and the Mediterranean wine trade, became irrelevant. With Atlantic coasts and a great seafaring tradition Spain and Portugal were well placed too, but they had home-grown drink industries to protect. Their colonies were forbidden from commercialising their products. England's and later Britain's colonies were founded by private companies and were self-governing, whereas Spanish and Portuguese colonial ventures were subject to central control. The Dutch operated in a similar way to the English and they initially controlled a large slice of trade particularly with the East and the French wine trade. England's rise to a great mercantile power was based on copying the Dutch: the development of the London Stock Exchange, and most importantly the Royal Navy. Through naval might England was able to first challenge and then sideline the Dutch. Unlike England, relatively safe behind the Channel and protected by the Royal Navy, The United Provinces were vulnerable to France which in the 17th century developed into the Continental superpower.

When I outline these ideas to people some scoff and say, what about France? Surely France is the most influential country in the world when it comes to drink? Most French wine would have been drunk locally. The court in Versailles would buy from nearby Champagne or Burgundy at a stretch. A London merchant had access to a greater selection of wines than the King of France. Despite the wondrous diversity of the alcoholic drinks of France, most of its wines and spirits were only popularised by British, Dutch and German merchants. The problem with the French is, to paraphrase George Bush Junior, that they don't have a word for entrepreneur. The wines patronised by the British became copied and sought after around the world. There are other French wines which were fine enough to become world famous such as the sweet reds of the Roussillon and the muscular wines of Gascony but without the renown in

London, they stayed as local specialties, and they remain so to this day. The intrinsic quality of wine was less important than how easily it could be shipped to Britain and the rest of the world. This is why so many traditional wine regions are on the coast or on easily navigable rivers with access to the lucrative British market.

This gets to the crux of the story. Britain was rich. By the 18th century London was by far the biggest city in Europe. Britain pulled in the best the world had to offer and this included wine. But my story isn't just about wine and Europe, it takes in home-grown drinks such as beer and whisky which from Britain would spread across the world, as well as the drink that was produced by Europe's collision with the Americas, rum. Through the medium of drinks, we can chart the rise of British power from a small corner of Europe to global preeminence taking in the Royal Navy, slavery, India, the Enlightenment, the Industrial Revolution and, of course, many wars with France. It's a story that features some of the great names of British history such as Nelson, Drake and Wellington, but also shines a light on some of the forgotten heroes such as merchants, scientists, distillers, brewers and entrepreneurs. Some of the brightest minds of the age were engaged in finding, making or selling alcoholic drinks. Many of the descendants of these men are still involved in the business and many firms are still in family hands. The success of drinks such as sherry and whisky relied on the foresight of older generations laying down stocks to mature that would not be drunk in their lifetime. Thankfully these traditions have, on the whole, survived intact.

British traders formed colonies not just in the Empire, but across southern Europe wherever there was money to be made from drink. While they rarely assimilated completely, they neither did nor could remain entirely separate. All over Europe, hybrid communities developed.

British and Irish merchants intermarried with local people as well as with fellow, usually Protestant, merchants from Holland, Denmark, Germany and France to form a sort of merchant aristocracy network. In the case of the merchants of Bordeaux the majority weren't actually British and yet they created an English-speaking community who played tennis and cricket, and set up clubs like proper English gentlemen. Some of these communities have now died out. The last British in Marsala sold up in the 1920s, and in Jerez in the 1980s. Yet despite the corporate buy-outs some of these families not only exist, but are thriving and still live halfway between two countries. In this book we'll meet families such as the Bartons in Bordeaux, the Sandemans and Symingtons in Oporto, the Blandys of Madeira and the Hines of Cognac who provide a living link to the past. They are no longer entirely British but, through intermarriage, have created a unique merchant class. Furthermore, even where the actual British have disappeared, the influence lingers in the dress, the institutions, the language and, of course, in the wine itself.

This is not a history of the British wine trade, so sadly the great wines of Germany (Rhenish to Shakespeare) so popular throughout the Empire and a favourite of Queen Victoria will only be mentioned in passing. It's a similar story with Burgundy. White burgundy was the light to claret's dark. The dominance of Chardonnay as a world grape has a lot to with the British and later American love of Burgundy, but the trade in these wines wasn't dominated by Britain nor were they developed to reflect British tastes. My interest is in the roots of modern drinks so the story will start in the 17th century. I will try to keep technical stuff to a minimum but, as the book is a celebration of the wonder of these drinks as much as anything else, I will endeavor to describe how they would have been made. There will be some talk of grape varieties but I'll keep the soil analysis to a minimum. At the end of each chapter there will be a short passage on present-day versions of these famous drinks for those who want to taste their way through the book (one could even treat the book as an extended drinking game.[1]) Though I will be looking at alcohol's destructive power both at home and on colonised populations not used to strong drink, this is not primarily a study of the effects of drink on people and cultures. It is more the effect of people and cultures on drink. It is the drink itself, how it tastes, how it has changed and the story that it tells that interests me. In some ways this story is the antithesis of the current trend for *terroir* in not just wine but beer and spirits. This is a very French idea that wine is a product of place more than anything: soil, climate and native flora. My story is about how drinks were created by culture or more accurately by cultures colliding, intermingling or fighting. Each chapter will be a drink (or two) and a time and place in British history. Chapters will overlap but the cumulative effect will be a (very personal and episodic) history of modern Britain told through drink as well as a history of drink told through Britain's history. It will end in the 1920s as the effects of Prohibition on Scotch whisky are too interesting not to mention. This point marks the beginning of the American cultural dominance and the decline of the British Empire. If we look at drinks popularised after the First World War such as Coca-Cola or cocktails, it's all about the American influence.

The changing drinks of the day are reflected in literature: from Falstaff's love of Sack to Samuel Johnson and port and rum in Robert Louis Stevenson's *Treasure Island* and Charles Dickens on gin. British culture, literature, science, philosophy and religion all can be seen through the bottom of the glass. A side effect of Britain uniting, conquering,

---

1   Idea for future venture – Empire of Booze as a board game for adults.

colonising, legislating and taxing was the creation of classic drinks. Britain's legacy of empire has been much argued over and years after the events modern politicians are still apologising for the wars, slavery and famines. The lasting gifts to the world of the English language, railways and organised sports are much noted but perhaps our greatest legacy might be alcoholic. One can literally taste Britain's history. I've had port from 1863 that was still delicious. But it is not just rare wines that speak across the generations, every time you order a drink in a bar or visit a wine merchant, you are raising a glass to the Empire of Booze.

I

CIDER, SCIENCE AND CHAMPAGNE

One of the most delightful things to happen in the last ten years has been the renaissance in British cider. For a long time cider was a bit of a joke. No article on the subject was complete without a mention of teenagers and tramps drinking in parks and bus shelters. Now, however, a good cider has become fashionable. Oddly this revival was sparked by a bland mass-market drink called Magners launched in 2004. People started drinking cider again but some also began to discover traditional styles and appreciate old apple varieties. Old producers have been revitalised and new ones have sprung up. Good quality cider is now available in supermarkets and most pubs. One man who kept the cider faith going even during the dark days was James Lane at Gospel Green in West Sussex. Like champagne, Lane's ciders (or cyders as he calls them) undergo a secondary fermentation in the bottle which produces carbon dioxide bubbles. He doesn't use cider apples which are tannic (think of the mouth-coating texture one finds in red wine and tea) because he is aiming to create something that tastes like champagne.

This seems an audacious thing to do, but it is cider, not champagne, that is the original fizz. Much of the technology that would create sparkling champagne came from the cider industry. Lane's cider is a revival of a style that has its roots in the very English Enlightenment of the 17th century. The method requires very strong glass, as the pressure in the bottle of sparkling cider is something like the tyre pressure of a London bus. Drinks such as this only became possible with the invention of a new kind of glass. The man credited with this discovery was Sir Kenelm Digby. A painting of him by Van Dyke graces the wall of the National Portrait Gallery in London. A balding mustachioed man in an ornate suit of armour, he looks a louche sort of fellow, the archetypal cavalier. One can imagine puritans muttering their disapproval as he rode past. Opposite him is his wife (also painted by Van Dyke), Lady Venetia Anastasia Stanley, who in the great tradition of 17th century beauties seems rather plain to modern eyes.

Sir Kenelm's life story spools out like a picaresque novel. His father was implicated in the gunpowder plot of 1605 and had been hanged, drawn and quartered. Sir Kenelm himself had a varied career as a privateer, soldier and academic. In his unreliable memoirs he claimed to have been propositioned by Marie de Medici, widow of Henry IV of France. She was 47, he was just 18. He was even accused, in 1633, of murdering his Lady Venetia – Van Dyke was on hand to paint her death portrait. He dabbled in alchemy and was best known in his own time for inventing a substance called the "Powder of Sympathy" that was said to have magical healing properties.

When I wrote an article about him a couple of years ago, someone commented that it was extraordinary that a man so colourful invented something as humdrum as the wine bottle. It was as if Orde Wingate invented the vacuum cleaner or Francis Drake the tin can. But without this invention wine as we know it would not exist. Previously wine bottles were used like modern day decanters for serving wine. They were much too delicate for storage purposes. With the new bottles wine could be stored safely and transported easily. The bottle provided an inert container, transforming wine by helping to protect it from oxidation so, as long as it was sealed properly, wine which previously would have gone sour shortly after the vintage could now be stored. It was possible to keep bottles of port and claret at home and follow their development. We can therefore date the birth of modern wine connoisseurship to this invention. And of course strong bottles also meant that a wine could sparkle. Only Digby's new bottles were strong enough to take the pressure produced during bottle fermentation.

Sir Kenelm Digby, engraving after Anthony Van Dyck

In 1660 Charles II was crowned King of England. Along with loose morals and ludicrous wigs, Charles's reign ushered in an explosion in learning. In November of 1660 the Royal Society of London for Improving Natural Knowledge, better known simply as the Royal Society, was founded by Sir Kenelm Digby and, amongst others, Christopher Wren, Robert Boyle and Robert Hooke. The Royal Society promoted a robust empirical approach to studying science. These men weren't specialists in the manner of modern day scientists but polymaths, equally at home in architecture, theology and engineering. These British thinkers were steeped in the works of John Locke, the philosopher who espoused a method based on experimentation and observation rather than metaphysics. This can be contrasted with the French love for theoretical thought. One thinks of the probably apocryphal line about the French engineer who asked, "it works in practice, yes, but will it work in theory?" Robert Hooke, of Hooke's law fame and architect of some of the most beautiful churches in the City of London, laid out the creed in his *Micrographia* of 1665:

> "It is now high time that it should return to the plainness and soundness of Observations on material and obvious things."

Science was a social activity amongst educated men. Whereas Elizabethan and Jacobean men would have gone to the theatre, for the Restoration man about town nothing was more *à la mode* than an interest in the natural sciences. The coffee houses of London were full of excited chatter about new discoveries. Many members of the Royal Society itself were dilettantes, amateurs or just curious gentlemen. Samuel Pepys, that most curious of gentlemen, was certainly no scientist, yet he joined the Society in 1665 and acquired a 12-foot telescope in order to look the part. Later, in 1684, he became the president and was even credited in the title page of Newton's *Principia Mathematica*.

It wasn't all learning; with the stability of the Restoration came frivolity too. The theatre was resurrected after the strictures of the puritan years, social mores were relaxed and Charles's court became notorious for its loose morals. This licentious mood is captured in Sir George Etherege's comedy the *Man of Mode* of 1676:

> "To the Mall and the Park
> Where we love till 'tis dark

Then sparkling Champaign
Puts an end to their reign
It quickly recovers
Poor languishing lovers
Makes us frolik and gay, and drowns all sorrow
But, alas, we relapse again on the morrow."

Note the mention of "sparkling Champaign" (sic). To our ears this sounds a commonplace sort of luxury but, in fact, this is the first mention of sparkling champagne in literature. The wines of Champagne were introduced to the court of Charles II by a French aristocrat, Charles St-Evremond. St-Evremond was a political exile from France who achieved posthumous fame as an essayist and is buried in Poet's Corner in Westminster Abbey in London. In his lifetime he was something of a libertine and during his exile became a fixture on London's wild social scene. He was a favourite of Charles II and was even given a playful job as "Governor of the Duck Islands" (an island of game birds in St James's Park), which came with a £300 a year salary.

At this time there was no regular trade with Rheims, the capital of the Champagne region, as there was with Jerez or Bordeaux, so St-Evremond acted as an importer. He supplied wine for the notorious *Petites Soupers* (parties or orgies attended by nobles and people of dubious virtue) of Charles II's court. This wine would have sparkled in England but in France champagne would have been flat. Getting a wine to sparkle deliberately is a difficult process, one that would take all the ingenuity of the Royal Society to master.

The honour of creating sparkling champagne is traditionally given, at least by the French, to a monk called Dom Pérignon who lived from 1638 to 1715. The story of the blind Dominican friar working away in his cellar and creating a sparkling wine beloved of Louis XIV is a powerful one. Moët et Chandon, the world's largest producer of champagne, now own the name Dom Pérignon and the Abbey at Hautvillers where he worked and they promote him as the inventor. Their prestige cuvée is named after him. It's a great tale and surely helps shift bottles of fizz but it isn't true. The real story of who first deliberately put bubbles in wine is more convoluted. Dom Pérignon, ironically, laboured very hard to keep bubbles out of the wine. Fizz would have been a fault.

These bubbles would have occurred naturally. Champagne is about as far north as grapes can be properly ripened to create wine. At harvest time in October it would be cold and sometimes the fermentation of the wine would finish and there would still be live yeasts and unfermented sugar within it. The following year when the weather warmed up the wine would start to referment producing carbon dioxide. This is something that has been noted for many years. There is a reference to it in the Bible: "Neither do men put new wine into old skins; else the skins break" (Matthew 9:17). If this wine is bottled and allowed to referment the bubbles are absorbed into the wine and then released when the wine is opened. Voilà! Champagne. However, all French wine, in fact, all wine throughout Europe, would have been delivered in wooden casks so this carbon dioxide would simply dissipate. Furthermore, bottles at the time were not strong enough to take the pressure of fermentation and would have exploded. Glass had been used since Roman times for serving and drinking from, but only in England was there a tradition of bottling wine and, thanks to the Royal Navy, English glass was the strongest in Europe.

One of James I's admirals, the Welshman Sir Robert Mansell, a veteran of the Spanish Armada, was worried about not having enough wood for shipbuilding.[2] At the time glass was made by burning charcoal from trees.

2   Approximately 6,000 trees were used to make *HMS Victory*, Nelson's flagship.

Mansell pioneered glass fired from coal and was given a royal monopoly of this new product. As this new glass was created at a much higher temperature, it was stronger than the charcoal-fired stuff. Impurities such as iron or manganese within the coal made the glass stronger still. In 1623 Mansell was given a monopoly by the King to set up a glassworks that made his fortune. Ironically many of the skilled glassmakers were Huguenots[3] fleeing religious intolerance in France. The bottles that came out of Mansell's works, though stronger than normal glass, probably would not have been strong enough to withstand the pressure of fermentation. A man who did make bottles of sufficient strength was the aforementioned Sir Kenelm Digby.

Sir Kenelm was a key figure in the early years of the Royal Society and its forerunner, Gresham College. In the 1620s he was best known for his "Powder of Sympathy" (probably iron sulphate) that was said to have miraculous healing properties. He claimed to have learned the secret from a Carmelite friar in Florence which sounds like something out of a Dan Brown novel. The lines between science and alchemy were still being drawn up and much of what were then thought of as real discoveries strike modern scientists as mere quackery. Digby also had a brief career captaining a ship that preyed on French, Spanish and Venetian ships in the Mediterranean, a licensed pirate, with the English under James I attempting to grab a slice of the lucrative Levant trade.

By all accounts the death of his wife affected him deeply.[4] Digby immersed himself in his experiments. He worked with another polymath, the glassmaker, and later writer

3   The mercantile flair of the Huguenots would prove a great asset to England and loss to France. Names such as Tanqueray in gin and Delaforce in port are Huguenots.

4   He was cleared of murdering her but he may have killed her inadvertently by dosing her with so-called viper wine - a youth balm made from the internal organs of a viper. Because you're worth it!

and historian, James Howell.[5] Howell was able to take Sir Kenelm's laboratory experiments and apply them on an industrial scale. Together they worked out that tunnels going into the glass furnace would increase the heat further still and, the higher the temperature, the stronger the glass. This worked by drawing oxygen into the fire making it burn more fiercely, though the reason why it worked was not understood at the time. Such furnaces were considered high technology in the late 18th century, so much so that Diderot included a diagram of one in his *Encylopedie*. Sir Kenelm's brilliance combined with James Howell's practical knowledge to develop a new stronger bottle. The new bottles were bulbous with a deep punt (indentation) on the bottom from where the blowpipe was fixed. They were dark from the coal smoke with a long cylindrical neck. They looked a little like an onion. You can see bottles like them in the Vintner's Hall in the City of London.

Under licence from Mansell, Digby opened a furnace at Newnham-on-Severn near the Forest of Dean where there was a plentiful supply of coal. Here he pioneered production of the new strong glass bottles. Sir Kenelm never patented his invention and other contemporary glassworks began making similar bottles. The new bottles were not only stronger but, because they were made in quantity, they were cheaper too. In one year 36,000 were made in Mansell's glassworks in Newcastle alone. After the Restoration in 1661 a glassmaker called James Colnett tried to obtain a patent from the new Royal government for these strong bottles but was opposed by a group of peers, John Vinian, Robert Ward, Edward Percival and Robert Sadler, who insisted that it was Digby's

---

5   Later Howell was to feel the full effect of Digby's "Powder of Sympathy". Howell was seriously wounded when he tried to break up a duel and Digby treated him with the magic powder. Howell wrote later how a "pleasing kind of freshnesse, as it were a wet cold napkin did spread over my hand".

invention. This sort of glass became known in France as *verre anglais* and German sparkling wine producers still refer to the thick material needed for their products as English glass.

Meanwhile imported wine to put in these new bottles was becoming increasingly expensive. England's expansionist and commercial ambitions put her at odds with her neighbours. For much of the 17th century England managed to be at war with France, the Netherlands and Spain, often all three at the same time. In order to break the Dutch commercial grip on England, Cromwell passed the Navigation Act of 1651. It meant that only English ships would be allowed to bring goods into English ports. This was designed to punish the Dutch but, as they controlled the trade in all German and a great deal of French wine, it made these wines very scarce in England.[6]

Following the Restoration, Charles II instituted his own series of Navigation Acts in 1660 which were to endure until the 19th century. In 1667 all wine from France was prohibited completely from sale in England. By early 1680 the official importation of French wines was practically nil. Of course wine would have been smuggled in but this contraband would have been expensive. Even when wine was available some argued that England should be self-sufficient. What was needed was an alternative to wine.

Cider had been made in Britain since the Romans introduced apple trees but now producers, especially in the south-west of the country where growing conditions were ideal, started to make something akin to wine from apples. One cider enthusiast, John Evelyn, put together a book entitled *Pomona* that became a sort of bible for the new wave of cider. In it he wrote, "Our design is relieving the want of wine, by a succedaneum of Cider."

---

6   Scotland could and did still import claret as they weren't at war with France or the Netherlands.

Cider was classed as farm produce and so didn't command any taxes at all. Cider would also free up grain for bread from beer-making duties. Growing apple tree orchards was becoming a patriotic duty. Just as Dom Pérignon was experimenting with the best grape varieties, so these West Country notables experimented with apple varieties. The best of these was called Redstreak, also known as the Scudamore Crab after Sir John Scudamore Viscount of Sligo and Ambassador to the French Court. He picked up an interest in French fruit and cider whilst fulfilling his ambassadorial duties. Redstreak was inedible as it was very high in tannin and extremely hard, but it was perfect for making fine ciders designed for keeping. A visiting Italian prince referred to this cider as "Vin de Scudamore".

In the 17th century cider wasn't the cheap drink that it is today as apples were difficult to press. You needed a powerful mechanical press to extract the juice which only the rich could have afforded to own in 17th century England. There were no commercial cider producers. James Lane at Gospel Green showed me his press from the 1860s which would have been very similar to ones used by Scudamore and others. It's an enormous contraption of wood and iron and can take half a tonne of fruit at a time. Before pressing the apples have to be crushed into a purée and spread on the press layered with hessian sacks. James Lane uses a machine not dissimilar to a wood chipper to mash the apples, but this would have to have been done by hand in Scudamore's day. It was long and labour intensive work compared with brewing beer or making wine.

Scudamore was the archetypal leisured English gentleman. His income from his vast estates gave him time to pursue his own interests. In some landowners these might have been some sort of debauchery or perhaps hunting, but for many of the day it was the pursuit of scientific discovery. While on the Continent proto-scientists would have been affiliated with universities or the state, British science owes much to wealthy amateurs such as Scudamore, Digby and, much later, Charles Darwin. Thomas Sprater, Bishop of Rochester, in his *History of the Royal Society*, referred to members as "gentlemen, free and confined". Free in many senses of the word, but mainly free from having to labour and free from interference from the Crown. Their security both financial and otherwise came from a changing attitude to the land that was peculiar to Britain. Previously nobles or gentry would have been lords over the land, owing allegiance to the king and at the same time a responsibility towards the peasantry. They didn't in the modern, legal sense own the land; it belonged to the Crown and they could be deprived of it at any time. By 1640, however, the last ties of feudalism had been cut. Much of the money that had been paid by landowners to the Crown now came from an excise on beer which was mainly paid for by the working classes. This became the standard way of raising money and persists to this day. Whenever governments need money, the first thing they tax are the pleasures of the working man. Locke's *Treatises of Civil Government* of 1689 proclaims the victory of the absolute ownership of land.

Scudamore's high quality cider would have been made from the first pressing of the fruit, as the best wines, olive oils and indeed ciders are produced today. Other sophisticated techniques used at the time included frequent racking[7] to preserve some unfermented sugar. The apples could also be left to dehydrate either outside or in barns to concentrate the sugars rather as some grapes are left to dry to create sweet wines. Scudamore's cider was high in alcohol, probably about 11 percent, with an elegant flavour. Its reputation quickly spread. John Worlidge in his book *Vitum Brittanicum or a treatise on cider* of 1676, a book that advocated cider

---

7   Moving to a new barrel and leaving yeast in the bottom of the old.

as Britain's answer to wine, mentioned how "a barrel of Redstreak surpassed the best Spanish and French wines". He went on to note that a Hogshead (110 gallons) of this cider went for £8 or £20 if it was two or three years old. This was a similar price to the best Canary sack.[8] Cider was not only commanding high prices, but was improved with age like the best wine. There are stories of competitions between vintners and cider-makers where their respective products would be tasted blind, with the home-grown product triumphing unanimously.[9] The lower orders were either given the good stuff watered down or drank something fermented from apples that had already been pressed mixed with water known as Ciderkin. Most modern ciders are closer to Ciderkin than good 17th century cider which was normally spelt Cyder. This is how James Lane at Gospel Green spells the name of his product, as do Aspall's in Suffolk.

Thanks to the new bottles, these West Country cider lords were able to experiment with making their product sparkling. The next bit of high technology needed to capture the bubbles was oddly enough the cork. At the time champagne did not have corks. They had been used by the Romans, but the technology had been partially[10] lost, and instead the Champenois would have used paper and wax to "cork" their bottles. Portugal was and still is the world's largest producer of cork and Britain's good relations with the Portuguese later enshrined in the Methuen Treaty of 1703 meant that there was always a plentiful supply of it. Digby experimented with corking bottles and leaving them to mature. This would have

8   Strong sweet sherry-style wine from the Canary Islands.

9   I was sceptical about these competitions because surely wine is so different to cider that you can't really compare them. Then I tried Gospel Green from Sussex which most people probably wouldn't even recognise as cider.

10   Corks were being used further south in France in Limoux to make a distinctive sparkling wine that you can still buy today. In fact the Limounais claim that they "invented" sparkling wine.

been impossible with the old style bottles as forcing a cork in securely could well have broken the bottle. We know that Lord Scudamore also experimented with bottles and corks. There is a drinking glass in the Museum of London that belonged to him which looks suspiciously like a champagne flute, a glass designed to capture expensively created bubbles. It was made in London some time between 1642 and 1660 with an "S" for Scudamore and some exquisitely drawn apples engraved upon it.

Digby was one of the pioneers of this rarefied new cider as outlined in his snappily-titled *The Closet of the Eminently Learned Sir Kenelme Digbie Knight Opened*.[11] In this book he describes how to make a strong sparkling cider for bottling. Naturally Redstreak is the preferred apple and, after corking, he outlines methods for storing the bottles, keeping them cool to minimise the risk of explosion. In cold weather they were to be kept in hay to stop them freezing, in hot weather kept in sand to prevent the fermentation getting too vigorous. In *Vitum Brittanicum*, Worsley also mentions techniques for keeping the fermenting cider cool by storing it in running water and even describes a method of placing it upside down in order to catch the spent yeasts in the bottleneck a full 150 years before Madame Clicquot pioneered this technique in Champagne.

Digby and others also experimented with distillation to make cider brandy. This was a West Country speciality that has been revived today by Julian Temperley of the Somerset Cider Company. He told me about an intriguing drink called Royal Cider that was like a kind of port made from apples. A hogshead of still fermenting cider would be mixed with a hogshead of cider brandy to create something very sweet and strong.

---

11 Interestingly enough this book contains a recipe from our old friend St-Evremond for *Potage de Santé*.

Other members of the Royal Society took an interest in cider and winemaking. John Locke himself, the father of empiricism, travelled through France and wrote extensively about the vineyards of Bordeaux. The greatest minds in the country turned themselves to studying and perfecting alcoholic drinks. It was as if Stephen Hawking's real interest was not astrophysics but homebrew. It was soon noted that the bubbles would be all the more vigorous if extra sugar was added to fuel the secondary fermentation. John Beale from Herefordshire cider country and formerly of King's College, Cambridge, read a paper to the Royal Society on 10th December 1662 where he described putting a "walnut of sugar" into bottled cider. This is about 20 grams of sugar, roughly the *dosage* of (amount of sugar added to) modern dry champagne. A paper on cider was read to the Royal Society by Sir Paul Neil on the 8th July 1663. This was concerned with how much leftover yeast should be left in the cider when bottled: too much and the fermentation would be too violent; "it may be possible to drive out the corks, or break the bottles."

The man who is credited with applying these techniques to wine rather than cider was Christopher Merret. Born in 1615 in Gloucestershire in the heart of cider country, Merret was educated at Gloucester Hall, Oxford, the same college as Sir Kenelm Digby. He trained to be a physician and was another founder member of the Royal Society. There are mentions of Merret in Pepys's diary. In one meeting on 11th January 1666, along with John Wilkins another founder member of the Royal Society, Pepys describes his time with Merret as being "so sober and so ingenious". The other mention shows Merret a little worse for wear on the 22nd January at the Crowne Tavern in London where they stayed "late till poor Dr. Merret was drunk, and so all home and I to bed".

Like Sir Kenelm Digby, Merret was interested in the production of glass and contributed much to creating strong glass through his 1662 translation of Antonio Neri's *The Art of Glass* – a seminal Venetian work on glass making. But it was a paper that he gave to the Royal Society on the 17th December 1662 called *Some Observations Concerning the Ordering of Wines* that stakes his place in history. In this paper he describes some faults that appear in wines and how to remedy them. Some seem a little unusual to modern ears such as adding beetroot[12] to red wines that have lost their colour, whereas others are still normal practice such as adding egg whites to wines to remove impurities. Amongst these helpful hints, there is this line:

> "Our wine coopers of recent times use vast quantities of sugar and molasses to all sorts of wines to make them drink brisk and sparkling."

This is how champagne is made. It would appear that Merret himself did not invent the technique as the way he describes it suggests that it was common practice to do this at the time. He was, however, the first person to write about it, hence his reputation as the godfather of champagne. There is an English sparkling wine made by Ridgeview called Cuvée Merret. By the late 17th century all the ingredients were in place in England to make a drink much like modern champagne. Wine from Champagne would have been brought over to England. The English market would have preferred the white wines made from the Chardonnay grape that had a greater propensity to sparkle rather than the red or reddish Pinot Noir-based wines suitable for ageing that Dom Pérignon strived for. Thanks to Sir Kenelm Digby the wines could then be bottled safely in the new strong glass and would either have had sugar added to them as per Merret's described method or left to referment naturally in the bottle. Due to

---

12 Sugar from sugar beet is an essential ingredient in most French wines nowadays.

the writings of the cider lords, experimenters with bubbles would know of the value of storing these wines under cork in a cool stable environment. These were the first sparkling champagnes mentioned in Etherege's comedy.

These wines, however, were not reliable. Sometimes there would be no fizz and sometimes the bottles would explode. It would have to wait until the 19th century for the ingenuity of Madame Clicquot in Champagne and the work of the scientists Louis Pasteur and Jean-Antoine Chaptal with yeast and sugar to perfect the technique. The English may have been the first to deliberately make them sparkle, but it was the French who perfected the technique and enabled champagne to be mass-produced.

Merret's life ended in disgrace when he was accused by the Royal College of Physicians of stealing property from them during the Great Fire of 1666. And what happened to the aristocratic ciders? Despite all the papers written, they were never more than a minority interest. They were also an answer to a problem that had largely gone away by the time they were created. By the time William III took the throne in 1688, England was importing significant quantities of wine from her oldest ally, Portugal. This special relationship was codified in the Methuen Treaty of 1703 which led to the establishment of a British colony in Oporto and the creation of a new drink, port, in which powerful Portuguese wine was made stronger still by adding brandy: much more to the English taste than 10 percent cider.

DRINKING THE EMPIRE

Cider has a bad reputation in England as it's used for what are essentially cider-style drinks made from concentrate, flavouring and water with no whole apples. Avoid anything that isn't made from whole apples. The ambition to make a serious cider never entirely went away. There were adverts in the *Calcutta Gazette* for strong ciders especially for the Indian market. Bulmer's used to make a "Super Champagne Cider de Luxe". Drinks such as these died out or were bastardised by mass production methods in the 1960s. Now, with the explosion of interest in cider, they're back. A number of producers around the country are now making ciders inspired by Digby and Scudamore.

Ashridge Devon bottle-fermented cider
It tastes nothing like champagne; instead it is a very elegant West Country cider complete with some tannin and a little scrumpy-like funkiness, but with the most elegant little bubbles and the taste lingers in the mouth beautifully.

Kingston Black Burrow-Hill bottle-fermented cider
This is probably quite close to what Digby et al were striving for. It's vinous with well-developed bubbles, but also has some quite firm tannins that cry out for a piece of mature cheddar.

The company that makes this is called the Somerset Cider Brandy Company. The owner, Julian Temperley, has revived the tradition of making top quality spirit from apples. He also makes a drink called Pomona which is a blend of unfermented apple juice and cider rather like Pommeau produced in Normandy and Brittany.

Gospel Green Sparkling Cider (it's a vintage drink – I tried the 2013)
This is very different from the West Country ones as it's made from eating and cooking apples rather than bittersweet cider apples. At 8.5 percent it's dry, elegant and beautifully balanced and considerably closer to a wine than a cider. It's much nicer than most proseccos and cavas and, indeed many champagnes. The company that can produce

something of this quality but in Moët-like quantities and market it as England's answer to champagne will be rich. It just needs a catchy name.

Aspall's
The Chevallier family from Jersey tried to grow vines in Suffolk and failed, so planted apples instead in 1728. They do sometimes make a bottle-fermented cider, but it's not available that often. Their ubiquitous dry Cyder, note spelling, is an excellent wine-style drink tasting of clean green apples.

Finally, I should mention that England now makes some good home-grown sparkling wines from the classic champagne varieties, Chardonnay, Pinot Noir and Pinot Meunier. The best of these wines can be superb, especially with some bottle age. Some, however, can be searingly acidic without much pleasure. None are cheap. Good producers include Henners, Nyetimber, Ridgeview, Gusbourne and the appropriately named Digby.

2

PORT WINE AND POLITICS

When I was a boy we used to holiday in Portugal every year. Like thousands of British people, my grandparents had a holiday home in the Algarve. My father would tell us on the drive from Faro airport that Portugal was England's oldest and best ally. It was as if there was a direct line from John of Gaunt's daughter, Philippa, marrying King John I of Portugal in 1387 and us turning up with a bottle of Johnnie Walker Black Label to give to Alessandro, the manager of the Penina Hotel, so that we could use his swimming pool. Portugal and England share a similar history. They are both small countries that have had a disproportionate effect on world affairs (there are far more Portuguese speakers in the world than French speakers). The Portuguese often define themselves in relation to their much bigger neighbour, Spain, as England has done with France. England and Portugal were two of Europe's oldest nation states assuming roughly their present borders in the 10th and 13th centuries respectively. And, of course, both were great maritime powers. Henry the Navigator, the instigator of the golden age of Portuguese exploration, was the half-English offspring from King John and Philippa's marriage. Earlier still it was English Crusaders on their way to Palestine by a roundabout route who helped drive the last of the Moors from the Algarve thus giving the country its modern shape. At various periods in history the English have shown up to fight the Spanish, the Moors, or just get drunk and meddle in Portuguese affairs. The insult *Bebibo Inglez*[13] (English Drunk) is an ancient one. The fact that Portugal survived as an independent country against so powerful a neighbour as Spain is much down to its turbulent and not always amicable alliance with the English. We haven't always been great friends. Nevertheless the fates of these two small countries have often been tied together. So when problems with Spain and France interrupted the usual supply of wine to England, it was inevitable that England would turn to her old ally. The result, eventually, was port wine.

Supply of French wine had been intermittent under the Commonwealth and the Restoration, but England's great rival then was not France but the Netherlands. The Navigation Acts that interrupted wine supplies were designed to take trade away from the Dutch. Charles II leaned towards France where he had been in exile. Charles hoped, as his father had done so unsuccessfully, to limit the power of Parliament, and imitate his cousin in France by turning his realm into a centralised despotic state. Louis XIV was the envy of all European monarchs for the power he exercised. Charles was also thought to be a crypto-Catholic (which he probably was, as he was received into the Roman Catholic church on his deathbed) and his Portuguese wife Catherine of Braganza was treated with some suspicion. England hadn't fought a major war against the French since the end of the Hundred Years War in 1453.

This all changed when a Dutchman, William of Orange, became King of England in 1688. He had, with the support

---

13 Much later Palmerston (Prime Minister 1859–1865) noted how sober Portuguese soldiers were in comparison with their British counterparts: "The love of ardent spirits was more common to the northern than to the southern nations, and occasioned great excesses. Hence punishments for this offence were rare among the Portuguese in our pay."

of Parliament, overthrown Charles's brother James II. Parliament was worried that James, as a Catholic, was hoping to introduce French-style absolutism to England (which he probably was). James fled to France and with French support plotted to regain his throne. Many Jacobite[14] loyalists fled to France after James II's defeat at the Battle of the Boyne in 1690 including one John Lynch from Galway whose son would go into the wine trade, acquire the Bages estate in Pauillac, later Lynch-Bages, and whose grandson would become Mayor of Bordeaux. We'll hear more about him later.

Holland was no longer a threat; France was now England's great rival. In 1693 William III, as he now was, put up the duty on French wine. By 1698 duty on French wine was £47 a cask when the wine itself only cost £12. By 1700 French imports had trickled to almost nothing. From 1688 until 1697 the English fought the Nine Years War against France and then from 1702 until 1714 the War of Spanish Succession. Conflict between the two countries would persist sporadically until the defeat of Napoleon in 1815. The harsh duty on French wine lasted even longer. It was finally repealed by Gladstone in 1860. Lack of claret had previously been a temporary aberration, now it was a permanent problem.

The 1654 treaty under Oliver Cromwell had given English merchants in Portugal special privileges. They had their own judges, laws, consuls and were allowed to practise their own religion. They were like a diplomatic community above most Portuguese laws. In return England promised to defend Portugal in the event of an invasion. Spain and Portugal had been united under the Hapsburgs from 1581 until 1640 and the Spanish still eyed their little neighbour

---

14 English Jacobites called themselves "Tories" after an Irish word for a brigand. It's amazing now to think that Tories identified with Irish rebels.

covetously. The 1661 marriage of Charles II to Catherine of Braganza (the Portuguese royal house) cemented the alliance between England and Portugal. As part of the marriage deal, England acquired Ceylon, Bombay and Tangiers which has to go down as one of history's great dowries. By the end of the 16th century there was already a sizeable English, Irish and Scottish merchant community in Lisbon and Oporto.

The English also had something that the Portuguese wanted – cod. Salt cod or *bacalhau* is, with pork, the most important ingredient in Portuguese cooking. There was a triangular trade between Britain, Newfoundland and Portugal. English woollens would go to Newfoundland to be exchanged for cod, which would be taken to Portugal in exchange for wine. Many of the grand old family names of the port trade started off as general merchants dealing in fish and cloth as well as wine. Everybody was happy except the English who weren't that keen on the wine they were getting.

Portuguese wines had been imported to England since the 16th century. They would have been from Minho in the north of the country. If you've ever tried red vinho verde or reds from Galicia[15] in Spain, you'll have some idea of what they would have been like: highly acidic, light in body but not in colour, tannic and tasting of raw grape skins. Vinho verde can be red or white. The name refers to young ie green wine rather than its colour. It's just the thing to drink straight after the harvest with a fatty Portuguese stew. These wines weren't much to the English taste which ran to strong Falstaffian wines such as sherry, malaga or Canary sack. The wines also struggled to survive the sea voyage to England without turning to vinegar.

---

15   A region linguistically and culturally closer to Portugal than Spain. During the 19th century most labourers in Oporto were Galicians.

Even the wine from around Oporto – as the English called it O Porto, literally The Port – would have been thin weedy stuff. Vines were grown in a coolish foggy climate not dissimilar to that of San Francisco, in fertile soils and trained up trees or over other crops. They are still grown like this in some parts of northern Spain and Portugal. What the English wanted was something a bit stronger. The climate up the Douro from Oporto was very different: baking hot in the summer and freezing in the winter. The soil, mainly schist, is so poor that only vines and olives would grow. Stronger wines from up country, often from monasteries, would occasionally come back to Oporto. These were much more to the English taste. Intrepid explorers set off to find the source of these burly wines. Even today the vineyards of the Douro feel a long way from Oporto. You have to cross a mountain range to get there, the Serra Maroa. This range protects the valley from rain which is why the climate is so dry. With modern roads, it's a two hour drive on vomit-inducing switchbacks or three hours on the most beautiful railway line in the world. In the 18th century it would have taken days to cover the hundred miles. Until the building of the railway, this region was cut off from the rest of Portugal. Early travellers told stories about the old gods still holding sway up the river. The food was awful, the inns full of bed bugs with one merchant describing how he had to sleep on the table to get away from the nasty creatures, "sleeping on ye tables for reason of ye vermin". Thomas Woodmass, a merchant who wrote one of the first accounts of the Douro, tells of how he was captured by brigands who stole all his clothes apart from his hat and coat and then tied him and his companions to a tree. Coming back down by the rapid, rock-strewn river on boats laden with pipes of wine was no less treacherous. Special flat-bottomed boats with one sail were used called *rabelos*. They looked a bit like small Viking boats. There were dangerous currents and whirlpools and many merchants were drowned. The river was dammed and tamed in the 1980s, so it's hard to imagine the river in all its terror now that it's as tranquil as a lake. The rewards of trading in wine must have been more than sufficient to make such hardships bearable. In 1678, 408 pipes (approximately 224,400 litres) of Vinho do Porto were shipped to England.

Finding good wine was difficult, but making sure that it arrived back in Britain in a drinkable condition was harder still; the wine would have been made in primitive conditions by small farmers. Viticulture was a long way from the systematic techniques used in Bordeaux or Jerez where a proper industry had grown up around the wines. They would not have known which grape varieties they were growing and different types were grown alongside each other.[16] The climate in the Douro was changeable, and a good crop could be destroyed in a single afternoon by hail. Often the wine that came down from the region was thin, weedy and made from under-ripe grapes, no better than the Minho wine that was so unpopular in London. Adding brandy to it made it fiery, but did nothing to improve the taste. The wine was then usually transported in goat skins which gave it a pronounced goaty taste. Animal skins were still used to transport lesser quality wines in Iberia well into the 20th century. They look horrible with their bodies grotesquely swollen with wine and runty little legs sticking out. One of the oddest things about studying the history of port, the wine, is how many writers say that it wasn't very good. This book is meant to be about how the British created delicious drinks, but in the case of port, people are tripping over themselves to tell us quite how vile it was. Perhaps the most famous poem about port, written by Richard Ames in 1693, is very unflattering:

16 Many vineyards including some that go into the finest wines are still mixed in the Douro. It is only since the 1970s that growers began to plant varieties individually.

"Mark how it smells, methinks a real pain,
Is by the odour thrown upon my brain.
I've tasted it – tis spiritless and flat,
And has as many different tastes, as can be
found in compound pastes,
But fetch us a glass of any sort,
Navarre, Galicia, anything but port."

Scottish drinkers in particular were not impressed. Boswell complained: "A bottle of thick English port is a very heavy and very inflammatory dose. I felt it last time that I drank it for several days, and this morning it was boiling in my veins." But there was more to it than simply disliking port on aesthetic grounds. Port had assumed a symbolic importance in the conflicts that divided Britain: the battle between Parliament and the Crown and more broadly the battle between Liberal Enlightenment values and despotism, and finally the wars of religion between the Reformation and the Counter-reformation. The battles that wracked Europe and killed millions of people in Germany (over a third of the population died during the Thirty Years War) were acted out by drinkers in Britain. It was a patriotic duty not to drink French wine or rather it became a patriotic duty to drink port if you supported the Protestant accession. The Jacobites, English Catholics, Scottish Highlanders and Irish Catholics would toast their precious claret to the "King over the Water" in France (James II and later Bonnie Prince Charlie[17]). This political identification with a lost cause persisted until very recently. In his autobiography, *The Moon's a Balloon*, David Niven is serving with the Highland Light Infantry in Malta in the 1930s:

---

17 The current Stuart "pretender" to the throne is Franz Prince of Bavaria.

"After the port completed its circle, a toast was given to 'the King'. Many of the glasses I noticed were ostentatiously passed over the top of a glass of water on their way to the lips in a rather juvenile gesture to show that Highlanders were still drinking to the exiled Stuarts – the King over the Water." There were even rumours that port was a plot to hit the Highlanders where it really hurt, under the kilt, as this poem alludes:

> "Firm and erect the Caledonian stood;
> Sound was his mutton, and his claret good;
> 'Let him drink port!' the English statesman cried:
> He drank the poison, and his spirit died."

Not all Scots, however, spurned port. Most just wanted to make some money and to drink good wine. As with most aspects of Britain's empire of trade and indeed the Empire full stop, Scots were over-represented. Some of the biggest names in port such as Cockburn, Graham and Sandeman were Scots. One of the most enduring firms was started by George Sandeman of Perth. He set up business in 1790 in the City of London shipping wines from Oporto. He operated from premises on St Swithin's Lane. The building now houses a restaurant called The Sign of the Don, named after the logo adopted by the Sandeman company in 1928, the Don. You can eat in the cellars where Sandeman would have stored his port. The Don, whose presence is all over Oporto, is the most famous port logo, recognisable even to those who have never tried port wine.

In the early days it was found that the best wine was made by the monasteries.[18] Priest's port commanded a premium

18 This is often the case. Burgundy before the French Revolution was a monastic wine. One of the Lebanon's best wines, Chateau Ksara, was also originally a monastery.

in 17th century London. They may also have been the first to fortify the wine. In 1678 two Liverpudlian merchants came to a monastery near Lamego and, impressed with the wine, asked how it was so strong and smooth and were told that it was the brandy that made it so good. It was not an unusual practice to fortify wine by adding spirits for long sea voyages, but the difference was that the monks added the spirit during fermentation so that it killed the yeasts and left some sugar unfermented. Yet this sweet port took a long time to catch on. Most port would have been dry as the brandy was added later. George Robinson in his 1754 book *Port* complained of a grower who "is in the habit of checking fermentation of the wines too soon, by putting brandy into them while still fermenting; a practice which must be considered DIABOLICAL". This debate as to the nature of port would rage well into the 19th century. Whether the brandy was strictly necessary to preserve the wine is a different matter. It would have naturally been about 15 percent alcohol, enough to keep it for the short voyage to England. It can't have hurt that the English liked their wine strong. So it may have just been fortified because that is how the customers demanded it. In a good vintage the wine would have been called "blackstrap". It would be dark, tannic, powerful, dry and not particularly sophisticated. It would bear some resemblance to today's more rustic table wines of the Douro.

Thomas Woodmass arrived from London in 1703 to seek his fortune in the Douro. He introduced English expertise in barrel making: "Ye English cupers (sic) are a drunken lott (sic), but ye natives now know how to make casks", he wrote. He went into partnership with a Peter Bearsley, son of Job Bearsley who owned the Ram Inn in Smithfields, London. Bearsley was one of the first Englishmen to go up country himself in search of good wine. The company founded by Bearsley would later become Taylor, Fladgate & Yeatman, one of the great names in port wine. Merchants such as these were generally the sons of middle-class professionals or gentry. One of the unusual things about England in Europe at that time was the system of primogeniture and the absolute sanctity of private property. In France when someone died his estate had to be by law divided amongst his family. Chateaubriand wrote of how a large estate could be reduced in two generations to "a pigeon, a rabbit, a fowling piece and a gun dog, although they still remain the noble chevaliers and mighty seigneurs of a dovecote, a swamp and a warren". But in England a man's property was his to do with as he wished after his death. Generally most of it went to the eldest son with small amounts given to other offspring: either a dowry for the women or for men to be trained in a profession, to buy a commission in the army or to be set up in trade. They often went into the wine business. Part of the character, not to mention the dress code, of the British wine trade is because of this influence. Along with the army, the law, and the church, the wine trade was something respectable sons of good families could aspire to. The British had a sizeable middle class, something that didn't exist in Portugal or indeed in most of the world. In 1814 Patrick Colquhoun in his *Treatise on British Empire* wrote:

"In most countries, society presents scarcely anything but a void between an ignorant labouring population, and a needy and profligate nobility ... but with us the space between the ploughman and the peer, is crammed with circle after circle, fitted in the most admirable manner for sitting upon each other, for connecting the former with the latter, and for rendering the whole perfect in cohesion, strength and beauty."

The close relationship between England and Portugal was enshrined in the Methuen Treaty of 1703. This treaty, protecting Portugal from Spanish or French aggression, also cemented what was already a sizeable trade and alliance with Portugal. English woollens could be imported into Portugal free from duty. Wine was an important factor in the treaty:

"That is to say, that her sacred Majesty of Great Britain shall in her own name and that of her successors, be obliged for ever hereafter to admit the wines of the growths of Portugal into Great Britain; so that at no time, whether shall be peace or war between the kingdoms of Great Britain and France, anything more shall be demanded for these wines, by the names of customs or duty ... than shall be demanded for like quantity or measure of French wine, deducting or abating a third part of the custom or duty."

The treaty ushered in a first golden age of port wine.

The British merchants in Oporto set about trying to make a more consistent high quality product. They sent men up river with the technical expertise to improve things. They built terracing for vines along the steep banks of the river. These terraces would have been cut from solid rock using only hand tools. It must have been hard, dangerous work. Later dynamite made things easier though hardly less perilous. Much of the terracing that makes the Douro such a dramatic region today was constructed in the early years of the 18th century. Wealth from the new plantings spread from the merchants to the growers. John Croft (founder of the port house that bears his name) notes disapprovingly how the peasants had started to ape the fashions of the British:

> "It has often been seen and noticed at Oporto
> that the meanest Labradores, or Farmers of
> the district or territory of Sima de Douro, after
> having, in a good year, sold their Wines well
> and profitably, have come down to the city, and
> bought cloaths (sic) of the richest brocades of
> France and strutted with them in the streets
> like so many Peacocks... "

The British didn't mix with the Portuguese and were mocked for their terrible grasp of the local language (which even the Portuguese admit is extremely hard to pronounce). In the 18th century, British adventurers, soldiers and colonists were "going native" all over the world. Early administrators from the East India Company[19] adopted Indian dress and Islamic customs and mores. This was before Victorian cultural rigidity set in. So the lack of interaction between the two populations may have been as much the Portuguese shunning the British as the other way round. Portugal at the time was a rigid aristocratic and chivalric country. The British traders who were generally middle class would have been looked down upon as common. There was very little native middle class and, of course, the British wouldn't have intermarried with the Portuguese peasantry (who probably wouldn't have had them anyway). As for the British, Portugal would have seemed incredibly alien to them. The claustrophobic Catholicism of the culture, the almost theocratic governance too, would have baffled the Protestant British. The Portuguese Inquisition would on occasion kidnap British children in order to raise them in the true faith. It's not a surprise that the British, in the early days, largely stayed apart from Portuguese. The British seem to have got on better with the Muslim rulers in India than Catholics in Iberia.

Instead the British tried to create their own insular little world. In 1790 the Factory House was built in Oporto in a Georgian style. This was the headquarters of the British merchants of the city. Here they would meet to socialise, but also to consolidate their control over the trade. Foreigners were not allowed to join.[20] The building would be more

---

19 There's an excellent book about this world called *White Mughals* by William Dalrymple.

20 This has been relaxed slightly in that Portuguese may join, but only if they're employees of a British-owned port house.

at home in Bath or Cheltenham than at the edge of Iberia. The British merchants formed a colony in Oporto on Rua Nova, now called Rua Infante D. Henrique. They married amongst themselves and imported black servants from America because they didn't trust the locals who were too familiar with their servants. Just as in Bordeaux, the British built warehouses outside the city, on the opposite bank of the river at Vila Nova de Gaia. It's still a separate city. This was to avoid the taxes levied by Oporto's rulers. Even today there are definite British houses and Portuguese houses.[21]

Sandeman used to be a thoroughly British house, but it's now owned by a Portuguese family firm, Sogrape, who made their fortune through Mateus Rosé.[22] It's still managed, however, by a relative of the first George Sandeman, also called George Sandeman. He is half English and half Spanish and was brought up in England and Jerez. He speaks English and Spanish fluently, but he told me that he is still teased by his wife, who is from Oporto, on his imperfect Portuguese. The Sandeman logo, the Don, shows the cosmopolitan nature of the company. The cloak is a traditional Portuguese student's cloak and the hat is a Spanish sombrero.

The town of Oporto these days is defined by its mixture of British and Portuguese traditions. I was lucky enough to be there for the annual boat race where the port houses race, extremely slowly, *rabelos* laden with wine, down the Douro. The crews are largely Portuguese, but the atmosphere of competitiveness dressed up as jovial amateurishness is pure English country fair. And on the sails are those old British names, Cockburn, Graham and Offley.

---

21 The main British houses are the Symington Group that includes Dow, Warre and Graham amongst others, Taylor Fladgate who own Taylor, Fonseca, Croft and Delaforce, and Churchill Graham.

22 Despite being something of a joke in the wine world because of its 1970s connotations, it's actually quite nice.

Our boat was captained by George Sandeman dressed in a cloak and round his neck was a polished silver bowl. Originally this would have been used by British merchants to assess the quality of the wine when going up country. The wines that sold best on the British market were the strongest and the darkest, and so many merchants simply bought wine on colour. There was the perennial problem of adulteration as there simply wasn't enough high quality port to go round. This led to conflict between the British who set the price of the wine as they had a near monopoly when it came to shipping it, and the growers who wanted more money for their product. In imitation of good vintages, elderberries (*baga* in Portuguese and now the name of the very tannic dark grape variety from nearby region of Bairrada) would be added to boost the dark red colour and sugar was added to sweeten it and mask the taste of the elderberries.[23] The winemaker at Sandeman told me that up until quite recently it wasn't unusual for elderberries to be used. He added that in order for it to look as if the *lagaars* (stone troughs used for treading grapes) were full of grapes which take up much more space, they used dwarves to tread them.[24] The growers in turn insisted that it was the British who were adulterating the wine in their warehouses at Vila Nova de Gaia. Instead of elderberries even stronger wines such as Alicante would be added. Baron d'Archenholz, a German historian in the 18th century, wrote "it is their attachment to strong liquors that make them so very fond of port wine ... In London they liked everything that is powerful and heady." Certainly Bordeaux for the English market was usually adulterated.

---

23 This might be the origin of the grave insult used by the French in Monty Python's *Holy Grail* – "your mother was a hamster and your father smelt of elderberries" ie he adulterated wine, a grave insult coming from a Frenchman.

24 At the time I wrote this down virtuously, but on reflection I think he must have been pulling my leg. The Portuguese have a very dry sense of humour.

Whoever was doing the adulterating, and it appears that both parties were involved, the price and reputation of port collapsed.

The British refused to buy wine from the growers and wrote an angry letter accusing them of adulteration. The shippers were sitting on stocks of wine so were in no hurry to buy. The growers, fearing ruin, wrote to the Prime Minister of Portugal, Sebastião José de Carvalho e Melo, later the Marques of Pombal. His response was in 1756 to form the slightly long-winded Companhia Geral da Agricultura e Vinhos do Alto Douro. From henceforth farmers would sell their wine to the Company who would set the price and then sell it on to the shippers. The British merchants would only be allowed to ship wines to Britain or British colonies. The Company also set grades of wine: the top grade for export, the next best for Brazil and the cheapest for the home market. Pombal's next step was the most enduring in that he demarcated the boundaries of the port region. The French didn't come up with similar laws for their wine regions until 1935. Stone posts were erected around the borders of the region. It was a capital crime to bring in grapes from outside the region or grow elderberries. He also cannily made sure that his vineyards were within the demarcated region so that the wine would be worth more. Pombal's original boundaries have been extended today, but the original area is still the most prestigious. These reforms meant that the Company, as it was known, even had a monopoly on the brandy for fortification.

Pombal's reforms challenged the British monopoly and, as you might expect, the British merchants hated him for it. Rather than buy wine at rock bottom prices from growers, they had to buy at prices dictated to them by the Company. Many thought that the new regime would bankrupt them. Pombal ignored British complaints, the price of port went up, but port was now such a fixture at home that demand didn't slacken for a moment. Exports from Portugal boomed and it ushered in another golden age for port. Overall Pombal's reforms turned out to be a good thing for the shippers as it greatly improved quality of wine. Pombal, however, wasn't entirely honest and his policies did make him extremely wealthy. He became so powerful that he was for a while virtual dictator of Portugal and the prisons were overflowing with his enemies. He fell from favour when Queen Maria I took the throne in 1777 and he died in 1782.

The wines from Pombal's time would have been very different from modern port. For a start they would have been dry. It's hard to know exactly when port became sweet. There is a theory that the changeover happened because of the 1820 vintage which was a summer so hot that the grapes became so ripe that they never fermented fully. The resulting wines with their residual sugar were greatly appreciated in Britain.[25] Such was the demand for similar wines that growers began adding the brandy sooner to arrest fermentation just as the Portuguese priests were doing in the 17th century. Well into the 19th century debate raged about the nature of port. Joseph James Forrester wrote a paper decrying sweet port in 1844 called *A Word of Two on Port Wine, shewing how and why it is adulterated and affording some means of checking adulteration*. He complained that port is now a "nauseous, fiery compound of sweets, colours and alcohol". Forrester is a titanic figure in the history of port wine. He mapped the Douro, catalogued the different vines and, unusually for an Englishman, spoke excellent Portuguese. Until Forrester growers would have had no idea

---

25 There's an interesting parallel to this in California with the 1997 vintage. Because it was such a large crop, some grapes were left to hang on the vines because there wasn't space to process them. They became super ripe and the resulting wines were so popular with customers and certain critics that it became the accepted style for Californian wines. Previously Napa Cabernets were noted for their elegant Bordeaux-esque style; 97 ushered in the era of the blockbuster.

what sort of varieties they were growing. To this day some growers still grow grape varieties intermingled without knowing what they are. His broadside against the mixed quality and dubious practices of the industry made him extremely unpopular, but did little to change the direction port was heading. The oldest port I've ever had, an 1863 tawny from Taylor's, was definitely a sweet wine. Forrester later fell victim to the Douro rapids when the *rabelo* he was travelling in overturned and he drowned. Legend has it that it was his money belt that sank him and that his female companion, Dona Antonia Adelaide Ferreira,[26] was only saved by her enormous crinolines which enabled her to float down the river.

Port inveigled itself into the British consciousness like no other wine except perhaps claret. It influenced British attempts to grow grapes in the colonies, hence Australian "ports" which we will read about in a later chapter. For much of the 18th and 19th century wine in Britain was port. A look at the inventory of the wine cellar of a bookseller in Pall Mall called Robert Dodsley in the 1760s shows how dominant port had become. He has nearly ten times as much port as claret. Dodsley published Samuel Johnson's book *London* and invested in the dictionary. Johnson himself was an enormous port enthusiast: "I have drunk three bottles of port without being the worse for it. University College has witnessed this." Johnson's love of drinking port to excess was such that he eventually had to give up drinking it entirely and turned to tea. But Johnson's port consumption was nothing compared to some Georgians'. William Pitt the younger, the Prime Minister, would drink a bottle before giving a speech before the House of Commons. Drinking three bottles a day was not unusual. This does seem an extraordinary amount

---

26 Another great port house. They make a very good dry Douro red named in her honour.

of wine, but these were pint[27] bottles and the wine would not have been fortified as much as modern port. It would probably have been about 16 percent. It's still more than the British Medical Association would recommend, but it's certainly not as inconceivable as drinking three 75cl bottles of 20 percent wine. The prize for rowdiest port drinker goes to a Shropshire squire called John Mytton who drank between four and six bottles of port a day. He was thought to have been permanently drunk for most of his adult life. He once set fire to his nightshirt in order to cure hiccups. When he arrived at Cambridge University he took 2,000 bottles of port with him. He left without any port or a degree. Briefly MP for Shrewsbury, he was more famous for his drunken exploits. Mytton's biographer, Charles James Apperley, wrote: "He once rode this bear into his drawing-room, in full hunting costume. The bear carried him very quietly for a time; but on being pricked by the spur he bit his rider through the calf of his leg." Mytton died aged 37, his enormous inheritance nearly spent (mostly on port).

John Mytton riding a bear into a dinner party, by Henry Aiken

---

27 And the pint was smaller in those days. It would have been about the size of a modern American pint, 473ml, rather than an Imperial, 568ml.

The English love of port continued throughout the 19th century. Port found its way into songs. At the bottom end there was cheap ruby port drunk in pubs with lemonade which is certainly the drink referred to in the music hall song *Down at the Old Bull and Bush*,

> "Come, come, come and make eyes at me
> Down at the Old Bull and Bush.
> Come, come, drink some port wine with me
> Down at the Old Bull and Bush."

At the top end, vintage wines were being appreciated. Wellington, when he was in Portugal during the Peninsula War, dined with George Sandeman. They both drank the 1794, "the finest ever known" according to Sandeman. The 1815, known as the Waterloo vintage, was another famous one.

This appreciation of vintage wine was enabled by the evolution of the wine bottle. Digby's bottles, which had been shaped like an onion, then evolved into a squat, almost square, bottle and then into something like the modern form. These newer shapes could be laid on their sides so that the corks would be kept moist, necessary for long ageing. Heavily tannic alcoholic wine such as port softens and mellows over time in bottle. Port aficionados could buy a pipe of port, have it bottled and binned (placed in a designated compartment in their cellar) and then appreciate its evolution over time. The best wine's ability to change and improve in bottle would probably have been discovered by accident. But once enthusiasts discovered this property, wines were made specifically to be kept. All the ingredients were now in place for that most British of fine wines, vintage port. Here is P Morton Shand, an early 20th century writer and gourmand, on the subject:

> "A properly matured Port is rightly considered

unequalled as the test of the pretensions of a
county family to proper pride, patient manly
endurance, Christian self-denial, and true
British tenacity."

Port can mature in the bottle over a considerable number of
years. At the *rabelo* race I took part in, one of the crew had
brought from his own collection a bottle of 1935 Sandeman.
It tasted magnificent. It's really the most nostalgic of wines.
When my daughter was born in 2011, it happily coincided
with an excellent vintage. There's a case of Churchill under
the stairs waiting for her 21st birthday. I hope that she lets
me have a glass. This tradition of keeping and drinking
vintage port is still very much alive in Britain and America.
The next chapter in contrast looks at a wine with a history
as colourful as port and a strong British connection, but
that is almost completely forgotten today.

DRINKING THE EMPIRE

The Portuguese and the British remain separated by the kind
of ports they enjoy. The British worship at the altar of vintage
port whereas the Portuguese prefer a tawny. Tawnies are
aged long in wood until they take on nutty characteristics.
They are then blended and sold by age statements: 10, 20, 30
or 40 years. The younger ones combine youthful fruit with
a nutty character whereas the older ones are all about dried
fruit, tobacco and spicy flavours. A 20-year-old tawny from
a company such as Sandeman offers an amazing amount of
complexity for the money. Also to complicate matters you
can buy wines known as Colheitas which are from single
vintage, but aged in wood like tawnies. The Dutch house of
Niepoort specialise in these.

Vintage ports are only offered in exceptional years such

as 1985, 1977, 2011 etc. Generally the port houses agree on which year is a vintage, though some go rogue and release a year that no one else does such as Cockburn in 1978. For the proper vintage experience you should buy them young and keep them for at least 20 years, though some American collectors like to drink them young and indeed vintage ports are kind of amazing when you can still taste all that youthful fruit. The greatest examples of vintage port are generally considered to be Graham's, Taylor's, Fonseca and Dow's with Quinta do Noval's Nacional forming its own little group as the wines are made in tiny quantities and incredibly expensive.

Highly regarded old wines from top producers eg Taylor's 45 are also expensive, but generally ready-aged vintage port is surprisingly affordable and, because it is fortified (and therefore stable), you stand a much better chance of getting a good bottle.

Other categories of port:

Ruby
These are made up of a blend of cheaper wines. The best, like Sandeman's Ruby, are simple, sweet and fruity.

Reserve
Ruby port with some older wines blended in and consequently have a little leather about them. Fonseca Bin 27 is consistently one of the best.

Late Bottle Vintage
Port from a single year, aged for at least four years in wood and sold ready to drink. Some aren't that different to reserve ports, but others have some real vintage character, will improve with age and need decanting as they are not filtered. Churchill's is a particularly good example.

Crusted Ports

These aren't seen very often. They're a blend of years and bottled unfiltered with the year of bottling on the label. They improve with age and, as the name suggests, form a crust and need decanting. The Wine Society is one of the few merchants who still sell this style.

Single Quinta Ports

Vintage ports from a single vineyard (quinta). They function as second labels for the port houses and are generally released in years when a proper vintage is not released. They're normally approachable at about ten years of age. Graham's Quinta dos Malvedos can be excellent.

Finally I should mention that the table wines of the Douro are remarkably good. They are some of the most distinctive wines around and quality is high. Casa Ferreirinha, the table wine arm of Ferreira, offers a full range right from budget Esteva to the stratospherically expensive Reserva Especial and Barca Velha. Perhaps Forrester was thinking of wines such as these when he campaigned against sweet fortified port. Other good names include Quinta do Crasto, Churchill, Poeira and Niepoort. Most of the port houses now have a table wine arm.

3

PURITANS!

It is perhaps an irony that in 1644 the great puritan, Cromwell, lowered the duty on spirits imposed by the Scottish Parliament. Furthermore it was Cromwell who agreed the 1654 treaty with Portugal, being the unwitting instigator of the trade in a highly alcoholic wine, port. But puritans would not have shunned wine, only an excess of wine. Cromwell himself apparently liked a drink. There is a good story, perhaps apocryphal, of Cromwell getting drunk at his daughter's wedding, throwing wine around and dancing until dawn. Puritans were mainly puritanical about religion: they wanted to remove any trace of Popishness from the church. They were also puritanical about sex, dancing, theatre and lewd behaviour in general. However, they were generally pretty relaxed about alcohol. John Milton, the poet laureate of Commonwealth, wrote a paean to the joys of beer in *L'Allegro*:

> "And young and old come forth to play
> On a sunshine holiday,
> Till the live-long day-light fail;
> Then to the Spicy Nut-brown Ale."

Methodists now shun alcohol but the founder of the movement, John Wesley, drank wine and was a beer connoisseur. His brother Charles Wesley, author of some of the finest hymns in the English language, was famous for his fine cellar. The stereotype of the tight-lipped unsmiling Calvinist is an enduring one, yet John Calvin himself wrote, "We are nowhere forbidden to laugh, or to be satisfied with food ... or to be delighted with music, or to drink wine."

The first crisis of the Pilgrim Fathers when they arrived in America was that they didn't have any beer to drink. They immediately set about trying to brew something out of the native flora. John Winthrop, founder of Massachusetts, landed at Salem in the *Arabella*, a ship groaning under the weight of forty-two tonnes of beer. Drunkenness was frowned upon by religious New Englanders; punishment for overindulgence included wearing a D around your neck or a day in the stocks, but alcohol per se wasn't. Rum was a currency in colonial America. The American Revolution started in a tavern. Benjamin Franklin wrote: "Behold the rain which descends from heaven upon our vineyards, there it enters the roots of the vines, to be changed into wine, a constant proof that God loves us, and loves to see us happy." This is now normally misquoted as "Beer is proof that God loves us and wants us to be happy".

The link between Protestantism and abstinence is actually a recent one. It has its roots in the temperance movement of the 19th century. Nowadays many Protestant sects especially in America consider alcohol un-Christian. They even have a school of pseudo-scholarship designed to prove that Jesus wouldn't have drunk wine. It's something to do with there being many Hebrew words for wine and some of them also mean unfermented grape juice. How this grape juice was stored in the days before refrigeration so that it didn't either ferment or turn to vinegar is not explained. It would have been much easier and healthier just to let it turn to wine. Jesus was, of course, a Jew and there's no tradition of abstinence in Judaism. Unlike many other things, the message from the Bible on alcohol is pretty clear and consistent: drink good, drunkenness bad. Puritans took the Bible literally which is why Winthrop, Milton et al were all happy to have a drink or two, or in Cromwell's case, nine.

4

MARSALA, NELSON'S WINE

From the top of the tower I could see right across the vineyards of Marsala, across to the Mediterranean and the nearby island of Mozia. The tower I was standing on was built, according to its present owner, Giacomo Ansaldi, by the Spanish in the fifteenth century. It was used to keep a look out for "Saracenas" – pirates from North Africa. Marsala in Sicily is only about 100 miles from the coast of North Africa. The tower had been built into a fortified courtyard known as a *baglio*. The word has the same derivation as the English word "bailey", as in a mott and bailey castle. It now generally means a winery. Just as in Bordeaux, a winery is also a castle. The *baglio* I was standing on, now known as the Baglio Donna Franca, used to belong to one of the largest producers of marsala wine, Vicenzo Florio. The Florio company would have had *baglios* like this all over western Sicily to harvest grapes and make wine that would be sent to Marsala, blended, fortified and then exported around the world. I was so captivated by the view across the sea that I didn't notice in the foreground a peculiar looking ruined building until Giacomo pointed it out. With its elegant Georgian lines, it looked for all the world like a chunk of Regency Bath had been dropped onto the parched earth. This was the ruins of a *baglio* that belonged to the firm of Woodhouse, another big marsala firm, now defunct. Giacomo wants to buy and renovate it just as he had Donna Franca, but it's owned by at least twenty people and trying to negotiate with all of them has proved impossible. According to Giacomo some of the owners would rather see it ruined than have someone else make money from it. Having had this particular ruined *baglio* pointed out to me, for the rest of my trip I noticed ruined *baglios* dotted all over Trapani province.

An experience like this functions as a lesson in Sicilian history: standing in a Spanish tower amongst the vineyards, that was used as a look-out for Muslim pirates, with a Sicilian winemaker whilst all around are the decayed relics of a once prosperous and now moribund industry. There's a lot of decline in Sicilian history. The great Sicilian novel *The Leopard* by Giuseppe Tomasi di Lampedusa is about the declining powers of an old aristocrat and indeed the declining powers of the old aristocracy. Sicily is like that; it's a melancholy place. Parts of Palermo look like the Second World War only ended recently, there are bridges that lead nowhere, and the main road from Corleone to Agrigento suddenly peters out into a dusty track as if it has been stolen by the Mafia. It was ever thus: "How lamentable to see so fine an island so totally neglected!" wrote W H Thompson in his book, *Sicily and its Inhabitants. Observations Made During a Residence in that Country, in the Years 1809 and 1810.*

As the largest island in the Mediterranean, Sicily has had more than its fair share of invaders. It has been fought over and ruled at various times by Greeks, Romans, Arabs, Byzantines, Normans, Catalans, Spaniards, Venetians, Neapolitans and, following conquest in 1860, became part of the new country of Italy. Sicily's many rulers, invaders and colonists have left their legacy around the island, in the buildings (the great Norman[28] cathedral at Monreale is a good example, built for a Norman king by Greek and

---

28 The Norman period when Sicily was ruled by Roger I is seen as the golden age. The decline set in from then on.

Arab craftsmen), in the food, and in the language. "Marsala" means Port of Allah; the classic local dish is couscous with fish. Sicilian, the language, is quite different from Tuscan (standard) Italian containing as it does elements of Greek, Arabic, Spanish and Catalan.

Sicily was the breadbasket of Rome, vital for keeping the mob placated. Later it was one of the centres for pasta production. The first place in Italy where the process was industrialised. Before the Neapolitans, the Sicilians were the first *mangia maccheroni* (macaroni-eaters). Messina was one of the great ports of the Mediterranean before trade shifted to the Atlantic in the 17th century. Sulphur, lemons and *barilla*, a plant derivative used in the making of washing powder, have all been major industries.

The British were here only very briefly in the late 18th and 19th centuries, but then there was talk of Sicily becoming a British colony like Malta or Cyprus. "It would be the jewel in the Empire crown after Ireland", as one notable remarked, which seems bitterly ironic considering how British rule in Ireland is remembered. There's very little to see to remind visitors of the time when the island was occupied by the British beyond some ruins dotted across western Sicily, but you can taste it in marsala wine.

The marsala story traditionally starts in 1773 with the arrival of a merchant from Liverpool called John Woodhouse. Apparently he was there to trade in *barilla* but some say that he was actually looking for wine to export. Either way he tried the local wine and noticed a similarity with madeira and, being a canny Scouser, saw an opportunity. In the 18th century madeira was big business. There was huge demand for madeira-style wines, not least from America, and growers and producers were struggling to keep up. A great quantity of ersatz madeira was made in Cyprus, South Africa, Australia and Sicily. This was how marsala was first sold to the world, as Sicilian madeira, rather than on its own terms. To ensure the safe journey back to England, Woodhouse fortified it with brandy, two litres per hundred of wine. He sent 8,000 gallons back to Liverpool in 1773.

Sicilians, however, would say that the marsala story starts long before the arrival of John Woodhouse because the Marsalans had been making a unique style of wine since antiquity. It was known as *vino perpetuo* or everlasting wine. It would have been made mainly from Catarrato and/or Inzolia white grapes, though red grapes may have been used too.[29] It was made by topping up barrels of wine with the newest vintage so the wine was continuously blended. A little space was left in the top of the barrel so the wine would gently oxidise and develop flavours of almonds. The resulting wine would contain minute quantities of very old wine. It may have also been sweetened with *mosto cotto* – cooked, unfermented grape must. It certainly would not have been fortified until the British came along. In fact, it is unlikely whether this proto-marsala would have actually needed fortifying to preserve it for the sea voyage to England, seeing as it was quite strong and already partially oxidised. Woodhouse may just have added brandy because that's how his customers expected their wine. Giacomo Ansaldi keeps a nursery of old unfortified marsala in his cellar at the Baglio Donna Franca. He let me try some from a barrel started in 1957 by an old farmer who wanted a wine to pass on to his grandchildren, but they're now pursuing professional careers in the north of Italy and don't have the space or interest to look after an enormous *botte* (traditional Italian barrel holding about 1,000 litres of wine though they

---

29 The classic marsala grape, Grillo (meaning cricket – the insect not the sport), is relatively recent. It was created by crossing Catarrato Bianco and Muscat of Alexandria (known as Zbiddo in Sicily). It is now the only one used in the best marsalas.

can be much bigger) of old wine. The smell filled the room, initially a little musty and then almonds and spiced oranges. It didn't taste like marsala, but instead was more like a very old table wine. There was none of the caramel or alcoholic burn that I'd come to expect from marsala. It was fascinating to try a wine that Woodhouse would have recognised on his first trip to Sicily.

The great ingredient, however, that the British brought to marsala was not brandy but capitalism. As Giacomo Ansaldi put it to me, "the British were experts in the market, the Sicilians were sleeping". He was echoing *The Leopard* here, perhaps consciously:

> "Sleep, my dear Chevalley, eternal sleep, that
> is what Sicilians want. And they will always
> resent anyone who tries to awaken them, even
> to bring them the most wonderful of gifts."

And indeed the British were resented at the time and there are still traces of that resentment when one speaks to some marsala producers.

In 1787 Woodhouse's 21-year-old son, also called John, came out to Sicily. He too noted the similarity to Madeira not just in the wines, but also in the soil and the climate. Confusingly John Woodhouse the younger was later known as Old John or Il Vecchio. He founded the Baglio[30] Woodhouse in Marsala, taking over an old tunnery – tuna packing plant. Woodhouse (junior) seems to have been homosexual: there are sly references in letters from business rivals to him taking a shine to certain handsome men who worked for him. He also had a penchant for getting drunk on his own supply, stripping naked and running through

---

30 Baglio refers here not to a fortified winery but to a wine cellar rather like a Lodge in Oporto or Bodega in Jerez.

the vineyards around Marsala, which rather bemused the natives. There's a bust of him at the Baglio Florio in Marsala. Contrary to such behaviour, he looks a stern, joyless sort, like someone's idea of Ebenezer Scrooge. He died in 1826 at the age of 52, but looked much older. The gout had taken its toll and in his last few years he hardly ate at all. At his death he was severely emaciated.

Even with John Woodhouse's entrepreneurial flair marsala might have remained a local speciality if events had not intervened. The French Revolution of 1789 brought about an intensification of the long war − a war that had raged intermittently since 1688 − between Britain and France. The French revolutionary armies and the later Imperial armies under Napoleon destroyed all before them. By 1810 almost all of mainland Europe was either under direct French control, controlled by puppet states or forced into an alliance with the great man. Napoleon was triumphant on land but Britain still ruled the waves. The Berlin decree of 21 November 1806 set up the Continental System which barred anywhere in Europe from buying British goods. It proved almost impossible to enforce. In fact, trying to enforce the unworkable system led Napoleon to invade first the Iberian Peninsula and later Russia. In trying to strangle Britain's empire of trade Napoleon would sow the seeds for his own downfall.

In order to break Napoleon's dominance, Britain needed to keep control of the Mediterranean. She held Gibraltar, Minorca and Malta, and could trade through Salonika and Constantinople in the Ottoman Empire. Sicily, as it had been throughout its history, was of vital strategic importance. It was also important as a source of lemons needed by the Royal Navy to combat scurvy. At the outbreak of the Napoleonic Wars, Sicily was ruled by one of the Bourbon family (the same royal family as the unfortunate Louis XVI): King Ferdinand I, known as "the nose" on account of his amazing Bourbon nose. His wife Maria Carolina was the sister of another unfortunate, Marie Antoinette of France. As you can imagine, they weren't very keen on revolutionary France. They ruled from Naples and took very little interest in affairs across the water in Sicily.

In 1799 a French force invaded Naples in support of a Jacobin government. Though many Neapolitans supported this so-called Parthenopean Republic, it was in effect a puppet regime. Horatio Nelson was in Naples at the time enjoying his celebrity and his affair with Lady Hamilton, the wife of the British consul. In contrast to Lady Venetia Stanley, from the portraits of Lady Hamilton in her prime, it's quite easy to see her appeal. She seems to have bewitched every man she met. Goethe, echoing Enobarbus's description of Cleopatra in Shakespeare's *Antony and Cleopatra*, has this to say about her performing in a play:

> "One beholds these in perfection, in
> movement, in ravishing variety, all that the
> greatest artists have rejoiced in being able
> to produce. Standing, kneeling, sitting, lying
> down, grave or sad, playful, exulting, repentant,
> wanton, menacing, anxious – all mental states
> follow rapidly one after the other."

Nelson was at the height of his celebrity at the time having just defeated a French fleet at the battle of the Nile. When the French invaded, the Bourbon king and his court fled across the Straits of Messina to their other capital at Palermo. Naples was swiftly retaken by Neapolitan forces abetted by Nelson who blockaded the city. Sadly Nelson then behaved rather badly and had many of the Jacobins executed including, after a show trial in front of Neapolitan troops, Admiral Caracciolo, who he had hanged from the yardarm of his own ship, the *Minerva*. Questions were asked in Parliament in London about Nelson's conduct. One notable Whig, Charles James Fox, referred to "the atrocities at the Bay of Naples".

For his loyalty to Ferdinand, the Bourbon king, Nelson was made Duke of Bronte in Sicily. He wore the badge displaying the honour at Trafalgar; you can see it on his coat at the Maritime Museum in Greenwich. Bronte was a small and rather impoverished town near Mount Etna in the east of Sicily and Nelson did not visit often. In this sense he acted like the perfect Sicilian absentee landlord. The Naples episode brings out a side to Nelson that we don't often hear about. We think of him as the brave and inspiring leader of men from the Nile and Trafalgar, the saviour of Britain and the face on a thousand pub signs. In southern Italy, Nelson was petulant, vain, cruel and his very public affair with Lady Hamilton whilst his wife and children remained in England made him extremely unpopular, not least with his wife.

George Romney – sketch of Emma Hamilton

This is just a sideshow, however, to the really interesting part of Nelson's time in Naples and Sicily. In 1798, just after the Battle of the Nile, Nelson met John Woodhouse (the younger) in Naples. He records the meeting in his diary and ordered two hundred pipes (each holds about 550 litres) of Woodhouse's marsala wine. He signed the contract for the wine "Nelson Bronte" in a rather shaky script as he was writing with his left hand since he'd lost his right at the Battle of Tenerife. It proved a lucrative market for Woodhouse. The Royal Navy's normal supplies of madeira and rum had been disrupted by the war. The two men also became friends. They must have made an odd pair, the dour businessman Woodhouse who detested parties and frivolity and Nelson the libertine hero. John Woodhouse named one of his houses in Liverpool "Bronte", after Nelson. Nelson wrote to his superior Lord Keith extolling the virtues of marsala: "The wine is so good that any gentleman's table might receive it, and it will be of real use for our seaman... "

Whereas port was the product of long-term diplomacy, marsala was created by strategic expediency. Woodhouse was canny in promoting his association with Nelson. Up until the 1920s white marsala for the British market was known as Bronte Nelson just as port producers made much of the Wellington connection and the 1815 vintage. In fact, when Woodhouse heard of the victory at Waterloo, he set aside one solera of the finest wines for VIPs which he christened "Waterloo". The names of other great Woodhouse soleras show his gift for marketing – Nelson, Vergine, Garibaldi, Trinacria and IP (Italian Particular – the cheapest sort). The Royal Navy bought both marsala and red wines from eastern Sicily which were fortified to make a sort of Sicilian port.

Woodhouse's success paved the way for other British businessmen to come out to Sicily. The greatest of them was Benjamin Ingham who arrived in Marsala in 1806. He was from a little town in Yorkshire just outside Leeds called

Ossett. His namesake and relative founded a Methodist sect, the Inghamites, who are still going in parts of America. Ironically, considering how Benjamin Ingham made his money, the Inghamites are teetotal. Ingham arrived on the island just after the British occupation. He was partner in the family firm and he was there to sell woollens (of course – it's what British traders always turned up with and were often bemused when the hot climate natives didn't want to buy). He was completely captivated on his arrival in Palermo.[31] He described the setting of the city as "more beautiful than the Garden of Hesperides". It must certainly have been a sight after grimy old Leeds. By this stage, Ingham was trading on his own account as well as the family business, and not just wine but also *barilla*, sumac, olive oil, citrus fruit, rags and sulphur. In early paintings he looks quite the Regency dandy with his fashionable haircut growing over his ears, but in later pictures he cuts a more severe figure, looking more like a no-nonsense Yorkshire mill owner. Like Woodhouse, Benjamin Ingham had no children though not for the same reason as Old John. It seems that Ingham was not romantically successful, having been spurned not once but twice. Later in life he eventually married a Sicilian aristocrat, Duchess of Rosalina, but had no children. Instead he employed a series of nephews bearing both the names Ingham and Whitaker – his sister Mary married a Joseph Whitaker. There's a story, possibly apocryphal, that when one of these nephews, William Whitaker, died in 1818, Ingham wrote to the boy's mother saying, "your son is dead, send me another". The letter, if it ever did, no longer exists.

---

31 Sadly it's now hard to imagine the beauty of old Palermo. It was destroyed first by Allied bombs during the War and then by the Mafia during a building boom afterwards known as the so-called Rape of Palermo. It's still a city crammed with fascinating buildings in a dramatic natural setting, but it's lost its harmony especially compared with its great rival in the east of the island, Catania.

Ingham may not have been successful romantically but he was a businessman of genius. He involved himself in every aspect of marsala from grape-growing to winemaking. His brother Joshua went to Spain and Portugal to learn about how to make fortified wine. Ingham built up the export business, not just to Britain, but to America and the Empire. Unlike in Oporto or Jerez where the merchants remained solidly middle class, the Inghams and the Whitakers became fabulously wealthy. The Whitakers are still a wealthy family in England, their fortune all stemming from Benjamin Ingham's hard work. There are country houses in England that bear the name Whitaker. The Giuseppe Whitaker Foundation of Palermo owns the island of Mozia which I could see from the Baglio Donna Franca.

In 1809 Benjamin Ingham visited Boston. As with madeira, America became a major market for marsala. Inevitably Thomas Jefferson has something to say about it:

"I received that Hogshead of Marsala wine you
were so kind to send me ... I perceive it to be
an excellent wine, and well worthy of being laid
in stocks to acquire age."

The nephew of Benjamin Ingham, also called Benjamin Ingham, wrote to his uncle in 1837: "Barclay and Livingstone (their New York agents) sell more wine, sale on commission than any other ten houses here." Ingham invested heavily in the US. He owned three percent of the New York Central Railroad valued at $23 million. When he died his estate was worth £9 million (about £1 billion in today's money depending on how it is calculated). Ingham had his own ships, one being the first to bring spices directly by sea to Sicily from the Far East.

The French invaded Naples again in 1806 and Napoleon placed his brother Joseph on the throne. So, from 1806, until Napoleon was defeated in 1815, Sicily came under direct British rule. A French writer, Louis Simond, wrote about Sicily under the British occupation:

"The English, it must be acknowledged, have left here no honourable monument of a power paramount to sovereignty ... the roads, the prisons, the hospitals, the corrupt and barbarous administration of justice, remained just in as wretched state as before they interfered. It is true they saved the island from French dominion; from the violence and plunder which attended it at Naples and in Calabria; they kept strict discipline; they paid honestly and liberally for all they had; but they did not mix cordially with the people. The continued meddling, teaching, ruling, with a high hand and a supercilious pride, till all classes were tired out; and yet all classes regret them, simply because they saved them from Naples for a while."

All sounds very reminiscent of the British in Portugal and Madeira, but it's not entirely fair. The British merchants, at least, did mix with the Sicilians. Unlike in Portugal, there wasn't really enough of a colony for the British to remain aloof. As we've seen, Ingham married a local, and various Whitakers also married Sicilians. The Inghams and Whitakers all spoke Italian, Ingham with a strong Sicilian accent. Ingham was made a Baron and identified himself as Sicilian. A note sent by sulphur mine owners and merchants protesting against duty on sulphur has Ingham's name is on it, the only British one, because he genuinely saw himself as Sicilian.

Simond is also wrong about the British investment in infrastructure. Before the British occupation there were only 250 miles of roads suitable for carriages on the whole island. People travelled around by *lettigas*, odd-looking sedan chair type things strung between two mules. They made the traveller extremely sick. There were the usual tales of terrible roads (and terrible inns and bedbugs and fleas etc.)

that will be familiar to readers from the Portuguese chapters (there should be a sub-genre of history, the uncomfortable inn travel writings) so the British invested in a proper road being built from Palermo to Messina, across the north coast of the island. John Woodhouse started an agrarian revolution in the west of Sicily. Ingham lent money to local farmers to plant grapes on land that had previously been used for wheat or lemons. Unlike the British in Madeira, who just bought the ready-made wine and sold it on, the Inghams were involved with all aspects of viticulture and winemaking. Ingham even wrote a book on viticulture. They built roads and a long jetty at Marsala. This was the same jetty that Italian nationalist leader Garibaldi landed at in 1860 with a thousand men all dressed in red shirts known as The Thousand. Much to the world's amazement he succeeded in conquering the island, overthrowing the Bourbon rulers and eventually united Italy under Piedmontese rule. Whilst in Marsala, Garibaldi sampled the wines and rather let the side down by preferring the sweetest marsala to the dry ones loved by the cognoscenti. Even now one of the cheapest marsalas you can buy is called the Garibaldi dolce and is from Cantine Pellegrino. It was something of a boom time for the island. Due to the needs of the Royal Navy, marsala became big business and some Sicilians even hoped that Sicily would become a British colony (which gives you some idea of how misruled the island had been that being a colony seemed a better option).

It was Lord William Bentinck, commander of British forces in Sicily, Plenipotentiary and Envoy Extraordinary, who I quoted earlier about Sicily becoming the new Ireland. The comparison between Sicily and Ireland is a good one. They were both neglected by the colonising power, the British or the Neapolitans, but also by the native aristocracy who preferred to play rather than manage their estates properly. Before the British left in 1816 and handed the island back to the Bourbons, Lord Bentinck imposed a constitution on the island that would abolish feudalism, guarantee the rights of the Sicilians and give them a good degree of autonomy. It was quickly suspended by Ferdinand when he regained the throne. He was always suspicious of the British community and their designs on his island. Following the quiet of British rule, Sicily became extremely turbulent. There were revolutions in 1820 and 1848 – when Ferdinand was forced briefly to give up the island. There were major outbreaks of lawlessness and disease. For example, the 1837 cholera outbreak in Palermo led to over 40,000 deaths. There were then riots directed mainly against the hated Neapolitans who were thought to have caused the outbreak and which led to another eighty deaths. The resulting clampdown by the authorities brought another hundred and fifty fatalities. During these periods of instability and terror, gunships would arrive in Palermo from Britain, America and France and take aboard the expats from those respective countries until things quietened down and business could resume. The British community tried to keep a low profile during periods of unrest. During the 1848 revolution Joseph Whitaker sent his wife Sofia and their children to Malta for their safety.

The British were sympathetic to the Sicilians' cause. Ingham wrote: "the Neapolitans have been too long accustomed to oppress and squeeze out of her every dollar they can, to relinquish the power that they have over her. Hence the poverty and wretchedness to which the country has been reduced." And yet they were businessmen, so preferred the oppressive peace of Bourbon rule to the potential anarchy of Sicilian. As such they were treated with some suspicion by the native population who felt that the British had encouraged them in their yearning for self-rule – or perhaps as Lampedusa suggests, they were just angry at having been woken up – through the constitution, but had then done nothing to support them once they did rise up.

It's a familiar story which is repeated again and again right up until the present day.

And yet despite all the unrest, the marsala trade boomed and Ingham's nephews founded an Anglo-Sicilian dynasty. Fortunes were made and the great marsala families were not afraid of spending their wealth either. Mansions were built and great balls were held with hundreds of guests. You can see how big the marsala business became by looking at the present-day harbour front at Marsala. Looking out to sea one can see the enormous jetty built by the British where Garibaldi landed. Turning the other way, the most striking building is the vast Florio warehouse. There are barrels of all shapes and sizes up to the ceiling. One monster is the size of a house and was built for the 1915 San Francisco World Fair. From the outside the building looks very Italian with its white stucco and shutters, but it is in fact built in a hybrid Moorish/British style, Moorish because it uses traditional Arab techniques to channel cold air from the sea into the warehouse to keep the barrels cool. The limestone floor absorbs moisture so the air is dry. Unlike madeira, marsala is generally stored somewhere cool. The floor may be Moorish, but above the arches are pure Gothic like one might find in an Oxford college. To the left of the gleaming Florio building is an enormous, ornate, dilapidated, yellow stone building. This was the Baglio Woodhouse. On the other side, the building with the tall chimney was the Baglio Ingham. The entire harbour front – about two miles – was devoted to warehouses of marsala wine. The Florio warehouses alone stretched over half a mile. The present cellars, vast as they are, are much smaller than the original operation. There is something of Ozymandias about the crumbling Woodhouse warehouse at Marsala – "look on my works yea mighty and despair." Now it is only Florio left.

The decline in the demand for marsala wasn't really the fault of the younger Whitakers. Even if another Benjamin

Ingham had come along, the marsala market would probably have deteriorated anyway. As with madeira and sherry, the producers reacted to fluctuations in the market by creating a cheaper product through planting inferior grape varieties, over-cropping, irrigating and then sweetening heavily to mask deficiencies in the base wine and lack of ageing. Cooked grape must with its caramel colour and flavour is a poor substitute for slow ageing with oxygen. Marsala went from being a wine created in the vineyard to a product made according to a recipe. Most still is. The Florio family sold out to Cinzano in 1924, the Whitakers and the Woodhouses in 1927. The low point came in 1969 when wines flavoured with eggs, almonds and bananas were allowed to be sold as marsala. Marsala is now only widely available in debased form as a sweetened liqueur wine used in Italian cookery. Say the word "marsala" now to most British people and they will think of Chicken Tikka Masala. Some might dimly be aware of something sticky essential to 1970s dinner party stalwarts, tiramisu or zabaglione. Americans will know it from such classic American Italian dishes as chicken in marsala sauce.

We can mourn the decline of these wines, but people nowadays just don't have the taste for oxidised wines. They like fresh, fruity wines, the sort of wines that are a product of refrigeration rather than oxidation. Port, sherry and madeira are never going to be big business again, but at least they've kept their reputations. Marsala's reputation has gone. Or almost has. Even in Italy, real marsala is rare. This makes it all the more appealing for me: a wine that one can read about, but not actually try. In the internet age, one can have an opinion on film, books and even paintings, from the comfort of one's armchair, but with wine, you cannot really understand until you taste. Wines that are obscure or hard to find build up a certain mythology. There are still a few producers making something like the real thing. One is

Florio, who makes a vergine (unsweetened) wine from 100 percent Grillo called Terre Arse.[32] I brought a bottle back from Sicily in the distant past when you were allowed to carry wine in your hand luggage. I think it cost me about eight euros. I was amazed by its nutty, exotic flavour.

Even better are the wines of Marco De Bartoli.[33] He was a member of another great marsala family, the Pelligrinos, but he hated what had happened to the wine he loved so he set up his own business in 1980. Like Giacomo Ansaldi he was able to buy up stocks of good old wines cheaply. Mr De Bartoli had a grudge against the British for ruining his native wine by sweetening and fortifying it. He's not alone: writing in 1833 the Duke of Buckingham stated that the wine

> "is good in itself though very much injured by
> the quantities of brandy which they put in it
> both for the British and American markets".

The British influence in Sicily has proved ephemeral and once those ruined Baglios crumble it will be impossible to discern. And marsala wine may well also die out soon. The Grillo grape, which makes the majority of marsalas, is now mainly used in the production of dry, modern, white wines which bear a certain similarity with the Albariño from northern Spain. The big Sicilian marsala firms, Florio, Pellegrino and Rallo, make the majority of their money from table wines. De Bartoli, now under the management of the children following the death of Marco in 2011, are the only producer making marsala in the traditional manner: hand-harvested grapes from their own estate, solera ageing and

32 LOL

33 There's a pleasing connection to Florio here as Marco De Bartoli was a car enthusiast and raced in the Targa Florio, the race founded by Vincenzo Florio in 1906, winning his class in the 1972 race driving a Lancia Fulvia.

no cooked grape must. Even they make most of their money from table wines, but theirs are a little bit different from the norm. I tried a 2011 Grappoli de Grillo from them recently. Imagine a white burgundy slowly morphing into a very light amontillado sherry and you're almost there. It was quite superb and so distinctly Sicilian. I felt like the future of a unique Marsalan wine is safe in De Bartoli's hands, even if traditional marsala dies out.

DRINKING THE EMPIRE

Where bureaucracy and Italy collide the results will always be complicated and, indeed, the various types of marsala are not easy to grasp. I'm not going to go through them all, but instead offer a few tips for buying. Vergine means unsweetened, the only thing added will be brandy. These are normally the best kind as there's no room for producers to cover up faults in the base wine by adding sugar. Superiore wines are sweetened and aged for at least two years and Superiore Riserva for at least four years. With all the logic you would expect, Fine is the worst sort and semi-secco is actually sweet. Here are a few good producers:

Florio
Along with Pellegrino, Florio is the best commercial marsala house. It now doesn't own any vineyards and so buys in all the grapes. The premium wines are all vintage rather than being a blend of vintages as is traditional in marsala. I tried the 2000 Terre Arse (literally burnt lands – a good description of Sicily in August) recently, with a name like this you can see why it's not more popular in Britain. It's a lot of wine for the money with notes of cinnamon, orange and lots of almonds. A couple of drops of this adds remarkable depth to sauces. I'd also recommend another vergine, Baglio

Florio. This is every inch the luxury product. It's exceedingly rich. In fact, it tastes more like a cognac than a wine.

Pellegrino

This company make the ubiquitous Garibaldi Marsala Dolce which is fine for cooking, but they also do some very good vergine wines. The vintage-dated and the solera vergines are worth trying, but the Riserva del Centenario really is exceptional. I tried the 1980 and I was impressed by its concentration and harmony.

De Bartoli

De Bartoli's signature product is a wine that he claimed reflects Marsala's pre-British wines. It is called Vecchio Samperi and because it's not fortified he's not allowed to call it marsala. Instead it's sold as a *vino liquoroso*, which it isn't. It has the most wonderful aroma of oranges, spices, caramel and vanilla. It smells sweet, but it's very very dry, and much lighter and more delicate, than you'd expect. There's some lemon and orange, lots of freshness and then a taste of almonds that goes on forever. De Bartoli do a full range of fortified wines and some excellent table wines from the Grillo grape. Mr Bartoli's opinion of British tastes was so low that for a time he refused to export his wines to these shores. He died in 2011; his children are continuing to make marsala in the time-honoured fashion, albeit without their father's gift for controversy.

5

LE STYLE ANGLAIS

A familiar sight at wine tastings in London is the dapper figure of Javier Hidalgo from the sherry family of the same name. I asked him where he had his suit made, a natty Prince of Wales check three piece complete with pocket watch and chain. He told me that he buys the cloth in Scotland and has it made by his tailor in Seville. This sort of sartorial elegance is pretty much mandatory in the sherry business. The head winemaker at González-Byass, Antonio Flores Pedregosa, sported a light tweed jacket when I met him on a recent trip to Jerez. I was in Jerez for the annual Feria, originally a horse fair but now the one time a year when the Jerezanos get drunk. I noticed that the women wore traditional Andalucian dresses but the men all looked like swarthy Bertie Woosters resplendent in tweed, cream trousers and spotty ties despite the 36 degree heat.

Port shippers and Bordeaux merchants follow a similar dress code. The more aristocratic Tuscan producers too. In fact, the wine trade in general is one of the last holdouts for *Le Style Anglais*, that idealised version of English fashion developed in and around St James's, London. It consists of shirts from Jermyn Street, shoes from Church's, suits from Savile Row and a tweed jacket with red or mustard yellow trousers from Cordings of Piccadilly. At wine tastings in London often the most English dressers are the Portuguese and the Spanish. One of the most charming things about *Le*

Style Anglais is how the Europeans get it slightly wrong – everything is too new and too sharply cut with not enough smell of a dog blanket in the boot of a Volvo 240 estate. This uniform is a throwback to when the British dominated the global wine trade so it was fashionable to ape their look. In 18th century Porto some of the locals even affected speaking Portuguese with a British accent. Until very recently it seems that the British hold on the dress code of the trade was absolute. If you were in London selling your wine then suits or tweed ruled. Generally wine merchants are much better dressed than, say, journalists or publishers.

There are those, however, who see *Le Style Anglais* as evidence that the wine trade is too male, too stuffy, too out of touch. The red trouser is the symbol of that most reviled of species, the wine snob. *The Daily Telegraph* wine writer Victoria Moore explicitly outlined this in a column on the new wave wine merchants. She wrote that the wine trade has traditionally been "a bastion of red trousers and thick third sons". In New York the prestigious distributor Martin Scott Wines has recently ditched its dress code. Sales staff previously had to wear a jacket and tie, but now this is thought to be positively off-putting to a new generation of wine buyers.

In contrast to the stuffiness of the proverbial wine snob, the trendiness of some wine shops or bars these days can be like visiting a trendy record shop from my youth and no less intimidating. Some wines are cool and some aren't. For some, scruffy attire is a sign of egalitarianism. Now nobody likes equality more than me, but I wouldn't like to see the wine trade lose one of its most distinctive features. The big trade tastings held in London in the spring and autumn are a glorious time for red trouser and tweed spotting. It's a joy to watch men who dress with a sense of style and wit. When the trade get together, you can see how delighted some are to be around like-minded and like-dressed people. Long may this tradition continue.

6

THE DEVIL'S DRINK

One of the customers at the wine merchant I worked at in Headingley in Yorkshire would come in every day and buy two cans of Guinness and a half bottle of Captain Morgan rum. He would then sit on a bench opposite and drink. I suppose he was what's euphemistically known as a "street drinker" but he was always unfailingly polite and, despite the amount he drank, never seemed drunk. Indeed when his companion, who we dubbed Mr Belisha Beacon because of the way his head would light up after a few, caused a scene by standing in the middle of the road shouting, he would look embarrassed at this undignified behaviour. He was a favourite customer, not least for the outlandish stories he told about being in Naval prison with the manager of the shop. With his weatherbeaten skin, haphazard teeth and penchant for rum, it wasn't difficult to imagine him in the Royal Navy, though Nelson's Navy rather than the modern service. We called him Captain Morgan after his favourite tipple, but we learned later that his name was actually Rodney. Which is apt because there's another make of rum called Admiral Rodney named after a contemporary of Nelson's. Like Nelson, such was Rodney's renown that his surname became a Christian name. Both Nelson and Rodney are still popular names in the Caribbean.

Rum is a by-product of the Caribbean sugar industry which was once a source of so much of Britain's wealth.

Sugar cane came originally from India and was brought west by the Arabs who planted it in Egypt. Most of Europe is too cold to grow it except in the deep south such as Sicily. When European powers started venturing west in the 15th century they took sugar cane with them and planted it in places such as the Azores, Madeira and the island of Sao Tome and Principe off the coast of what is now Gabon. Madeira, before it became famous for wine, was a sugar plantation. When the European powers began acquiring chunks of the Caribbean and South America, they found that the tropical climate and soil were particularly good for growing sugar cane.

As cultured Europeans it was only a matter of time before they began making booze from sugar. Probably the first to do this were the Portuguese in Brazil who made a spirit out of the juice from the sugar cane, an early form of cachaça. The Dutch, though, soon discovered that you could make a spirit from molasses, the waste product of sugar refining. Being made from a waste product meant that rum could be incredibly cheap. What wasn't so cultured was the manner in which the cane was cultivated with slave labour from Africa.

British colonialism in America was to a large extent made possible by slavery. It paid for colonies, made fortunes back in Britain and made the luxury products of sugar and tobacco available to all. Even American colonies with little or no slave populations made money from feeding slaves with salt cod or salt pork, or processing molasses. Back home the cities of Bristol and Liverpool were the principal ports from which slave ships sailed and returned with sugar and rum. Rum was so profitable that on some plantations it covered the cost of the business so that the refined sugar trade would be all profit. Adam Smith wrote:

"It is commonly said that a sugar planter
expects that rum and molasses should defray

the whole expense of his cultivation, and that
his sugar should be all clear profit."

As rum is made from a waste-product, molasses, it doesn't
use up any food, unlike, say, whisky or gin, so there is no
danger of its production being restricted in times of drought.
Fortunes made on the back of sugar became legendary.
There's a play of 1771 by Richard Cumberland called *The
West Indian* where the title character is so wealthy he had
"enough sugar and rum to turn Thames into a rum punch".

The sugar cane was not only harvested by slaves, but
African slave traders were often paid in rum or brandy.
Alcohol oiled the transactions between Europeans and
African slavers; John Atkins, a Royal Naval surgeon, noted
that African slavers "never care to trade with dry lips".
Once in the Americas slaves were given rum as part of the
"seasoning" process. In this process the weak or disobedient
would die. An excess of rum might make sailors and
planters violent, but it was supposed to make slaves more
passive, amply demonstrating the hopelessness of the slaves'
position. Slaves were rewarded with extra rum or could
barter their rum for goods and services. They were given
days off to work their own land. The resulting produce
could be sold, not for money, but for rum. It functioned
as a currency across the Americas. Rum was even used as
a medicine and pick-me-up for slave owners to give their
slaves. Thomas Roughly wrote in the *Jamaica Planter's
Guide* of 1823: "in bad weather, a glass of good rum should
be given to each ... keeping them in heart and they will
work accordingly."

Rum was what united the varied islands and territories
in the Caribbean. It was, to begin with at least, a low status
drink. Brazilian rum, cachaça, was mainly drunk by the
slaves. If you smell the modern stuff you have some idea of
why. There's a stench of rotting vegetation combined with

sulphur; it's like opening a vent to a tropical island hell. The early proto-rums made by the Portuguese, French, Spanish and Dutch were all rough spirits. They all had native liquor industries, wine and brandy, port and madeira, to protect, so their rums were never commercialised. Portuguese and Spanish planters often had wine estates back at home so they didn't want to create any competition. The Portuguese made it illegal to sell rum and the Spanish were not allowed to make rum until 1796 in their colonies. In contrast to today, Cuba in the 19th century was notorious for the poor quality of its rum. The Spanish saw their colonies as places to extract gold and silver rather than as places to develop businesses. You'd expect the French to make good rum from their experiences in Cognac and indeed a Dominican friar, Jean-Baptiste Labat, on Martinique, was a pioneering figure in the evolution of rum. But his efforts were hampered by the French state. Rum exports were banned in 1715 to protect native brandy. Most rum, therefore, would have been cheaply produced and horrible to drink. This reputation persists to this day; there's a rum still made in Newfoundland called Screech because of the noise that people made after drinking it.

Barbados was not only the first place where rum began to evolve into something more sophisticated, but it's where the first written record of the drink's name comes from. The word "rum" probably comes from a Devon word "rumbullion", meaning a fight or a disturbance. It was first recorded on Barbados in 1665. A contemporary source wrote that "The chief fuddling they make on the island is Rumbullion, alias Kill-Devil,[34] and is made of sugar canes

---

34 The diabolical connotations of rum have persisted to this day. It is used in voodoo ceremonies in Haiti. Lee "Scratch" Perry, who produced some of Bob Marley's greatest early work, used to sprinkle white rum around his studio as a way of purifying it of "duppies" – evil spirits or vampires. "The duppies like the white rum," he said in a recent interview.

distilled, a hot, hellish, and terrible liquor." Barbados was first settled in 1627. Initially British colonists tried tobacco and then indigo, but they didn't grow successfully. Sugar cane, on the other hand, flourished. Soon the entire island was given over to cane production and they had to import all their food, often in the form of salt cod from the Grand Banks off Canada. There was a lively trade between the two colonies and this is the reason why one of the great Caribbean dishes, salt cod and ackee, has as its main ingredient a cold water fish from thousands of miles away. As with many things in the drink world, the British took an invention, in this case rum, refined and then commercialised it.

The island had a number of advantages that suited rum production. It had a good source of fresh water, an essential ingredient in distillation. In the early days, many of the labourers were indentured workers from Britain rather than slaves. They came from Scotland, particularly from the Scottish Borders, and from Ireland and brought with them a knowledge of distillation. One thing the island did lack was enough wood to fuel the stills. As sugar and rum production took off, the island was quickly stripped of trees and coal had to be imported from Britain. Much of what we know about the early days of Barbadian rum is from a writer called Richard Ligon who arrived on the island in 1647. He was a Cavalier who was ruined by being on the losing side of the Civil War, so he went to Barbados and wrote a marvellous book about his time there called *A True and Exact History of the Island of Barbadoes*. Ligon was something of a renaissance man, an architect, a gourmand and a writer. He notes in detail how the rum was made, "The drink of the Island, which is made of the skimmings of the Coppers, that boil the Sugar, which they call Kill-Devil."

Water would have been added to enable the molasses to ferment. The sugar content is too high otherwise for the yeasts to go to work. The air in the Caribbean is alive with wild yeasts. Apparently you wouldn't want to drink the fermented product before distillation because it tastes unpleasant and is a powerful laxative. It would have been about 15 percent alcohol. The key to the smoothness of Barbados rum is that it was double distilled just as with Scotch whisky. This produces less quantity, but a much better spirit than just single distilling. The first distillation makes a weak spirit of around 20 percent called low wine, the second produces rum, a spirit of around 70 percent. Distillation works on the principle that alcohol boils at a lower temperature than water, around 78 degrees centigrade as opposed to 100 degrees. The purpose of distillation is to separate alcohol from water, but you don't just have the two compounds, there are others created known as congeners. Some of these taste disgusting and some such as methanol are downright poisonous, but in small quantities congeners add complexity and interest to the resulting spirit. Otherwise you just have ethanol which doesn't taste of anything. The art to distilling is capturing some of these flavours, but without poisoning anyone or getting those horrible cachaça flavours I mentioned.

Barbados became famous for its rum and its rum-drinking. Improvements in distillation techniques meant that by the early 18th century rum was being appreciated for more than just its strength. It was becoming smoother with less of the vegetative notes. Barbados rum was considered superior to others. The Mount Gay distillery that still makes some of the best rum on the island dates back to 1703. Even the French agreed. Savary des Bruslons wrote that "Rum or tafia is one of the best branches of commerce of Barbados. It concedes almost nothing to the spirits of France." Another Frenchman, Pierre François Xavier de Charlevoix, a Jesuit priest and writer, wrote how he preferred Barbados rum because it does not have the "taste of cane which gives it a quite disagreeable aftertaste".

Oak ageing could turn the rum into something sublime. Wood tannins and with them flavours of vanilla and coconut would soften the fiery spirit. Nowadays old bourbon barrels are used. Rum would have been shipped in the oak barrels and the heat of the tropics would age it very quickly. They say that one year in the Caribbean is worth three years ageing in Scotland. Rum when it arrived in Britain would have had some sort of ageing, but, because of the extra ageing time, rum shipped via India would command a premium.

Richard Ligon noted how rum was a comfort against the harsh conditions on the island. "It is helpful to our Christian Servants (white indentured labour) too; for, when their spirits are exhausted, by their hard labor, and sweating in the Sun, ten hours every day, they find their stomach debilitated, and much weakened in their vigor every way, a dram or two of this Spirit, is a great comfort and refreshing to them." The West Indians drank an astonishing amount. Every adult male, free and slave, drank on average a pint a day.

In 1655, the English under William Penn captured the island of Jamaica from the Spanish. About twenty times the size of Barbados, it proved an even better place to make rum. The soil and the climate were perfect for the cultivation of sugar cane, there was plentiful water and trees to fire stills. Jamaica became a rum powerhouse able to turn out large quantities of high quality spirit – perfect for the Royal Navy. It was Samuel Pepys, when he was Chairman of the Navy board, who in 1688 suggested that the Navy take rum instead of brandy. Much more patriotic, as brandy was produced by the Dutch and the French.

With William Penn's invading force was a Francis Dickinson from Somerset. For his part in the capture of the island he was granted 6,000 acres of land. Part of this grant was a sugar plantation that became known as the Appleton Estate in the Nassau Valley. This is far inland about eighty miles from Kingston. Penn had three sons, Ezekiel, Caleb and Vickris, and the estate remained in the family until 1847. The first mention of this as a rum-producing estate was in 1749. It became famed for its quality. Today Appleton Estate is considered the finest rum in Jamaica, if not the Caribbean. They still use techniques that Richard Ligon would recognise. Fermentation takes place with wild yeasts, rum is distilled in pot stills and only sugar cane grown on the estate is used. Joy Spence, the master distiller, told me:

> "All Appleton Estate rum is produced on
> a single estate, in a small circumscribed
> geographic area. Consequently, Appleton
> Estate is one of the few rums in the world to
> claim a *terroir* (the sum of the effects that the
> local environment has had on the production
> of the product)."

Almost all other rums are made from molasses that can come from anywhere. Appleton uses "up to ten varieties of sugar cane grown which have been specially selected – the sugar cane produces rums that tend to have fruity and buttery notes". The resulting spirit is then aged in used bourbon barrels (like a lot of Scotch whisky). Joy Spence adds, "I don't think that the rums were aged for as long back then so they would not have been as smooth and refined." Another change is that nowadays, again like Scotch whisky, most of their bottlings consist of powerful pot still spirits tempered with rum from column[35] stills to create a lighter, less robust end product.

It's not Jamaica's most famous rum though. That honour goes to our old friend Captain Morgan.[36] It's named after

---

35 We will learn more about the different types of distillation in the gin chapter.
36 Captain Morgan black label rum in Britain has the words Jamaica Rum on the bottle. Not all Captain Morgans are made from Jamaican rum.

Edward Teach (aka Blackbeard) showing off his trademark beard
Artist: Joseph Nicholls

the pirate Captain Henry Morgan. He was notorious for his
brutal sacking of Spanish cities in Panama. His effectiveness
at targeting the Spanish led to him eventually being knighted
in 1674 and then becoming the Lieutenant Governor of
Jamaica. In 1669 Henry Morgan's flagship was destroyed
when carousing sailors accidently set the magazine on fire.
Pirates weren't subject to the enforced sobriety and strict
rationing of Naval sailors. In 1720 an engagement between
the pirate John Rackham and the Royal Navy ended up in
ignominy as his crew were too rum-fuddled to fight. The
pirate Blackbeard, real name Edward Teach, wrote this in
his diary: "Such a day; rum all out. Our company somewhat
sober; a damned confusion amongst us! Rogues a plotting.
Talk of separation. So I looked sharp for a prize (and) took
one with a great deal of liquor aboard. So kept the company
hot, damned hot, then all things well again." This scene
could be straight out of Robert Louis Stevenson's *Treasure
Island* and, indeed, Long John Silver is probably literature's
most noted rum drinker. It's a novel soaked in rum most

famously captured in the song of the pirates, "Fifteen men on the dead man's chest .../ Yo-ho-ho, and a bottle of rum/ Drink and the devil had done for the rest."

Originally sailors didn't just drink rum. Normally they would also be served beer, when it was available, and wine. Beer and wine would spoil quickly, so were generally only available at the beginning of voyages. One such wine was Mistela from Spain which sailors referred to as "Miss Taylor". The officers would have drunk good fortified wine such as marsala, madeira or port. Initially the rum would have been served neat only when the beer or the wine ran out. In 1731, however, it became standard practice to issue a daily rum ration. The Navy needed some way of measuring the alcoholic strength of the spirit so they came up with a crude but effective technique. Some gunpowder was mixed with rum and if it didn't ignite it meant it was less than 57 percent alcohol. If it exploded, it was significantly stronger. If it just lit, then the spirit was deemed to be 100 percent proof. This is the origin of the term Navy strength and why they are bottled at around 57 percent.

In 1740 Admiral Edward Vernon introduced a mixture of one part rum to four parts water flavoured with lemon juice and brown sugar. Vernon was known as "Old Grogram" because of the cloak he wore made of the waterproof fabric, grogram, hence this proto-mojito was known as grog. The lemon would have provided some much-needed Vitamin C to stave off scurvy. French sailors did not have grog, they just drank brandy so were less healthy than sailors in the Royal Navy. There's a theory that part of the reason for the British dominance over the French at sea was because the British weren't suffering from scurvy.

Every sailor in Nelson's Navy was given half of pint[37] of

---

37   Roughly a modern American pint, 473 ml.

rum a day. There was a certain amount of ritual around making grog. The grog would be mixed in a scuttlebutt (cask used for serving water) and when it was time to serve the piper would pipe: Up Spirits! British ships tolerated tipsy crews, but full-on drunkenness was dangerous and affected the Navy's ability to fight. Vernon referred to drink as "the formidable dragon". Grog was designed to keep crews relatively sober, but many worked out ways to get drunk. Sailors were given this irrespective of age, so younger sailors would often sell or barter their rations, or some simply saved up their tots and went on a spree. A sailor, George King of the *Melpomene*, wrote of one binge of 1809: "the morning following I was completely stupid with the grog."

The Navy's long relationship with rum has entered the English language. We still use the word groggy to mean a state of befuddlement. Sailors would try to smuggle rum aboard, hence the term "rummage" which originally meant to search for contraband booze. When Nelson was killed at Trafalgar, his body was pickled in rum and brought back to England. Along the way, so the story goes, most of the rum was drunk by thirsty sailors and so "Nelson's blood" became a term for rum. In the early days rum would have been bought on an ad hoc basis, but by 1780 one company, E D & F Man Ltd, had the contract to supply Navy rum. Their rum was a mixture of Demerara rum from British Guiana and rum from Trinidad with others blended in. Naval rum had become an institution. H Warner Allen, classical scholar and wine writer, wrote in 1931:

> "Rum is the Englishman's spirit, the true spirit
> of adventure. Whiskey belongs to Scotland and
> Ireland, Brandy to France, Gin to Holland, but
> Rum is essentially English despite its tropical
> origin. The very word calls up heroic memories
> of the iron seamen who on lawful and

unlawful occasions built up the British Empire
overseas, and if ever Rum were to disappear
from Navy rations, a great tradition would be
tragically broken."[38]

For both pirates and the Royal Navy rum was essential
for the smooth running of the ship. As it did throughout
the Americas, it functioned as a currency. Sailors would
often be paid in rum which they could drink or barter for
goods and services. There was a chronic shortage of money
in the American colonies. Settlers used Spanish, French,
Dutch, Portuguese and, oddly, Austrian coins. The Thaler
was Austrian and via the Dutch word *daarler*, we have the
root of the word dollar. It was often simpler, though, just
to use rum. Rum functioned as a currency in the Northern
Colonies. Adam Smith wrote in *The Wealth of Nations*:

> "In the province of New York, common
> labourers earn three shillings and sixpence
> currency, equal to two shillings sterling a day;
> ship carpenters, ten shillings and sixpence
> currency, with a pint of rum worth sixpence
> sterling, equal in all to six shillings and
> sixpence sterling."

As well as being used to pay labourers, a piece of land
in Kernersville, North Carolina, sold for four gallons of
rum. This rum would have been made all over the North
American colonies from molasses shipped from the West
Indies. New England was a good place to distill as there
was plentiful water and wood to fire stills. It didn't taste
so good though. West India rum sold for twice as much.

---

38   The tradition finally ended on 31 July 1970. It was known as Black Tot day.

When George Washington ran for election to the Virginia House of Burgesses, at one campaign event he served up 28 gallons of rum. This was for a county with only 391 voters. The average colonial American drank about four or five gallons of rum a year. The pre-revolutionary states of America had a great tradition of rum-based drinks such as hot toddies, eggnogs and spiced, buttered apple cider made with rum, drinks which persist to this day. There's one drink that involves sticking a red hot poker in an eggnog type construction to cook the component parts.

All this rum was dependent on cheap molasses coming in from the Caribbean, but the British didn't want the colonists buying it from the French West Indies so, in 1733, they put a tax on molasses imported from non-British colonies. This was designed to enrich Caribbean plantation owners at the expense of New Englanders. It was widely ignored and molasses was simply smuggled in from French colonies. The French were selling their molasses at giveaway prices since the French Royal Degree of 1713 banned importation of rum and molasses to France to protect the brandy industry. French molasses was so much cheaper that the tax proved impossible to collect. Smuggling became the norm in North America. Everyone was involved in it, not just gangsters but respectable citizens. Peter Faneuil of Boston, who built the Faneuil Hall in 1743, one of Boston's great landmarks, had one of his ships seized in 1736 for illegally trading with the French. For a long time Britain turned a blind eye to its colonies flouting the laws, but things changed with the conclusion of the Seven Years War fought between Britain and France between 1754 and 1763.

This war was fought between Britain and France in Europe, India and America. It was a triumph for Britain as it ousted the French from North America and India. Britain was now undisputed top nation, but this victory had been won at huge financial cost. In order to fight the war Britain had employed 45,000 troops in North America, roughly five times the number of French. Britain was now dangerously indebted. The British government thought that, as the war had been fought partly to protect the British colonies in America, the Americans wouldn't mind paying some taxes to fund the aftermath of the war. They were wrong. Britain lowered the duty on molasses, but this time actually tried to enforce it. By British standards, taxes on the colonists were very low. The problem was that now that the French were not a threat, the colonists didn't see why they should have to pay for the British Army.

The revolt sparked when the British tried to collect their taxes. It led to rioting and the boycott of British goods. The Boston Tea Party was, in fact, a group of wealthy smugglers protesting against cheap tea from the East India Company undercutting their stock. The resulting War of Independence was a fiasco for the British. Britain won military victories but was never able to subdue the revolt. Opinion at home was sharply divided over the war with many MPs openly siding with the rebels. It seems that Britain's heart wasn't really in the war and in 1783 admitted defeat. This marked the high point of rum in America. After independence, rum became associated with the colonial days. The new Americans drank whiskey made from corn (maize). This was the drink of the west, of exploration and the frontier. Corn grew in massive quantities and whiskey was the best way to preserve it. The revolution was partly fought so that Americans could spread west. The British had forbidden settlements west of the Appalachian Mountains.

The native inhabitants suffered greatly as America expanded. When the British arrived in North America they found, though they did not know it, a continent that had already been severely depleted by disease. The unholy trilogy of rum, disease and guns would kill millions more. Most tribes had no knowledge of alcohol whatsoever and so went completely to pieces when they encountered strong spirits. William Penn wrote in 1683, "The Dutch, Sweed and English have by Brandy and Specially Rum, almost Debaucht the Indians all. When Drunk, the most Wretched of Spectacles." Some Indian chiefs pleaded with British colonial authorities for rum not to be sold in their territories such was its terrible effect. Laws were passed in many colonies forbidding the sale of alcohol to Indians but as Europeans headed west, these became impossible to enforce. With independence, they were increasingly ignored. In fact, rum was sometimes used as a weapon to undermine native communities. Benjamin Franklin wrote: "It (rum) has already annihilated all the tribes who formerly inhabited the sea-coast."

Back in Britain, the plight of African slaves was galvanising public opinion. Abolitionism was inspired by evangelical Christians both in the Church of England and amongst non-conformist sects such as Quakers, Baptists and Methodists. It was led by William Wilberforce who was devoutly evangelical. His Christian awakening was driven in part by his disgust with the loucheness of Georgian London. He was great friends with William Pitt the Younger, who served as Prime Minister from 1783 until 1801 and then 1804 to 1806, and friends also with Pitt's great rival Charles James Fox, but following his conversion sought to distance himself from his old, rather dissolute life. He wrote of his new moderation: "Never more than six glasses of wine ... to be in bed by eleven and be up by six o'clock." With Wilberforce in Parliament, the campaign was led on the ground by Thomas Clarkson who travelled around the country speaking to thousands of people. Massive petitions were presented to Parliament with over 60,000 names on them. These had to travel around the country and were taken very seriously by Parliament. It is estimated that 1.5 million British people in total signed anti-slavery petitions when the population was around 12 million. It was a popular genuinely reflected the will of the British people. Thomas Clarkson wrote that abolition "spoke the national voice". It was particularly strong amongst working-class and middle-class women (unlike say Suffragism which was mainly an elite concern). Jane, a Quaker abolitionist, writes in 1836, "Our subscribers and most efficient members were all in the middling and working classes but they evince great zeal and labour very harmoniously together."

The slave trade was eventually abolished by Britain in 1807, but slavery persisted in British colonies until 1834. Now, however, sugar cane wasn't so profitable. Cheaper sugar could be obtained from sugar beet grown in the damp soils of northern Europe, though you can't make rum from it as it gives off sulphurous compounds when distilled. The success of sugar beet was a side effect of the Royal Navy's blockade of the Continent during the Napoleonic wars. The French scientist Chaptal pioneered the development of this crop. Sugar cane was now no longer as profitable without protectionism. Adam Smith argued that slavery wasn't cheap at all as people working for themselves worked harder and "whatever work he does beyond what is sufficient to purchase his own maintenance can be squeezed out of him by violence alone, and not by any interest of his own... " The West India lobby, once all powerful especially in the House of Lords, waned as sugar became less profitable.

The Caribbean, previously vital to Britain's wealth, became something of a backwater, no longer fought over by the major powers of Europe. It was heavy industry, steel, coal and shipbuilding, not sugar that would prove the motor of British power in the 19th century. The Caribbean languished but, unlike in the United States, the rum business carried on. Rum sat slowly maturing in the island heat. Of all the drinks in the book rum has the most violent and unpleasant history. It's also perhaps the most emblematic of the story, being a direct product of the European discovery of America and subsequent exploitation of African labour. It's hard to imagine that all that misery created something so sweet and delicious.

DRINKING THE EMPIRE

Rum is still sold on its traditional links with the Royal Navy, piracy and tropical islands. In the past very broad stereotypical images of former slaves were also used – there was one unforgettable make called Nigger Head Brand – but now they tend more towards beautiful Jamaican women dancing to reggae at dusk. Much more palatable.

The French divide rum into two classes: *rhum agricole* which is made from sugar cane juice and *rhum industriale* which is made from molasses. They do this because most rums from the French Caribbean are the former and it sounds better and therefore it relegates most rum from former British colonies as industrial. A great way of getting one over on the old enemy. *Cachaça* is in the former category and it's horrible neat. Many *agricole* rums have quite a pronounced vegetal taste especially when young. I tend to prefer the molasses one and not just for patriotic reasons.

There are three broad styles of rum, white rum which is unaged, aged rums of various colours and then dark rum such as Captain Morgan, which is coloured with molasses. There are also rums flavoured with coconut, pineapple, vanilla, spices etc. which, while not particularly serious drinks, can be delicious in rum punches. The ones I'm interested in are the aged rums designed for sipping neat. Here are a few to try.

Pusser's British Navy Rum
A blend of rums from around the Caribbean and bottled at Navy strength. This is apparently what they used to serve onboard ships and, if that's true, then being in the Navy certainly had its perks. It is a quality drop.

Admiral Rodney Extra Old

Named after the great Royal Navy admiral, this is from St Lucia. It's a smooth one, but with a nice spicy quality and a dry finish.

El Dorado 25-Year-Old Demerara Rum 1986

This is from Guyana which is a former British colony on the mainland of South America. It has a wonderful flavour of vanilla, dark chocolate and red fruit. Long, harmonious and best enjoyed like a single malt whisky with just a splash of water.

Doorly's XO

From Barbados, the birthplace of quality rum, this is made in a pot still using techniques that wouldn't surprise Richard Ligon. It's aged in oloroso sherry casks for a truly superior drop.

Appleton Estate 12 year old

This estate in Jamaica is one of the legends of the rum world. They make some very expensive, rare spirits. This is at the more affordable end, but it's still luxurious with flavours of smoke, tobacco, leather and honey.

Penny Blue Batch No 2 Single Estate XO

Unusually this is not from the Caribbean, but from Mauritius in the Indian Ocean. It's very different from the big, sweet stereotype of rum, being light bodied and peppery like a Highland single malt.

Barbancourt 5 star

From Haiti this is a *rhum agricole* and is considered by many to be among the world's finest. It's aged in Limousin oak, the same as used by cognac producers.

7

EVERLASTING WINES

About ten years ago a friend of mine inherited a country pile near Hull from a misanthropic great uncle. The place was a bit neglected so he planned to sell off some of the family treasures in order to pay for renovations. A man came from Christie's to assess the collections. His verdict was damning. Regarding the paintings there were some good names but they were all minor works. There was nothing of any great value. It seems that Stubbs, famous for his horse paintings, wasn't very good at painting people. There was more disappointment in the cellar. Most of the good wine had been drunk leaving just assorted ordinary clarets, port from lesser vintages and, worst of all, supermarket Liebfraumilch from the 1980s. There was nothing that would pay for the badly needed roof repairs. And yet it wasn't all bad; amongst the dross my friend found some Malartic-Lagravière claret 1961. The bottle we tried was remarkably good and vigorous. Better still there was a bottle with the words Blandy's Terrantez 1795 stencilled on the bottle. Could it really be that old? From the capsule on the bottle it looked like it had been bottled in the 20th century, probably before the war. I did a bit of research and found that there was little reason to doubt that the wine, a madeira, was genuine. Even if it wasn't from the 1795 vintage, then it was likely to be very old. My friend is now saving it for a special occasion.

With any other wine it would be foolish to keep it, but the magical thing about madeira is that it lasts. I've never tried anything quite as old, but at Berry Bros wine merchants in London a couple of years ago I tried an 1875 Malvazia (Malmsey) from D'Olivera which if anything tasted a bit young. It was crammed with sweetness with that famous madeira tang to it. More than any other wine, madeira is one where you can taste history. You can try wines that Thomas Jefferson would have been familiar with. It's like hearing a voice from the past. What is this wine that can last for ever?

Like most of the drinks in this book, madeira owes its fame principally to an accident of geography. The island off the west coast of what is now Morocco was first colonised by the Portuguese from the 1420s. It is in the perfect place for ships to stop off at on their journeys from Western Europe to North America. The trade winds from the northeast would take ships past Spain, down to Madeira, the Canary Islands and the Azores, and then across the Atlantic to North America. The voyage back to Europe would go across the top via Iceland. The New World had things that the English were greedy for, principally sugar and tobacco, but also cod from Newfoundland. No ship's captain wanted to undertake a potentially risky voyage to America without a cargo to trade so a triangular[39] trade developed where cloth would be taken from England and sold in Madeira for wine, the wine was then sold in the British colonies of North America or the Caribbean for sugar or tobacco, the cargo would then be taken back to Britain where there was great demand for such things. The risks were high but then so were the potential profits. The Atlantic in the 18th century

39 Triangular trade suggests that the routes were straight and undertaken by one ship on each leg. Instead it was a complicated system of overlapping and crisscrossing routes between Europe, Africa and America.

was the equivalent to railways in the 19th century: it was the engine of trade. Previously a voyage to America had been a journey into the unknown; now people and goods regularly took the six week voyage to America.

Part of the reason why the English settled America was in the hope that this new land could produce some of the Mediterranean goods that they craved such as cooking oil, silks and wine. They were to be disappointed. Good wine couldn't be made on the east coast of North America. The vines that settlers brought over died and the native ones didn't make terribly nice wine. The characteristic tasting note is foxy and not in a good way. Nobody knew why the European vines didn't thrive in America. Much later scientists would discover it was due to a tiny little insect called phylloxera, but not before it had crossed the Atlantic and caused havoc in the vineyards of Europe.

As well as Madeira, wine would have been bought in the Azores or the Canary Islands for sale in America. Canary Island wine was very popular in Britain; there's a mention in Shakespeare of Canary sack. It was a sweet wine normally made from the Malvasia grape. There was one thing about madeira wine, however, that made it special. It's the reason it is still appreciated today when Canary isn't and why it became the most popular wine in British America and later India: it improves when it is heated. Wine, as a rule, needs to be kept cool. If it gets too warm it starts to taste baked. It's why you should never buy a bottle of Dom Pérignon from a corner shop. It will have been sitting on a hot top shelf for years. In the little wine merchant I worked for in Leeds we would wince when someone bought a dusty bottle of top shelf burgundy as we knew how sweltering it was in the shop in the summer. Most quality wine these days is shipped in refrigerated containers to prevent this happening. Madeira wine's peculiar affinity with heat was noted early on in the island's history. Sir Hans Sloane[40] who visited the island in 1687 noted:

> "the more tis expos'd to sunbeams and heat,
> the better it is and instead of putting it in a cool
> cellar, they expose it to the Sun ... no sort of
> wine agreeing with those hot places like this."

Madeira is the most famous sun-loving wine, but it isn't the only one. Vin santo, sacred wine, is made from raisined grapes in Tuscany and then stored in the eaves of farmhouses where it gently cooks. Some types of Banyuls and Maury, fortified reds from the Roussillon in France, are left out in the sun in glass demijohns where they take on nutty, fruity and slightly bitter flavours known as *rancio*, literally rancid. Noilly Prat vermouth is made in the south of France from wine that has had similar treatment.

The wine Sir Hans Sloane tried would have been made from some varieties that we would recognise such as Sercial, Bual, Verdelho, Tinta (red variety) and Bastardo (pink variety) but they would all have been blended together including the red ones. The colour would have been either white or a sort of rose colour known as partridge eye. It would have been dry, unfortified and unaged. In fact, it would probably have been rather harsh and acidic. Wines from Madeira are noted for their acidity which is partly why they last so long. Sercial, the grape variety, is known on the Portuguese mainland as Esgana Cao, dog strangler, due to its searing acidity. It now makes some of the best dry wines on the island, but it does need ageing to tame that acidity. Also, to confuse matters, Bual is known as Malvasia Fina on the mainland. There are many different types of Malvasia grown

40   Irish-born physician who gave his name to Sloane Square in London.

all over the Mediterranean and Iberia. Wines made from Sercial were known in 19th century Britain as madeira hock (a generic British term for wine from the Rhine after the town of Hochheim). A shipment of white wine would often be sent with a barrel of red wine alongside so that importers could colour the wine as per their customers' tastes. Wines arriving in the colonies or in London were given names to denote the class and the style of wine. The top was Malvazia which was very rare, and it was followed by the following blends: London Particular, London Market, New York, Virginia or Jamaica and West India (aka Common).

The exception to the blending of grape varieties was Malvazia or Malmsey which would have been sweeter and darker. It was rare, very expensive and also rather unstable as it contained unfermented sugar which might start fermenting at any moment. As yet brandy was not added to stabilise it. What was added was calcium sulphate[41] or gypsum which helped fermentation, bolstered acidity and also led to brighter, clearer wines. It was an essential ingredient in madeira. Right from the beginning madeira was a manufactured wine.

Initially ships' captains stopping on the island would just purchase wine speculatively, but soon a group of British merchants developed dedicated to supplying the needs of the burgeoning Empire. These shippers, as in Oporto, didn't own any vineyards or indeed make any wine. They would buy it from Portuguese growers and then market it under their names. The British brought commercial nous rather than viticultural skill. As usual amongst such merchants, Scots were over-represented. You only have to look at the

---

41 Interestingly calcium sulphate was the secret ingredient in the water that made Burton-on-Trent the brewing capital of England. It gave the beer its famous Burton bite. Later it was added to the liquor (brewing water) in the rest of the country to mimic that famous taste in a process known as Burtonisation.

names – Newton, Cameron, Gordon, Bissett, Duff and Scott. Of the British firms on the island in the 1810s four were Scottish, three English and one Irish. Many of these were youngest sons from prosperous families who wouldn't inherit, so sought their fortune in the wine trade. One such Scot was Francis Newton who escaped Scotland after fighting on the losing side at the Battle of Culloden in 1745. He found work as a bookkeeper on Madeira and eventually set up a firm with Thomas Gordon. As the distances involved with selling madeira were so long, wine merchants had to advance long credit terms to their customers. The whole business was based on trust. Wine was sold on a personal basis often to friends, family and countrymen. Newton had a brother based in Virginia who handled the wine at the other end. The Newtons sold mainly to fellow Scots who were doctors, lawyers or other trusted professionals. They in turn would sell to a network of friends and colleagues in America. There were little informal distribution networks all over the American colonies making sure that madeira was widely available. Newton and Gordon's firm became Cossart Gordon after William Cossart became involved with the trade in 1808. Wines are still produced under this name.

Oddly madeira never became that big in Britain despite the large British trading community on the island. It was in America that it reached its apotheosis. Frederick Marryat, a novelist and former officer in the Royal Navy, in his 1839 work *A Diary in America* thought that this was down to the climate:

> " ...where the Americans beat us out of the field is their Madeira, which certainly is of a quality which we cannot procure in England. This is owing to the extreme heat and cold of the climate, which ripens this wine; indeed,

I may almost say, that I never tasted good
Madeira, until I arrived in the United States."

You might even go as far to say that it was the wine that
built America. By the early 18th century the English
settlements had evolved into vibrant (more or less) self-
governing colonies. In one decade between 1727 and 1738
over three quarters of the wine going to Anglo-America was
madeira. Initially this wine would have been drunk young,
but gradually a taste developed for older wines. Colonists
in America noted how the wine improved if it was shipped
through the tropics. The action of the heat, the slowly
changing temperature and the rocking action of the water
all mellowed the wine into something quite remarkable.
Wine sent via the West Indies sold for £10 to £12 more
a pipe (approx 400 litres). People not only liked the taste
but they liked the story behind it. At this time we see the
beginnings of a connoisseurship not seen since Roman
times. It was a mark of status to have old vintages. The
American elite would keep the wine in their houses and note
how it changed over time. Houses in Savannah, Georgia
had special overground storage areas for keeping the wine.
There is still to this day a madeira club in Savannah who
meet to sample rare vintages. William Neyle Habersham, a
wealthy landowner and noted madeira connoisseur born in
Savannah in 1817, had special glasshouses built to channel
the hot Georgia sun into his wines. The fashion for aged
wine was well established by this time.

In order to fulfil the demand for old-tasting wines,
merchants began to blend vintages. In 1764 the Scots
merchant Robert Bisset wrote in a letter that he was
combining vintages in order to fulfill demands from
customers for older wines. In a letter of 1768 Francis
Newton explains how he added buckets of old wine to
the new vintage to improve them. Old wines lent weight

to lighter vintages and new vintages lent vigour and fruit to old and perhaps tiring wines. By the mid-18th century this sort of blending was commonplace. Producers were also starting to add brandy to their wine. There's a theory that this came about due to the difficulties of shipping wine during the Seven Years War (1754–1763). There were large stocks piled up on the island which were distilled in order to save space in warehouses. This was then blended into the wine. They may have also done this to boost alcohol in a light vintage or to stabilise the wine for long sea voyages. But it can't be denied that their customers, British and colonial, liked strong wine. Thomas Lamar, a madeira shipper, wrote that his customers liked "everything that is powerful and heady". There was good customer feedback for the strong stuff. Merchants knew their customers intimately through regular correspondence. In this way the demands of the far-off consumer could quickly reach the island. The merchants were reacting to the demands of the market. The more northern American colonies liked heavily fortified wine whereas the southern states and the Caribbean preferred lighter wines. Fortification, however, didn't become a standard part of the recipe for madeira until the 19th century, not least because good brandy, normally from France or mainland Portugal, was often in short supply when Britain and France were at war.

It was because of another war that madeira began to assume its modern form, the American War of Independence. George Washington was a keen madeira drinker as was Thomas Jefferson. The founding fathers would have toasted the Bill of Rights with madeira. The war with Britain meant that the wine could not be easily shipped to the colonies. France and Spain saw it as a chance to get one over the old enemy and so sided with the colonists, but Portugal remained loyal to the British. The Royal Navy's superiority meant that there was a wine shortage in America. Furthermore it was too dangerous to ship the wine via the Caribbean, but customers outside the rebellious colonies, not least in Britain itself, still wanted wine that had had the full tropical treatment.

A clever man on the island of Madeira had an idea. His name was Pantaleão Fernandes the Younger (he was in fact extremely old at the time of his invention) and he invented a system of heating pipes of madeira wine in specially designed rooms containing stoves, in Portuguese *estufas*. His technological brainwave was picked up all over the island. The *estufa* race was on. The idea was to artificially create the conditions on the journey of the wine through the tropics. Other merchants on the island thought that it was the movement of the boats as well as the heat that made madeira so good, so they built steam engines to rock the barrels mechanically as if they were on a ship. It took a while to get the *estufas* right as some merchants used too high a temperature and the wine would cook. Despite these teething troubles, by 1815 special heating rooms were ubiquitous across the island. Nowadays most madeira will have been *estufa* treated, though the very best are merely kept in especially warm warehouses. Long ageing takes care of the rest.

The American Revolution and the resulting war changed business for madeira merchants. Exports fell by two thirds so there was a backlog of wine on the island. Previously merchants would have dealt mainly in wine from the previous vintage. By the end of the war in 1783 their business had changed. Merchants moved from being brokers and selling to passing ships to holding stock and fulfilling standing orders. Their customers now had a taste for aged wines and providing these wines meant that merchants had to hold sizeable quantities of old wine. Large stocks and *estufas* all required capital so firms needed investors. They became bigger and acquired some of the trappings of modern capitalist enterprises: silent partners, stockholding, warehouses, multiple employees and, to organise it all, proper book-keeping. Madeira was becoming an industrial wine. It was at this time that many of the names that you still see on bottles today began. Blandy's, the shipper of my friend's wine, were founded in 1811[42] by John Blandy who was sent to the island in 1807 with General Beresford's army to help defend it against Napoleon.[43] Between 1640 and 1815 the quantity of wine produced on the island increased sixfold. William Johnstone, a madeira shipper, wrote: "a large stock of old wines requires much capital and is attended with much expense, but it is extremely desirable & absolutely necessary." Previously the British shippers were part of the Factory House on Madeira. This was originally set up to protect the British from the Inquisition, but by the 18th century was more of a business cartel designed to protect the interests of the members, nearly all of whom were wine merchants. They set prices for wine to be bought and sold. Increasingly they found themselves undercut by the new breed of brash trader such as Blandy and Johnstone, independent young men with new business techniques. Eventually the Factory House was dissolved in 1812. Nowadays the Blandy family, headed up by Chris Blandy, owns the Madeira Wine Company, the island's largest producer.

Change was also in the air in southern Spain. Sherry had

---

42 This may seem to contradict the vintage on my friend's bottle of Terrantez 1795, but there is no reason why Blandy's could not have bought up old stocks of wine. Shippers didn't actually make any wine. They just bought it, matured it, turned it into madeira and then sold it.

43 Or so the story goes, as with so much in this book. New evidence suggests that he was actually there like so many modern British tourists who travel to the island for a rest cure. He evidently liked the place, decided to stay and got a job with a counting house on the island. From there he moved into the madeira business.

been a popular wine in Elizabethan England. It was known as sack. The origins of this word are mysterious. It may come from the Spanish *seco*, meaning dry, though much sack was in fact sweet or from another Spanish word, *sacar*, meaning to draw out (from a barrel). Or it may come from the Spanish *saca*, meaning export goods. We can gauge how popular by how often it is mentioned in Shakespeare's plays. Rhenish wine is mentioned four times, claret and Malmsey (madeira) once each, but sack is mentioned an astonishing forty-four times. It's almost as if he was being paid to mention it. Falstaff says in *Henry IV Part II*: "If I had a thousand sons, the first human principle I would teach them should be to forswear thin potations and to addict themselves to sack."

The thin potations that Falstaff refers to would have been bordeaux. The sherry marketing board could not have come up with a better advert for their product. Sherry was a very different animal to the drink we know today. It would have been consumed as young as possible but, as with madeira, a sherry from a good vintage and properly kept could last. It even improved on tropical voyages. You can buy a sweet sherry made in this style by Lustau called East India Sherry. It's a blend of a dry oloroso sherry and a sweet PX. Lustau then matures it in a particularly hot and humid part of the warehouse to mimic the long journey around the tropics.

Since its Elizabethan heyday, sherry had been in decline. Trade with Britain had been severely disrupted by the War of Spanish Succession which ran from 1701 to 1714. By the mid-18th century sherry's place had been taken in British hearts by port and to a lesser extent by Málaga[44] from the south of Spain, a sweet Muscat also known as Mountain

---

44 Sadly the last classic Málaga producer, Scholtz Hermanos, originally a German firm, sold up in the mid-1990s and now there is no one making málaga wine in the old style. Their old bodega is now a department store.

Wine. Vineyards in the sherry region were uprooted and replaced with orange groves. The vibrant expat community in Jerez was long gone. By 1754 there was only one British shipper left, a man called John Brickdale.

The sherry business was further hampered by an organisation known as the *Gremio*. This was like a trade union of growers who controlled the price of wine which they often set too high. The *Gremio* limited the amount of wine that merchants could hold and forbade them from owning vineyards. It was designed to stop a situation like in Oporto or Madeira where the merchants had the upper hand over the growers and could dictate prices. What was good for the growers, however, was not necessarily good for the trade and the sherry business stagnated. Juan (or Jean) Haurie, a French shipper, took on the *Gremio* in 1772 in a court case and won. He could now control his sherry from grape to bottle and opened the doors to the modern sherry business. In a way, though, the years of stagnation had been good for sherry, the wine. It meant that merchants and growers, monasteries and middlemen (known as *almacenistas*) were sitting on large quantities of old wines. Sherry, like madeira and marsala, is a wine that can improve with oxidation and, if not quite as immortal as madeira, then is certainly very long-lived.

Sherry's customers developed a taste for mature wine and the Jerezanos invented a way of blending older wines into a new one called the solera. It was already in normal use by the time James Busby, the Australian wine pioneer, visited Jerez in 1831 and noted this technique. It's a more systematic version of the topping up technique used to make the "perpetual wines" of Marsala. It's best thought of as a triangle of barrels with three on the bottom, two in the middle and one on top of that. The wine in the bottom contains the oldest wine. Roughly four times a year a small proportion of the wine from the bottom is taken out to be bottled or blended with other soleras. It is then replaced by the wine from the layer above and this is in turn replaced by wine from the top barrel. This top barrel is then topped up with the new vintage. This process is known as "running the scales". In this way the resulting wine contains minute quantities of very old wine. The longer a solera is kept, the better the resulting wines are. On sherry bottles you will sometimes see a year and this is normally the year when the solera was started. The Del Duque solera at González Byass was started in 1835. Some vintage wines were also sold, usually of the better kind. Vintage wines are now released very infrequently. When they do appear it's because a bodega has something exceptional to offer that they don't want to lose in a blend.

Previously sherry was sold as soon as it had finished fermenting, but when it was left in barrel a funny thing happened. A thick layer of yeast, known as *flor*, grew on the top. This prevented the wine from oxidising and enabled it to age while staying fresh. You can think of it as like cling film over an apple which stops it browning. Adding younger wine keeps the *flor* alive and healthy. *Flor*-affected wines are known as finos. Sometimes the *flor* wouldn't develop and the wine would oxidise and darken. It was then known as an oloroso, meaning pungent or fragrant depending on who you ask. Both fino and oloroso would be bone dry. These two styles could only develop when the young wine was allowed to mature. They are sherries that we would recognise, but what was shipped to England was usually something a little different. It would have been subjected to what's known as *travail à l'anglaise* which involved taking a dry oloroso and liberally dosing it with brandy and sweetening it with sweet wine from the Pedro Ximénez grape. To this day, when many people in Britain think of sherry, this is the concoction, now known as cream sherry, that they think of. It's the sherry of vicars and maiden aunts.[45] The crisp fresh fino was not to British tastes and mostly would have been drunk in southern Spain. In fact, according to Antonio Flores Pedregosa, the winemaker at González Byass, wines that developed a *flor* used to be considered faulty and, not being thought fit for export, were used for home consumption only. There's a letter in the González Byass archives dated 7th August 1844 from their London agent complaining about being sent a "very pale wine", a fino, and enquiring, "where are my low-priced wines?" This was the nature of much of the wine exported to Britain.

Sherry today is made in the so-called sherry triangle between the towns of Jerez, Sanlúcar de Barrameda and Puerto de Santa Maria, although in the 18th and 19th centuries vineyards from further afield would have gone into the wines, and not always legitimately. Sherry is made from three grapes, Palomino Fino, Pedro Ximénez and more rarely Moscatel; however, other grapes including some red grapes would have gone in the wines too. These vineyards are all around Jerez. In contrast to port and madeira vineyards, these vineyards are owned by sherry companies rather than by small farmers who sell their grapes. González Byass have the largest holdings in Jerez and are self-sufficient in grapes. The best are grown on a chalky soil known as *albariza*.

In Jerez it's impossible to ignore the Arab past. The town of Jerez still has something of a Moorish feel with its Arab Alcazar looking over the González Byass bodega. The full name of the town is Jerez de la Frontera, on the border between Islam and Christendom. The music that you hear in the back streets and at bullfights, flamenco, sounds like something from Egypt. Lorca called Jerez "city of gypsies".

---

45 At one time you weren't allowed to write articles about sherry without mentioning maiden aunts and vicars.

The bodegas of Jerez with their arches and seemingly infinite patterns of repeating barrels stacked against the walls have something of the Mezquita (mosque) in Cordoba. Domecq's bodega is actually known as La Mezquita. The word alcohol comes from the Arabic *Al Kohl*. It's interesting how the fortified wines loved by the British were made at extremities of Europe, places either literally or culturally closer to Africa than Europe.

Sherry develops very slowly. Inside the González Byass bodega, it's stacked floor to ceiling with wine slowly maturing. The floor is watered to keep the air humid so the wines don't evaporate too much. The ideal humidity is around 75 percent in order for the *flor* to grow healthily. As well as a mosque, the other thing it reminded me of was the vast warehouse at the end of *Raiders of the Lost Ark* where the Ark of the Covenant is crated up and forgotten about. Indeed when González Byass were renovating recently they found a room unknown to them stacked full of ancient sherries. They have a series of soleras known as the Apostles, where each wine is named after one of Jesus' disciples. The Judas butt is vinegar – very valuable in Jerez. They have some old oloroso wines dating back to the early 20th century that are so pungent that they can only be blended. Antonio Flores Pedregosa refers to them as "handkerchief wines" because if you put a drop on your handkerchief you will be able to smell it all day. Sherry is undoubtedly an evocative wine. The best description of a very old sherry I've read described a particular Palo Cortado as "smelling like dark alleys and crime".[46]

By the late 18th century merchants from England, Scotland, France and Ireland were well established in Jerez and they now had a consistent product to sell. This

---

46 The wine writer Talia Baiocchi is quoting Ashley Santoro of sherry bar Casa Mono.

consistency made sherry particularly conducive to being sold as a branded product. This period saw the birth of some of the great sherry brands, some of which persist to this day. One such merchant was Thomas Osborne who arrived in Spain from Devon in 1772. The company he founded, Osborne (now pronounced Osbornay in the Spanish style), is responsible for those black bulls you see dotted around the Spanish countryside. They were originally adverts for sherry. For once the word iconic to describe them isn't hyperbolic. So powerful are these symbols of Spain that they are sometimes vandalised by Catalan nationalists. William Garvey came from Ireland and built the largest bodega[47] in Jerez at the time. It was over 600 feet long and 125 feet wide. Like many in the wine business, he was an Irish Catholic fleeing British persecution. As in Oporto and Madeira, British shippers came to play a major part in the industry. George Sandeman from Oporto set up a sherry business. If you walk around Jerez today you still see the old British names such as Garveys, Harveys and Osborne, though most of these once-family-run businesses are now in the hands of multinational drinks companies. Yet the British never dominated the trade to the extent that they did in Portugal. They intermarried with the Spanish and French shippers creating a distinctive Anglo-Spanish merchant aristocracy. González Byass are one of the few firms still in family hands. It was founded in 1835 by a Spanish merchant, Manuel Maria González Angel, who built up the business from scratch. In 1833, penniless and without any obvious prospects, he married Victorina de Soto y Lavaggi whose father was the richest man in Jerez. His prospective father-

---

47 It was demolished in 1997 to make way for a supermarket. Jerez is a bit like that. Grand old buildings butted up against modern monstrosities with no regard to views or heritage. From the González Byass bodega you can see a Moorish castle and a 1970s block of flats.

in-law was not keen on the match and tried to dissuade González by drenching him with water and setting the dogs on him when he came a courting. González was clearly a man of some determination and the business flourished. The British market was so important that in 1855 his British agent, Robert Blake Byass, became a partner in the firm which became González Byass. The Byass family sold up in the 1980s, but the head of the company is still a Señor González. They are now so big that they have bought up whole streets in Jerez as part of their bodega. There was a security guard at the gate who waved us cheerily in when we said we were from London. Perhaps he thought we were there to buy massive quantities of sherry.

The nascent modern sherry industry was interrupted by the Peninsula War fought between 1807 and 1814. It led to turmoil across Iberia and severely disrupted both the sherry and port businesses. Initially Spain was allied with Napoleonic France against Britain and Portugal. But by 1808, Spain was occupied by a French army and a nasty guerilla war (this is the origin of the term) began. This escalated with the landing of a British army and featured some of the bloodiest conflicts of the Napoleonic wars. Both Jerez and Oporto were occupied by French armies. One of the most prominent French shippers, Juan Carlos Haurie, the nephew of the man who had taken on the *Gremio*, was ruined by having been a little too close to the occupying French forces. For a long time after the war, travel within the Iberian Peninsula was dangerous and there were uprisings and civil wars in both Spain and Portugal between liberal and absolutist factions. It was easier and more profitable to export than to sell internally.

Domecq were González Byass's great rivals. Pedro Domecq Lembeye was a French aristocrat fleeing the revolution. He first went to London where he went into the sherry business[48] in 1809 with a wealthy investor, Henry Telford, and an agent called John James Ruskin, father of *the* John Ruskin, the critic and writer. In 1816 he moved to Jerez and in 1818 he took over the ailing Haurie business. When Domecq died in 1839 his estate was worth over £1 million, a huge amount for the time. The ninety bedroom Palacio Domecq[49] dominates the main square in Jerez. It was built in 1788 and bought by Juan Pedro Domecq in 1855. Writing in 1876 Henry Vizetelly notes how there was a butt of very old sherry in their bodega dedicated to Ruskin père. Ruskin junior didn't have such a happy time in Jerez. He fell in love with one of Domecq's daughters, Adela, who apparently laughed at him when he declared his feelings for her. His love life went downhill from here.[50] But at least the sherry fortune enabled him to pursue his career. He wrote a (not terribly good) poem about the horrors inflicted on Spain and specifically sherry by the Peninsula Wars. Here's a little extract:

> "Alas, and it filled me with grief
> To see there not promise of fruit
> For the insect was eating the leaf
> And the worm was at work on the root."

It goes on like this for four verses. Dickens did better justice to sherry, extolling the virtues of a fine amontillado in 1858:

---

48 They took over an Irish business, Gordon, Murphy & Co, who should not be confused with Patrick Murphy whose firm Jean Haurie inherited in 1762.

49 When Fortune Brands, owners of Jim Beam bourbon, bought the Domecq firm in 2005, they didn't realise that the palace was included in the assets until someone asked a Fortune executive what they planned to do with it.

50 He married Euphemia Gray, but the marriage was annulled in 1854 on the grounds of "uncurable impotency". Gray then married John Everett Millais and bore him eight children.

" ...we are away on the wing of the wind to the
region of your nutty, full flavoured, unbrandied
Amontillado sherry, the golden juice I have
so often held up to the light with ridiculous
affectation of knowingness; the stuff, to use
Binn's the wine merchant's affectional phrase,
that Falstaff grew witty and racy on, and called
his sherris sack... "

Note that his amontillado is unfortified. It marks Dickens
down as a connoisseur. This is to differentiate it from
spurious amontillado that was sold in London which
would have been made from cheap olorosos sweetened and
fortified. It would still have been strong, probably around 15
to 16 percent due to evaporation of water. All sherry now
has to be fortified by law. In Spain it would have been drunk
bone dry but even the best were usually slightly sweetened
for the British market. A shipper writing in the late 19th
century is quoted by Henry Vizetelly as saying, "Whenever
I receive an order for the driest amontillado I have, I always
put a gallon or more of dulce (sweet wine) into it before
shipping it, because I know that if I sent the wine in its
natural state I should be certain to have it returned upon
my hands." Walter McGee, writing under the pseudonym
Don Pedro Verdad (Sir Peter Truth), in 1875 campaigned
for pure sherry, unfortified, unfiltered and unsweetened.
Amontillado was the drink for the sherry aficionado. The
word literally means in the style of Montilla, a region next
to sherry that still makes sherry-style wines. An amontillado
is an aged fino. It has matured under *flor* and then the *flor*
dies off and the wine starts to oxidise. The most famous
literary hymn to sherry comes in Edgar Allen Poe's *A Cask
of Amontillado*. In this short story Montresor lures his
victim, the ironically named Fortunato, for reasons that are
not entirely clear, to his doom with the promise of a rare

amontillado. Montresor then bricks his foe up in a wall. It was made into a film starring Vincent Price. The director, Roger Corman, amalgamates two Poe stories so the two men become rivals in love.

My favourite cultural sherry lovers, though, are Niles and Frasier Crane from US TV sitcom *Frasier*. In times of need they always turn to the sherry[51] decanter. The sitcom is set in the 1990s, when sherry couldn't have been less fashionable. The brothers were terrible snobs and loved the rituals around wine appreciation. Their wine club, Frasier says, is "just about wine and clear constitutional procedures for enjoying it".

This kind of wine fetishism has its roots in the late 18th century. Madeira distributors in America sold not only wine, but accessories such as fancy corkscrews, silver decanter tickets, crystal decanters, and special little glasses. English glassware was fashionable in America and Portugal. It was prestigious, but was also made in large quantities at a good price. Quality glassware was used, even in quite modest households in remote parts of Canada. The Atlantic world was connected in a way that seems very modern. One could even buy glasses that showed your political allegiance, Jacobite or Whig. Having the right wine glasses and decanters marked you out as a gentleman and were part of a universalism in accent, dress and manners amongst the ruling classes across the English-speaking world. Your lifestyle signalled your status in life and trivial things such as how to hold a glass of wine became important. There's a story about George Washington laughing at a friend "for holding the wine glass in the full hand". How ghastly! An appreciation of old wine, in contrast, was seen as a sign of good taste. In Oliver Goldsmith's 1773 play, *She Stoops to*

51 Though sometimes the writers displayed their ignorance about the wines by having a character say an "Andalucian amontillado" when someone who appreciated sherry would never use that term.

Conquer, one of the characters, Mr Hardcastle, says: "I love everything that's old: old friends, old times, old manners, old books, old wine." The modern language of wine appreciation developed as wine became more durable. People would try old wines and different vintages over an evening and needed a universally accepted way to discuss them. Books about wine appeared in the late 18th century and in the following century, wine columns featured in newpapers. In 1788 *Treatise on the Wines of Portugal* by John Croft was published, an early classic wine book.

But for all these new pretensions, wine was becoming an everyday commodity across the English-speaking world. Sherry became the most popular drink in Britain. It would have been drunk with meals in middle-class British homes. By the middle of the 19th century roughly 40 percent of the wine drunk in Britain was sherry. In 1873 7.5 million gallons of sherry were exported from Spain and three-quarters went to Britain and the Empire. In this it was greatly helped by the evolution of the modern wine bottle. Rather than having to buy a barrel of wine, it could be imported in cask and then sold in bottle. Sherry entered a long boom period that persisted until the 1980s. Even imitators around the world could not dent the popularity of the real thing. Not even when a doctor with the Dickensian-sounding name of J L W Thudichum wrote a spurious article claiming that sherry was dangerous due to the addition of gypsum before fermentation. Just as with madeira and Burtonised ale, small amounts were added to bolster acidity. It was harmless. Nowadays sherry producers use tartaric acid instead. At one point in the 1920s it was estimated that a quarter of the wine shipped to Britain was sherry.

Whilst sherry boomed, madeira went into a long, slow decline. Once America was an independent country it lost its exalted place on the table. America was no longer subject to the Navigation Act, so she could therefore buy drink from whoever she wanted. Claret and sherry began to compete and eventually usurped madeira in the States. After California became a state in 1850, wine from this former Spanish colony began to trickle east. This opening up is reflected in Jefferson's cellar. After the revolution he spent time in Paris where his eyes were opened to the glory of continental wine. When he was US President his cellar contained Chambertin, Margaux, Champagne, Montepulciano and Aleatico from Tuscany and Nebbiolo from Piedmont. His attempts to grow wine himself, at Montecillo, were less successful. The imported vines kept dying because of the phylloxera louse. After 1815 madeira became a niche product. It did, however, find something of a home on the other side of the world in India, where its heat-loving properties were appreciated. Britain lost an empire with the colonies in America, but there was a new one developing in the east. After the American War of Independence, Madeira shippers reorientated their trade. Wine was now shipped to Sumatra, China, Bara, Madras, and Bombay. Before the revolutionary war only 2.5 percent of ships from Madeira went east. Between the American and French Revolution about 40 percent of trade was now going east to British colonies and ports. The East India Company started shipping wines from Madeira around 1700. Some of the wine would be taken to India and then sold in London where it fetched a higher price because the journey had improved it. Other wines such as claret were shipped to India, but nothing thrived in the heat like madeira.

DRINKING THE EMPIRE

Madeira
Madeira's problem today is that the grapes that make the best wine are in short supply. After phylloxera, most of

the island was planted with a variety called Tinta Negra Mole, which generally makes quite average wines (though I was speaking with one producer who told me that when grown on the right soils and with the yield controlled it can actually be quite good. Nevertheless most madeiras are not made from grapes grown this way.) The cheaper wines will have been heated in *estufas* and can taste rather cooked. It's worth spending at least £20 on a bottle. The grape variety on the label is a good sign of quality: Sercial being the driest, then Verdelho, then Bual and then Malmsey/Malvazia. There's also a very rare grape called Terrantez, which was until recently nearly extinct. The better wines will have an age statement and the most expensive a vintage.

Good shippers include Henriques and Henriques, Barbeito, Justino Henriques and D'Oliveiras. The Blandy family own the Madeira Wine Company whose brands, apart from Blandy's itself, are Cossart & Gordon and Leacock's. For the true madeira experience, you really want to try a very old wine. They're not hard to find at auction or from merchants such as Berry Bros & Rudd. They are never cheap, but for the age and the experience, they are not that expensive either. Here are a few more widely available ones to try.

Blandy's Madeira Sercial Colheita 1998
Lovely notes of hazelnuts and tangy fresh lemons. Such vibrancy! One for the fino sherry lover.

Justino Henriques 10-year-old Verdelho
This is nutty and floral with just a touch of sweetness. Really tangy, runs the whole gamut of citrus fruits. A great introduction to madeira.

Henriques & Henriques 20-year-old Terrantez
Wow, what a nose! Nuts, caramel and a sharp dose of

vinegar too, extremely long and complex. Definitely not a wine for madeira beginners.

Blandy's 10-year-old Bual
Layers of caramel, walnuts, molasses and vanilla. This manages to be very sweet, without being in any way cloying. A good one to drink instead of port.

D'Oliveiras Malvazia Colheita 1992
I love the combination of intensely sweet marmalade leavened with smoke, nuts and a sharp tang. A mere baby, this will age for decades.

Sherry
Fino and manzanilla
Finos in the 19th century would have been closer to how amontillados taste today. Fino sherry has changed considerably in the last thirty years. It's now filtered heavily and cold-stabilised to create a very clean, refreshing drink such as the most famous fino, Tio Pepe, made by González Byass. It's a lovely drop, but recently there has been a Sir Peter Truth type hankering for something with a bit more character. There's a trend for unfiltered fino *en rama*, literally meaning raw. The nearest thing to an old style fino is probably something like Hidalgo's Manzanilla Pasada which is much richer than a normal manzanilla (a fino matured in Sanlúcar de Barrameda). It's not expensive and is extremely good.

A company called Equipo Navazos, which specialises in rare sherry bottling, has created in conjunction with Niepoort, the port house, an unfortified table wine made from Palomino Fino with some *flor* influence. It's a vintage wine, bottled at around 12 percent and is probably similar to the sort of everyday wines drunk in Jerez in the 18th and 19th century.

Amontillado
Bodegas Tradición Amontillado Muy Viejo 30 Years Old
A wine so complex that it makes me quite emotional. I defy you to take a sip without imagining music in your head. It's very expensive but shows just how good sherry can be. It's also quite incredibly dry so needs to be approached with caution.

González Byass AB Amontillado
At the other end of the scale, this is something that only sherry can do, offer so much complexity for so little money.

Oloroso
Emilio Lustau Oloroso Pata del Gallina
Tastes of toffee, molasses and nuts, but totally bone dry. This is an *almacenista* sherry which means it comes from a sherry merchant, someone who holds stocks of sherry to sell to bigger firms, but doesn't make his own wine. Sometimes these rare wines are bottled on their own.

Blended sherry
González Byass Matusalem
Just to show that blended sweetened sherries can be amazing too. The classic Matusalem is a blend of very old oloroso sweetened with PX. Utterly delicious and a good sherry to convert the non-sherry drinker.

Pedro Ximénez
Montilla, the region next door to sherry, produces sherry-style wines only from this grape variety. In fact, their sweet PXs are allowed to be included in sherry. The oldest sherry I've ever had was a pre-First World War Montilla which was astonishingly raisiny but also fresh.

These wines are absurdly undervalued. Try the Alvear Solera 1927 for a taste of that ancient magic. 1927 is the date the solera was started and contains some very old wines. Like molasses and walnuts with amazing complexity, this is the acme of the PX style.

Palo Cortado
There's a final style of sherry that I haven't mentioned called Palo Cortado. This is an unusual style that is neither amontillado nor oloroso. The sherry companies like to preserve an aura of mystery around it but nowadays it is made quite deliberately. At González Byass they start off with the sort of delicate mosto (unfermented grape juice) that will make a fino, they let the *flor* grow, but only for a short time, before fortifying it to kill off the *flor*. The wine then ages oxidatively. You end up with a wine with some of the delicacy of an amontillado but with the weight and richness of an oloroso. I'm not sure if I was meant to tell you this. González Byass do some breath-taking vintage Palo Cortado which are very expensive. Fernando de Castilla Antique Palo Cortado is quite spectacular and at under £50 not bad value at all.

Own label sherry
Finally, these sherries from supermarkets and wine merchants can be of an amazingly high standard. Look for the name of the producer at the bottom of the bottle. Good names are Lustau, Barbadillo or Sánchez Romate. Currently my favourite fino is the one marketed by the Wine Society made by Sánchez Romate.

8

OLD SOLDIERS AND SAILORS

On Thursday 7th May 2015 a rare bottle of port was sold at auction by Sotheby's for 6,800 euros. It was a bottle of Ferreira from the 1815 vintage and it was auctioned to tie in with the 200th anniversary of the Battle of Waterloo. At the other end of the scale Fonseca released a special Waterloo Reserve port for around £12 a bottle. Very nice it was too.

The success of the auction is testament to how interest in the Napoleonic Wars never seems to flag. There are more books written about Napoleon than anyone else in history. For drinks producers, the Napoleonic wars have proved the gift that keeps on giving. It's the hook that sells booze. There's Napoleon himself and cognac, not a brand but a legally defined type of brandy, equivalent to an XO. The story goes that Napoleon was a great cognac drinker and had it sent to him when he was off conquering Europe. The Courvoisier bottle is known as the Josephine in homage to the shape of the Empress's neck.

Napoleon's maritime nemesis, Nelson, also does sterling work in the marketing department. As we have seen, after losing his life at the Battle of Trafalgar in 1805 his body was pickled in rum and sent back to England. Afterwards rum was known in the Royal Navy as Nelson's Blood. There are now a few different rum brands that feature Nelson on the label including one featuring a hirsute one-eyed sailor who looks more like Barry Gibb in his 1970s pomp. Nelson is a popular name for a pub. At one point near the Old Street roundabout in East London there were two pubs facing each other, one called the Lord Nelson and one called The Nelson's Retreat. And until the 1920s the Woodhouse marsala firm marketed a wine called Bronte Nelson after the estate on Sicily that Nelson was given by King Ferdinand.

When John Woodhouse learned of Wellington's victory in 1815, he set aside a solera of the finest marsala wine for VIPs which he christened Waterloo. The merchants of Oporto had even better reason to honour Wellington as he had ejected the French from their city in 1809. Whilst there he enjoyed the 1794 vintage with George Sandeman. The 1815 vintage, a notably good one, was christened the Waterloo vintage. I am sure that much port was spuriously labelled 1815 to capitalise on the Duke's fame (though not of course the Ferreira auctioned by Sotheby's, I hasten to add before anyone's lawyers get in touch).

Hidalgo Palo Cortado label featuring the Iron Duke himself

When the French forces occupied Jerez the commander, Marshal Soult, dedicated a cask of the oldest wine in Domecq's cellars to Napoleon by writing the Emperor's name in chalk upon it. When the British army arrived they in turn dedicated barrels of sherry to Nelson, Pitt the Younger and Charles James Fox. The prize for most shamelessly playing both sides goes to Hidalgo sherry who today market a Wellington Palo Cortado and a Napoleon Amontillado. According to Javier Hidalgo, this is because the Hidalgo family hedged their bets during the Peninsular War and sold wine to both sides.

But it's not only the marketing allure of Napoleon, Nelson and Wellington that has proved so enduring, the war itself had a direct influence on the development of wine, perhaps more so than any other war in modern history. Bordeaux, madeira, sherry and champagne were all changed irrevocably. The war led to the routine bolstering of alcohol levels with sugar. The Continental System designed to cut Britain off from her empire of trade also cut France off from the rest of the world including the Caribbean. The resulting sugar shortage was solved in some style by Jean-Antoine Chaptal, scientist and Minister of the Interior under Napoleon, by planting sugar beet all over northern France. This cheap sugar was then used to bolster the alcohol levels in French wine. This was not a new technique, it's mentioned in Diderot's *Encyclopédie* of 1765, but it became routine under Chaptal's guidance and is now known as chaptalisation. It is now standard practice all over France and northern Europe.

Spare a thought for poor old Marshal von Blucher, commander of the Prussians, whose intervention late in the day at Waterloo proved so decisive. He doesn't have any drinks named after him, although he is, like Wellington, immortalised in an item of footwear, the Blucher shoe.

9

WORLD BEERS

When I first started talking about the idea behind this book, my friends would try to shoot down my argument by asking me about beer and the British link. What the world drinks is what the British call lager and everyone else simply calls beer. The Bohemian golden lager exemplified by such delicious beers as Pilsner Urquell and Budweiser (the Czech and not the US one) is now brewed all over the world. When refrigeration enabled beer to be brewed anywhere, it was the Bohemian model that they took. They didn't brew brown ale. The most popular beer in America, Australia, Canada and South Africa, all the places where you would expect to find the British influence, is a pilsner-style beer.

Recently, though, this global domination by lager has been challenged. Old British beer styles have been resurrected and reinvigorated. Oddly, much of this stimulus has come from the USA. As a reaction against the blandness of normal American lager-style beers, a movement now known as craft beer started in the US and then spread back to the mother country. This has sparked off a revolution (and I don't think it's too strong a word to call it a revolution) in world beer. Where previously brewing was all about consolidation, now there are small breweries opening all over the world. Interesting beers are now brewed everywhere even in countries such as Japan with little brewing tradition, and it's the American-influenced British classics that most appeal. The charge is led by a beer called IPA, India Pale Ale. This is the beer of choice for trendy folk around the world. Most incongruous of all, I went to a craft beer bar in Paris where bearded Parisians were sampling English-style beers. Being French they were drinking them out of wine glasses and doing far more smoking, flirting and gesticulating than actual drinking. Funny how the French can get it so wrong. But still, they were drinking English beer! Who could have predicted that twenty years ago?

IPA is a beer that has passed into legend and many of the generally accepted facts about it owe more to myth than to verifiable history.[52] The background to its creation is the gradual British conquest of India. This began with the formation of the East India Company in 1600 at the end of Queen Elizabeth I's reign. It was founded in imitation of the wildly successful Dutch East India Company. James Lancaster sailed in 1601 to grab a slice of the lucrative spice trade. There was no intention initially to conquer territory or form an empire. In 1662 Charles II married Catherine of Braganza and received the port of Bombay, or good harbour as it meant in Portuguese. It was just a trading colony, but marked the beginning of English encroachment in India that would only end in 1947. In 1707 the last strong Mughal Emperor, Aurangzeb, died. The Mughals, who were originally Persians, governed much of the sub-continent. From the death of Aurangzeb, India was increasingly divided between smaller local rulers. The European powers saw an opportunity to grab a slice. In 1716 the East India Company signed a treaty with Emperor Farrukhsiyar allowing them to trade without

---

52 I speak from bitter experience after writing an article about it that was ripped to shreds by some online beer scholars. Still, one of them then emailed me with some helpful research tips for this chapter. As William Blake put it: "Without contraries is no progression."

duty in much of Mughal India. The East India Company had its own private army and was able to back up business with force. Gradually it squeezed out and defeated its rivals, both local powers and the French, the Dutch and the Portuguese. With the loss of the American colonies in 1783, Britain's imperial and economic gaze turned firmly to the east.

One of the first things that the British needed to do when exploiting or exploring a new country was to secure a good source of alcohol. The Mughals were surprised by the drunkenness of the Europeans. The Mughal Emperor Akbar who ruled from 1542 to 1605 issued a decree allowing Europeans special dispensation to consume alcohol because "they are born in the element of wine, as fish are produced in that of water and to prohibit them the use of it is to deprive them of life." Alcohol was thought by Europeans to prevent tropical diseases and indeed much of the time would have been safer than drinking water. It was thought that large quantities of alcohol helped acclimatise Europeans to the tropical humidity. In fact, it would have done the opposite. In the 18th century the life expectancy for company servants or soldiers in India was approximately three years.

One of the most notorious drinks these early imperialists drank was arak. This would have been a rough drink distilled from the sap of coconut palms. Aniseed and other flavours would have been added to disguise the taste. It may well have contained methanol and could therefore have been highly toxic. It's still a problem. In 2002 at Mecca eleven pilgrims died after drinking badly distilled illicit arak. The East India Company had terrible problems with their men going on binges. In 1756 after too much arak one of General Clive's men tried to take the enemy fort of Baj-baj near Calcutta on his own. An eyewitness account in *The London Magazine* stated that "he took it into his head to scale a breach that had been made by the cannon ... then after having given three loud huzzas, he cried out, 'the place is mine."' We've all been there. There's another account of an arak-fuelled party in Sumatra where two died from a "surfeit of immeasurable drunkenness". Arak is the parent of such drinks as ouzo and raki which the British still have a bit of a problem with when on holiday.

Arak would normally have been consumed in the form of punch to disguise the taste. Samuel Johnson's dictionary defines punch as "a liquor made by mixing spirit with water, sugar and the juice of lemons and formerly with spice", which is as good a description as any. He also gets the etymology right. The word punch is derived from "panch", meaning five in Marathi or, as Johnson[53] puts it, "an Indian word expressing the number of ingredients". Punch houses opened throughout British India. In 1707 in Calcutta alone there were seven hundred. These were often rather insalubrious places and of course the booze wasn't up to much. Much preferred to the ubiquitous punch were imported drinks. Large quantities of European wines, beers and spirits were shipped to India. Joseph Collet, servant of the East India Company and later President of Madras, and his team of nineteen in a month made their way through "74 dozen and a half of wine, 24 dozen and a half of Burton Ale and pale Beer, 2 pipes and 42 gallons of Madeira wine, 6 Flasks of Shiraz, 274 bottles of toddy, 3 Leaguers and 3 Quartes of Batavia arrack, and 164 gallons of Goa". The wine would probably have been claret.[54] "Shiraz" meant Persian wine not something from the Barossa Valley and

---

53 James Boswell, writing in his *Life of Johnson*, describes how his subject's Lichfield accent was mocked: "Garrick (the actor) sometimes used to take him off, squeezing a lemon into a punch bowl ... looking round the company, and calling out, 'Who's for Poonsh?'"

54 A certain Louis Gaspard d'Estournel made a fortune selling the claret from his estate – Cos d'Estournel – in the East. In tribute to the source of his money he built the magnificent building that still stands on the estate today in a fantasy Indo-Chinese style. The nearest comparison would be the Brighton Pavilion.

"goa" would have been a kind of punch. There is a record of William Kirkpatrick, known in India as Mir Ghulam Ali, Sahib Allum, another servant in the Company, ordering some raspberry and cherry brandy, garden peas, good coffee, a pipe of hock and some good red port". All the comforts of home. Rum too was very popular in India. There's a recipe that was served to British soldiers called the "Fixed Bayonet" that consisted of a chicken stuffed with chillies and then boiled in rum. Don't try this at home.

It was impossible to brew beer in most of India as it was too hot, so that also had to be imported. It would have been far healthier than arak or rum and safer to drink than the water. One of the myths about IPA was that it was a beer especially brewed to survive the six month journey through tropical seas because ordinary beer was too weedy to stand up to such rough treatment. Therefore IPA was packed with hops and alcohol to preserve it for the sea voyage and then on the journey it mellowed into something quite extraordinary, the madeira of beers. Hops, as well as providing a pleasant bitter taste, also function as a preservative. There are elements of truth here, but the key point in its development was that it wasn't brewed especially for the journey nor was it the only beer that made the voyage. Even small ale at four to five percent could survive the journey,[55] though I'd imagine that a stronger beer stood a better chance of making it in good condition.

The beer that became known as IPA was brewed by Hodgson's Brewery of Bow in East London. Hodgson's were not one of the big London brewers. They were used as suppliers because they were handy for the East India Company docks at Blackwall on the north bank of the

55 This also rather puts paid to the idea that sherry, port etc. were fortified in order to survive the comparatively short journey from Spain or Portugal to Britain. The alcohol was probably there because that is how the British liked their wine.

Thames. The beer shipped to India was originally a strong stock beer containing about 10 percent alcohol. This was a type of beer brewed in October and designed to keep. In England it would have needed a year to mature in barrel and a year in bottle before being sold. Sometimes these old beers would be blended with young fresh beers and then sent out by breweries. This October beer, as it was known, was shipped to Bombay via Madeira and Rio de Janeiro, Cape Town and Mozambique. After six months at sea it was found to have matured and improved into something quite special. It was the equivalent of years in a British cellar.

Servants heading out to India from Britain would fill ships full of goods to sell on their own account. They weren't supposed to do this, but on the whole the Company turned a blind eye. They were paid a pittance and this was their main source of income. Some became enormously rich. Ships would return from the East laden with cotton and spices but in the early days of the Company, the British didn't have much that the Indians wanted, so the goods on the outbound voyage would be for Europeans in India. It was therefore very cheap to ship directly from London to India as most of the business was the other way. Hodgson gave generous credit terms, 18 months, to East India men. The *Calcutta Gazette* from January 1801 carried an advert for "beer from Hodgson ... just landed and now exposed for ready money only". Even though Hodgson's beer wasn't especially brewed it to survive the voyage nor was it the only beer that could, it proved a hit with thirsty Company servants and soldiers in India. It dominated the market and even inspired songs:

> "Who has not tasted Hodgson's pale beer
> With its flavour the finest that hops ever gave
> It drives away sadness, it banishs fear
> And imparts a glad feeling of joy to the grave."

Hodgson's then got greedy. Frederick Hodgson and Thomas Drane had the idea of cutting out the East India Company and shipping their beer directly. So they raised their prices by 20 percent and refused to grant credit to East India captains. Piqued by this, Campbell Marjoribanks, a director at the Company, met with a Burton brewer called Samuel Allsopp. Previously Allsopp and other Burton brewers had specialised in Burton Ales which were particularly popular in the Baltic and Russia, though they were shipped to India too. Burton ale is something quite different to IPA; it's a thick sweetish beer something like a modern day Winter Warmer. Peter the Great was a big fan of English beer. He had picked up a taste for it while in London. This trade with the Baltic was wrecked first by Napoleon's Continental System and then, as it picked up after the war, by the Russians increasing duties on English beer in 1822. Allsopp's were looking for a new outlet. After his meeting with Marjoribanks, Allsopp brewed a prototype IPA in a teapot. It met with approval and the beer started to be shipped to India. The new beer went out in 1823 and it was preferred to Hodgson's. Hodgson's gamble had failed.

Burton breweries could ship beer by canal to Liverpool and from there to India. Other Burton breweries such as Bass & Ratcliff got in on the act. By 1832 Hodgson market share was down to 28 percent, with Allsopp at 12 percent and Bass at 43 percent. The water in Burton-on-Trent contains gypsum, calcium sulphate, which makes the beer brighter, clearer and paler and gives it a pronounced acidic bite. Another part of the legend of IPA was that a cargo of beer bound for India was shipwrecked off the coast of Ireland. The locals pinched it, liked it and so the taste for IPA spread to Ireland. It's a lovely story with shades of *Whisky Galore* by Compton Mackenzie, but sadly it appears to have been invented by a later writer called William Molyneux. However, IPA did start to be sold, not just for export, but across Britain where it became enormously popular, though the term India Pale Ale was not coined until later. Beer historian Martin Cornell dates the first use of the term to an advert in the *Liverpool Mercury* on 30th January 1835. Railways meant that it was now cheap to send beer from Burton to London and other cities.

Pale ale was made possible by a new kind of malt. In the malting process, barley is soaked in water, allowed to partially germinate and then heated in order to dry it out. This converts the starch into sugar, making production of alcohol easier. Previously beers were dark because the drying heat could not be finely controlled, so you ended up with a highly roasted malt, brown malt. The change was made possible by coke. Coke is fuel often derived from coal but with fewer impurities. It burns much cleaner than coal (whose noxious fumes tainted the malt) and the temperature can be controlled with precision. This process was invented in the 17th century, but didn't become widespread in the production of malt until the mid-18th century. Maltsters[56] could now produce a brown malt for porters and a pale one for pale ales. The rest of Europe only had brown malt. Until the 19th century lagers from Bavaria and Bohemia would have been brown. It was a Viennese brewer, Anton Dreher, who, following a visit to Bass in Burton-on-Trent in the 1830s, brought the secret of pale malt back to the Continent. Legend has it that he used a special hollowed-out cane to hold beer samples stolen on his brewery visits. Back in Vienna he used his new-found knowledge to make a new pale lager, the prototype of the world's bestselling beer type. So, in some ways, even lager has a British root.

Back in Britain bottled pale ale became fashionable.

---

56 Maltsters are people who make malt. This labour intensive process was generally done on a large scale by specialist companies, rather than by the breweries themselves.

Music hall star Tom MacLagan sang a song about young rakes with top hats and mutton-chop sideburns drinking Bass Pale Ale. They sound a bit like hipsters (surely it can't be too long before the mutton-chop revival kicks in) and their choice of drink hasn't changed much, though modern rakes would probably decry Bass for being a bit commercial. Pale ale would have sold for about twice as much as ordinary beer and was generally preferred to wine by the middle classes. Walter Besant, a novelist and historian, wrote in the 1880s that "beer was universally taken at dinner; even at great dinner parties some of the guests would call for beer."

The IPA made for the home market would have contained about half the hops as that destined for India as it didn't have the long hot voyage to mellow it. If you want to try something like a pre-voyage Indian Pale Ale try a big American IPA such as Goose Island. There's a very funny book by Pete Brown[57] about his attempts to transport a barrel of IPA by sea to India so he could taste the beer as it would have been drunk by old India hands. IPA when served on draught became known as bitter because of its taste and this is the archetype for most British beers these days. Burton became the capital of British brewing. In 1834 there were fifteen brewers brewing about 70,000 barrels a year and by 1888 there were thirty-one producing over 3 million barrels. By 1877 Bass was the largest brewery in the world. That famous red triangle was the world's first trade-mark. It became available in every corner of the world and provided a little bit of England wherever you were. It was a global brand in the way that, for example, Coca-Cola or Apple are today. You can see that famous bottle in Edouard Manet's painting *A Bar at the Folies-Bergère*. In 1881 students at the Oxford Union won the motion that bottled Bass had done

57   *Hops and Glory: One Man's Search for the Beer that Built the British Empire.*

more for humanity than the printing press. Equally hyperbolic was a tribute to Bass paid in the 1884 book *Fortunes Made in Business* that reminds me somewhat of John Lennon claiming that the Beatles were bigger than Jesus. It's worth quoting at length:

> "It is no extravagant assertion to say that throughout the world there is no name more familiar than that of Bass. A household word amongst Englishmen, it is one of the first words in the vocabulary of foreigners whose knowledge of the English language is of the most rudimentary description ... The word 'Bass' is known in places where such names to conjure with as Beaconsfield, Gladstone, Bright, Tennyson and Dickens would be unintelligible sounds. To what corner of the habitable world has not Bass penetrated? He has circumnavigated the world more completely than Captain Cook. The sign of the vermilion triangle is sure evidence of

A Bar at the Folies-Bergère by Manet

civilisation. That trade mark has travelled from 'China to Peru', from 'Greenland's icy mountains to India's coral strand'. There it is in Paris or St Petersburg, Madrid or Moscow, Berlin or Bombay, Brussels or Baalbec, New York or Yokohama, San Francisco or San Stefano, Teheran or Trichinopoly. You meet the refreshing label up among Alpine glaciers and down in the cafes of the Bosphorus; among the gondolas of the Grand Canal at Venice, the dahabeeyah at the first cataract on the Nile, and the junks of China. It has reached the 'Great Lone Land'. It has refreshed the mighty hunter camping out in Wyoming, Montana or Dakota. It sparkles before the camp fire of the Anglo-Saxon adventurer out in the wilds of the Far West, and its happy aroma is grateful to the settler in the Australian bush. When the North Pole is discovered, Bass will be found there, cool and delicious."

But IPA wasn't the only beer that was shipped out to India. It wasn't even the most popular beer in the East. IPA was the beer of choice for officers, colonial administrators and Nabobs. The ordinary soldiers and clerks, however, the backbone of the Empire, would have drunk porter. Soldiers were issued with a daily ration. There are records[58] that show that until the 1860s more porter was sent out to India than IPA. Whitbread, one of the biggest London porter brewers, in some years exported 38,000 barrels of porter. These East India porters would have been heavily hopped like IPA for the journey out to India. A Dr Dempster, writing in 1863

---

58   Uncovered by beer historian Ron Pattinson.

wrote, "It is difficult to keep ale imported from England. Porter keeps better." Like IPA was until very recently, Porter is currently a rather forgotten beer, but in the 18th and early 19th centuries it was *the* beer and London was world capital of brewing. A Swiss visitor to London, César de Saussure, wrote in 1727:

> "Would you believe it, although water[59] is to be had in abundance and fairly good quality, absolutely none is drunk. In this country nothing but beer is drunk ... Another kind of beer is called porter, meaning carrier, because the greater quantity of this beer is consumed by the working classes. It is a thick and strong beverage, and the effect it produces, if drunk in excess, is the same as that of wine; this porter costs threepence a pot. In London there are a number of alehouses where nothing but this sort of beer is drunk."

Porter was a strong dark beer. It would have been heavily hopped and around seven percent alcohol. When Saussure was writing it would have been brown rather than black. Originally porter would have been made from brown malt; later it would have been made mainly from pale malt like pale ale with some black malt (also known as patent malt) added for colour. It was named after the porters who were the lifeblood of commercial London. On the far right of Hogarth's print, *Beer Street*, of 1751, there's a porter

---

59 The English have long been notorious for shunning water. Sir John Fortescue wrote in the 1460s that the English "drink no water, unless at certain times upon a religious score and by way of doing penance." When Benjamin Franklin worked in London for a printing firm, he was mocked as the "water American" for his preference for water over beer.

drinking his beer from a tankard. These men were licensed to carry goods around the City and on and off ships. This powerful beer provided alcohol and refreshment, but also a significant number of calories. Many piecemeal workers such as porters were paid in the pub, so consequently much of their wages were spent here. Some apprentices were even paid in beer. Until the 1960s, workers doing particularly arduous jobs at Fullers brewery in west London, such as cleaning out the mash tuns, were given extra beer as a reward.

Porter was a beer that suited 18th century London, at that time by far the largest city in the world. Beer was difficult and slow to transport before railways, therefore, the breweries had to be situated in towns. Porter could be brewed on a bigger scale than any previous beer and at a higher temperature, so it could be brewed for more of the year. It would have then been stored in enormous vats containing thousands of barrels worth of beer. Here it was matured for up to two years when it would take on a wine-like tang. Sometimes old beer and returns would be added to the vat. This aged or "stale" beer would then be sent out to pubs with young mild beer where they could be mixed by the landlord (Guinness in Dublin was sent out this way until the 1950s). In much the same way that producers add old wines to madeira and sherry to add complexity, the pubs were aiming for a consistent product with a taste of the old beer, but cheaper and with the freshness of the young beer. Whereas before many pubs and larger households would have brewed their own beer, porter saw the takeover of London drinking by big breweries, because you can't brew porter on a small scale and you need enormous vats to age it in. This required capital. These vats were prone to accidents. On the 17th October 1814 a vat twenty-two feet high containing over 3,500 barrels of beer ruptured at Meux and Co brewery on Tottenham Court Road. A tsunami of black strong beer engulfed the surrounding slums killing at least eight people. London was literally drowning in drink.

The big porter brewers were Whitbread's, founded by Samuel Whitbread in 1742, and Truman, Hanbury, and Buxton,[60] whose enormous Black Eagle brewery on Brick Lane was producing 400,000 barrels of beer in a year. It closed in 1989 and it's now an arts centre with shops, bars and markets. The biggest of them all was Barclay-Perkins founded by a Quaker family. In 1867, Barclay-Perkins brewed 423,444 barrels. You can still see signs from these now defunct breweries above pubs around London. The families of these brewers became involved in politics. Samuel Whitbread was MP for Bedford. Henry Thrale, son of the brewer Ralph Thrale of Southwark, was MP for Southwark for twenty-three years. It wasn't just the porter brewers, both Allsopp and Bass were elevated to the peerage. There was a very influential beer faction in the House of Lords that became known as the Beerage. The Liberals blamed the loss of the 1874 General Election on the influence of the big brewers and distillers in the Conservative Party. Gladstone's Licensing Acts of 1870 had disturbed these vested interests. Gladstone wrote that "More immediately operative causes have determined the elections. I have no doubt what is the principal. We have been borne down in a torrent of gin and beer."

The big porter breweries were at the cutting edge of technology. Copper and iron vats began to replace wood and one of the first steam engines in Britain was installed in Whitbread's Chiswell Street brewery near the Barbican in 1787 by James Watt. This brewery was one of the wonders of the industrial age with an unsupported roof bigger than that of Westminster Hall. Instruments such as

---

60 They have recently been revived and are brewing from a site in Hackney Wick about three miles from the old site on Brick Lane.

the hydrometer took the guesswork out of fermentation. Breweries had early forms of refrigeration meaning that they could make beer even in the summer months. To put this into perspective, refrigeration in winemaking didn't become standard practice until long after the Second World War. Porter brewing was uniquely suited to mass production. It was one of the first businesses to be industrialised.

When people came to London for the Great Exhibition of 1851, they were eager to try the famous London porter, although at the Exhibition site itself no alcoholic drinks were on sale. In the late 18th century porter took off outside London, in Dublin, Glasgow and around England. Porter spread around the world. George Washington was a porter fan. There's evidence of a Philadelphia brewery shipping porter to India and indeed it is still brewed in Pennsylvania by Yuengling and Stegmaier. Everyone was trying to imitate that London taste. In 1904 in Denmark at the Carlsberg brewery a chemist, N Hjelte Claussen, finally discovered what gave porter its distinctive tang. He isolated a yeast that he named Brettanomyces, British yeast. The vats in London's breweries would have been infected with this yeast; it was the thing that set proper London porter apart and made it incomparable. In wine the presence of Brett (its usual abbreviation) is considered a fault. Sometimes you get the distinct smell of old socks. But in small quantities it gives wine a savoury, almost animal quality. Château de Beaucastel in Châteauneuf-du-Pape is famous for its Brett.

In the 1830s porter, however, began to lose popularity in London. The growth of the railways was key to this change. Beer could be brewed more cheaply in Burton-on-Trent and then sent overland to London. Pale ale, Burton's signature beer, was fashionable. It was a sign of status to be seen drinking bottled pale ale. The working classes turned to mild ale. These beers were cheaper to make than porter. They didn't require huge vats and they didn't need maturing for as long. Ale, both mild and pale, was far more profitable. Gradually porter began to die out in London. The big brewers ripped out their huge vats and moved over to ale production. Rather than be made from the old brown malt, porter was now made from a mixture of pale malt which could be more efficiently fermented, and black malt which just provided colour. Malt was heavily taxed so it made sense to use less. This new porter wasn't aged properly, it lost that acetic tang and just became a dark beer. People noticed the changes and complained. Porter began to decline in alcohol content too. During the First World War alcohol content of porters went down to three percent, a mere shadow of its 18th century heyday.

But porter never entirely went away. It continued to be brewed around the world often in the most unlikely of places: Canada, South Africa, Sweden, Poland, Sri Lanka, Finland, Denmark and even the Czechs carried on producing porters. But it was in the form of Guinness that porter continued as a true world drink. Guinness began as a porter brewery and are now famous for their stout. What's the difference between these two drinks? Initially stout simply meant strong and could be applied to any beer, but gradually it was only applied to porter. Breweries would list various kinds of porter. A special kind of high strength porter exported to the Empress of Russia was known as Imperial Russian Stout. There were high tariffs on Burton Ale in Russia, but not porter. Eventually the word porter was dropped and stout came just to mean a strong porter. After a while it stopped meaning that. Stout came to mean a dark or black beer. Nowadays the two seem to have swapped places in strength. Stout tends to be lower in alcohol, blacker and drier, whereas porters are stronger, browner and sweeter. The two words, however, can more or less be used interchangeably. Guinness have recently launched a porter that is lower in alcohol than their stout and a West Indies porter that is stronger. If you want to read a mass of contradictory evidence then Google "what's the difference between stout and porter".

While porter died out in London, in Ireland it became king. John Purser from Reid's[61] brewery in London, who until quite recently still made a stout that was a rival to Guinness, was sent to Dublin in 1776 to show the locals how to do it. Arthur Guinness,[62] an Anglo-Irish Protestant, founded a brewery at St James's Gate in Dublin in 1759. He probably began brewing porter around 1783. By 1799 he was brewing nothing but porter. He soon began selling his beer back to Britain and the colonies. In 1801, just over a year before he died, he came up with the recipe for a West Indies Porter, a blend of pale and dark malt with some brown. Porter was also made in Cork by Beamish, another Protestant family. Guinness and Beamish both exported to India and the West Indies. Just as in England, brewers became influential figures. Arthur Guinness II became Governor of the Bank of Ireland and William Beamish became an MP. By 1833 Guinness had overtaken Beamish to be the biggest brewery in Ireland. Between 1855 and 1880 sales rose sixteenfold. By the end of the 19th century Guinness were the biggest brewery in Europe. Largely they brewed two types of beer: Guinness Extra Stout for the home and British market, and Foreign Extra Stout, an evolution of West Indies Porter, for export.

Guinness adopted the harp as their symbol in 1862 to emphasise the Irishness of the company. Oddly for a brand

---

61 In 1961 Guinness paid Watney Combe Reid £28,000 to stop brewing Reid's Stout and take Guinness in their pubs.

62 I had a bit of an argument on the internet with an American who said I couldn't put Guinness in the book as it was Irish. First of all it's my book and so I can do what I like, but secondly from 1801 until 1922 Ireland was part of the United Kingdom. Furthermore the Guinnesses were an Anglo-Irish family and until 2005 their largest brewery was in Park Royal, West London, opening in 1936.

so associated today with great advertising, Guinness was pretty slow with the marketing. Guinness would be exported in cask and then bottled by independent companies around the world. Until the 20th century these bottlers would have a stronger brand identity than the drink inside the bottle. Customers would ask for drinks by the logo on the bottle: for example, the bottling firm of Johnson & Co of Liverpool used an elephant emblem. Often bottlers would work with both Guinness and their great rival for world beer status, Bass. These bottlers would then advertise both products alongside each other. Guinness resolutely refused to advertise, thinking that it was only for inferior products. Nevertheless, Guinness's ubiquity was astonishing. Guinness employed a number of people who were paid to explore the world checking on the distribution and quality of the beer, called travellers. One of these, J C Haines, working in the 1890s, mentioned how the locals in Cairo had taken to drinking Guinness: "I occasionally ... saw three or four Arabs sitting with a quart of Guinness before them." In 1898 an explorer, Ralph Patterson Cobbold, managed to find a bottle of Guinness in the high Hindu Kush for which he paid the extortionate sum of eight shillings. "The stout was excellent," he pronounced.

In 1929, due to stagnating sales in Britain, Guinness took the momentous decision to advertise. They engaged the services of the advertising agency S H Benson, who created some of the most charming and best-loved advertising ever. Those wonderful whimsical animals such as the Toucan were designed by John Gilroy. Some of the copy was written by Dorothy L Sayers:

> "If he can say as you can
> Guinness is good for you
> How grand to be a Toucan
> Just think what Toucan do"

Guiness poster from 1930s designed by James Gilroy

Another example of their eye for marketing was the *Guinness Book of Records*. It was originally created in 1955 purely as a publicity stunt. It was not expected to make money, but it has become a hugely successful global publishing phenomenon.

I don't find modern draught Guinness terribly exciting, but the Guinness Foreign Extra Stout is a direct link to the kind of beer that would have been brewed in eighteenth century London. It is descended from West India Porter which was first sent out to the colonies in 1801. The name was changed to Foreign Extra Stout in 1849. Brewed in Dublin for export, it's high in alcohol at 7.5 percent and crucially contains a proportion of "stale" beer and the aged beer contains traces of the Brettanomyces yeast which give the beer its distinct almost wine-like tang. It's a bit different from the original as it is now pasteurised and carbonated rather than being live. But it's still a wonderful beer and probably the closest thing to an old London porter that you can buy today. Whilst Britain was in full imperial retreat, Guinness were setting up an empire of their own, based on this Foreign Extra Stout.

In 1963 the first Guinness brewery outside Britain and Ireland was opened in Nigeria. This was followed by breweries in Kenya, Uganda, Tanzania, Sudan and Somalia. There are now breweries all over Africa as well as Jamaica, Canada, Australia, New Zealand, Singapore, Malaysia and many others. Most recently, in 2000, Guinness opened a brewery in Ethiopia. The legend "Guinness is Good for You" appears in Amharic on the label. African Guinness still makes this claim which they're not allowed to do in the rest of the world. Guinness, especially in Foreign Extra Stout form, contains a significant amount of calories so does function, like London porter, as a source of sustenance as well as refreshment. Just as in 18th century London, it is drunk in places such as Singapore by labourers who appreciate just this quality. So, in moderation, it probably is good for you. Cleverly Guinness went into partnership with local companies and employed mainly local people. Now African drinkers think of Guinness as their own. For these foreign-brewed Guinnesses, a concentrated beer called the rather unromantic sounding Guinness Flavour Extract is shipped out from Dublin and brewed with a beer made from local ingredients. Each Foreign Extra Stout is distinctly different depending on precisely where it's brewed. The concentrate makes up roughly two percent of the total. Both the Jamaican and Nigerian versions are widely available in London and are delicious.

So while lager conquered Britain after the war, a descendent of a half-forgotten London beer quietly spread around the world thanks to the vision of an Irish brewery.

DRINKING THE EMPIRE

Pale ale

Sadly the once mighty Bass has fallen victim to brewery consolidation. The old brewery is now owned by Molson Coors, but the brand is owned by another multinational, Anheuser-Busch InBev. Bass is now brewed by Marstons in Burton, but only small quantities and not widely distributed. A rather insipid version of Bass is also brewed in the US.

Some brands do come back from the brink though. Brewed since 1829, for a long time Worthington White Shield was one of the only bottle-conditioned pale ales widely available in Britain. It almost died out in the late 90s, but is now brewed by Molson Coors in Burton and its future looks secure. It's a lovely beer that has won the CAMRA's best bottled beer in Britain a record three times.

For the full no holds barred American IPA experience, a drink such as Goose Island from Chicago is hard to beat.

Jaipur by Thornbridge, based near Derbyshire, is a good example of the British response to the American version of an originally British style. It is another one in a big hoppy citrus style. It's only 6 percent but to me tasted stronger.

Porter and stout

Guinness Foreign Extra Stout (Dublin-brewed)
I've probably written enough about this already. Suffice to say that's worth seeking out as it's marvellous and has the true winey taste of old style London porter.

Guinness Extra Stout
This is ordinary Guinness without the nitrogen and I much prefer it as it's got a proper bite to it.

Samuel Smith's Oatmeal Stout
Sam Smith's are a Yorkshire brewery who for some reason

own a large estate of beautiful Victorian pubs in Central London. They only sell their own brand beers, wines and spirits. The oatmeal stout is available bottled.

Fullers London Porter
This is made with a large percentage of brown malt, as well as pale, crystal and chocolate malt. It's brewed to 5.5 percent and it is rich and chocolatey with a pleasant sweetness about it. It's probably similar to an unaged London porter. As an experiment I wish they'd age some and sell it at their brewery pub mixed with young beer for that authentic 18th century taste.

Porterhouse Brewing Company Celebration Stout
This is an Imperial Russian Stout from Ireland, the kind of beer that Catherine the Great might have enjoyed. This is malty and creamy with lovely balance. I didn't really notice the 7.5 percent alcohol.

Rodenbach Grand Cru
Not a porter or a pale ale, but a Belgian red ale aged for up to two years in oak *foudres* which are infected with Brettanomyces. It has sweet cherryish fruit and then a strong acetic tang.

10

GIN PALACES

I'm sitting in The Viaduct Tavern,[63] fabulously ornate pub near the Old Bailey in the City of London. It's one of those places that makes you marvel at the splendour of the Victorian age that put so much pride into something as prosaic as a pub. Compare it to the modern minimalist craft beer pubs that have started to spring up over the capital which are really just beer shops. The fug of warmth, beer and mulled wine in the pub on a cold December's night was intoxicating. But that's nothing compared with the baroque splendour of the interior. The bar is polished mahogany surrounded by etched glass, the beaten metal ceiling is high and the walls covered in elaborate frescoes representing Commerce, Agriculture, Science and Fine Arts. The first three are essential to the production of gin, the last less so. Gin is why this place exists. It's now a pub owned by Fullers, the Chiswick brewery, but it was originally built in 1869 as a so-called "gin palace". It's the last surviving actual gin palace in London although up the road is the Princess Louise which was built in the gin

---

63 When you read about The Viaduct, it will always be mentioned that cellars used to house prisoners from nearby Newgate Prison. This theory is almost certainly nonsense. It's been quite thoroughly debunked by London historian Peter Berthoud simply by pointing out that the tubes generally described as feeding tubes for the prisoners are in fact coal chutes. Premises all over London have similar chutes in the pavement that lead down to the cellars.

palace style, as is The Red Lion just off Jermyn Street, a symphony in etched glass.

Probably the first gin palace, the one that set the style, was opened by a firm of wine merchants, Thompson and Fearon's, on Holborn Hill built in 1831. It was designed by John Buonarotti Papworth who designed the Montpellier Pump Room in Cheltenham and the interior of the St James's gentlemen's club, Boodles[64]. Another well-known architect who designed gin palaces was Stephen Geary who is best remembered for Highgate Cemetery. None of the pubs designed by these men survive.

Their brief heyday was created by the budget of 1825 which saw a reduction in the duty on spirits. For a brief time gin was actually cheaper than beer. A young Charles Dickens wrote about the gin palace phenomenon in his *Sketches from Boz* for London's *Monthly Magazine*:

> "The primary symptoms were an inordinate love of plate-glass and a passion for gas-lights and gilding ... All is light and brilliancy. The hum of many voices issues from that splendid gin-shop which forms the commencement of the two streets opposite; and the gay building with the fantastically ornamented parapet, the illuminated clock, the plate-glass windows surrounded by stucco rosettes, and its profusion of gas-lights in richly-gilt burners, is perfectly dazzling when contrasted with

---

64 Boodles is also a make of gin that was part of the now-defunct Seagram spirit empire. It was named after the gentlemen's club. According to my late uncle who was a member, when Boodles found out that someone was using the name of their club for a gin, they wrote to Seagrams to complain. Happily a compromise was reached: Boodles gin were allowed to keep the name and in return every member of Boodles got a case – six bottles – of gin free a year from the company. It's a deal that persists to this day.

the darkness and dirt we have just left. The
interior is even gayer than the exterior. A bar of
French-polished mahogany, elegantly carved,
extends the whole width of the place... "

The term gin palace now has jocular connotations. One
refers to luxury yachts as floating gin palaces. The surviving
buildings built in the style seem so beautiful to our eyes that
it's hard to imagine that at the time they were considered
rather sinister. They were not the convivial places for a
quiet pint that they are now, but ruthless money-making
machines. They were built at great cost for the specific
aim of luring people in and they only sold gin. There was
no beer, proper food or pub games. Unlike old-fashioned
taverns they were not divided into sections with "snugs"
and private rooms upstairs. There was no seating. There
was nothing to distract from the purpose of inebriation.
The gin was sold under such catchy names as "butter gin",
"the out and out!", "the no mistake" and the "real knock-me
down". There was a kind known as "cream gin" which was a
mixture of gin, cream and sugar.

These drinks and the inebriation they produced
provided escapism from the grind of everyday London life.
The gin palaces themselves were exciting and welcoming
but most importantly, warm. The climate in the early 19th
century was particularly cold. The gin palace craze caught
the end of the Little Ice Age. The Thames froze almost
every year. London was a dark, cold, gloomy place. These
new drinking shops, in contrast, were lit by gas at a time
when gas lighting was a rarity. They must have seemed
like a visitation from another world. A good comparison
would be a casino in Las Vegas with all the neon, the grand
scale and the glamorous girls, who are all part of a ruthless
scheme to extract as much money as possible from their
visitors. There were even "showily-dressed damsels" in

some gin palaces to encourage men to spend their money. A well-placed gin palace could make a guinea (just over a pound) a minute, a massive sum at the time. The rough equivalent would be about £65 a minute so in a night, roughly seven until midnight, a gin palace could turn over the modern equivalent of £20,000.

Speaking to a House of Commons Select Committee on Drunkenness, a London grocer described a new gin palace that had just opened near his shop:

> "(The gin palace) was converted into the very
> opposite of what it had been, (from) a low dirty
> public house with only one doorway, into a
> splendid edifice, the front ornamented with
> pilasters, supporting a handsome cornice and
> entablature and balustrades, and the whole
> elevation remarkably striking and handsome ...
> the doors and windows glazed with very large
> squares of plate glass, and the gas fittings of the
> most costly description ... When this edifice
> was completed notice was given by placards
> taken round the parish, a band of music was
> stationed in front ... and when the doors
> were opened the rush was tremendous, it was
> instantly filled with customers and continued
> so till midnight."

Once you got beyond the superficial glamour, things weren't quite so elegant. Here's Dickens again on a gin palace at closing time:

> "It is growing late, and the throng of men,
> women, and children, who have been
> constantly going in and out, dwindles down
> to two or three occasional stragglers – cold,

wretched-looking creatures, in the last stage of emaciation and disease. The knot of Irish labourers at the lower end of the place, who have been alternately shaking hands with, and threatening the life of each other, for the last hour, become furious in their disputes, and finding it impossible to silence one man, who is particularly anxious to adjust the difference, they resort to the expedient of knocking him down and jumping on him afterwards. The man in the fur cap, and the potboy rush out; a scene of riot and confusion ensues; half the Irishmen get shut out, and the other half get shut in; the potboy is knocked among the tubs in no time; the landlord hits everybody, and everybody hits the landlord; the barmaids scream; the police come in; the rest is a confused mixture of arms, legs, staves, torn coats, shouting, and struggling. Some of the party are borne off to the station-house, and the remainder slink home to beat their wives for complaining, and kick the children for daring to be hungry."

Dickens's *Sketches from Boz* were illustrated by George Cruikshank. *The Gin Shop* from 1829 shows a typical Victorian gin shop, not quite a gin palace. All looks fairly normal until you notice that the gin is being served from coffins. In the back of the shop skeletons are dancing around a massive cauldron and the man and the woman drinking the gin are standing in a massive bear trap that could spring on them at any moment. The message is clear: gin = death. It's not particularly subtle, but it is effective.

It's very reminiscent of an illustration from almost a century earlier, *Gin Lane* by William Hogarth. The early

Victorian gin palace boom was almost a rerun of the first gin craze of the mid-18th century. Gin was based on a Dutch spirit called Geneva, meaning juniper. Originally this would have served a medicinal purpose: the juniper was thought to be a cure for stomach aches. Juniper bushes grow wild all over Europe. In fact, to this day they are not cultivated; the berries, which are really miniature pine cones, are foraged. As spirits began to be drunk for pleasure, the juniper was something easily available and with a taste strong enough to disguise the taste of the rough liquid.

This alcohol would usually have been distilled from grain but brandy would also have been used as a base. Other more exotic flavourings such as cardamom from the Dutch East India Company were also used but it was the taste of the juniper that predominated. Many Englishmen would have picked up a taste for Geneva when fighting alongside the Protestant Dutch in the religious wars that wracked Europe in the 17th century.

The Gin Shop by George Cruikshank

It really took off, however, when the Glorious Revolution of 1688 put Dutchman William of Orange on the throne. As we have seen, with William's accession came war with France. The new king was in need of money to fund his campaign. He saw breaking the monopoly of the Worshipful Company of Distillers and taxing spirits as the way to pay for it. Furthermore William's supporters in parliament were largely landowners who, thanks to a succession of big harvests, had a glut of corn. A profitable way to use this up was to distill it into spirits to be made into gin. The King lowered the duty on gin, but raised it on beer and other spirits especially brandy. So a combination of factors – good harvests meaning that there were large quantities of grain available for distilling, deregulation of the distilling industry and tax on French brandy – resulted in a tsunami of gin hitting London in the early 18th century. Gin was now made by a myriad of amateur distillers rather than by the old guild. It was the first time in history that large quantities of spirits had been cheaply available. After 1694 a glass of gin cost less than beer. Gin consumption rocketed from half a million gallons in 1688 to 19 million in 1742.

The result was the carnage that Hogarth recorded. A statistic that illustrates how much gin affected London was that the population didn't grow between 1728 and 1750 despite approximately 8,000 immigrants arriving in the city every year. The number of christenings declined. Stunted sickly children were being born to drunken mothers. Perhaps the saddest story associated with the gin craze was of Judith Dufour who took her 2-year-old son from the workhouse where he had been staying as she had been incapable of looking after him. Once out, Judith murdered the child for the clothes he had been given, sold them for 1s 4d and spent it immediately on gin. There were a number of Acts of Parliament designed to stop the drunkenness. The problem was that most of the MPs were making so much money out of the craze that it wasn't in their interests to stop it. Inevitably the bills were ineffective and the madness continued.

Henry Fielding of *Tom Jones* fame, who was also a magistrate, wrote in 1751 that gin caused a "new kind of drunkenness". This belief that drunkenness from gin is worse than other kinds has persisted to this day. People still say things like, I shouldn't drink gin because it makes me sad. As the gin would have been very crudely distilled, there is no doubt that these early gins could have had unusual effects. Many would have contained methanol, a dangerous form of alcohol, as well as other less harmful impurities. There is some debate, however, amongst historians as to what extent the gin scare was caused by gin and how much of it was tied up with a ruling-class fear of the mob and public disorder. Undoubtedly problems caused by gin were exacerbated by events such as the 1713 Treaty of Utrecht which deposited demobbed soldiers from the War of Spanish Succession on the streets who became robbers, beggars and highwaymen. It's therefore interesting to ask why it was only London that had a gin craze. All parts of Britain had the same combination of deregulated distillation industries and an excess of grain to be distilled. But there was something unique about London.

London was in 1716 the largest city in Europe with over half a million inhabitants. Many of the new inhabitants came to the slums of St Giles. This was the epicentre of the gin craze and it was where Hogarth's *Gin Lane* was set. This is the area south of Bloomsbury between the churches of St Giles-in-the-Fields, built in 1733 and still standing to this day, and St Martin-in-the-Fields, also still standing. The words St Giles became synonymous with desperate poverty. To "dine with St Giles and the Earl of Murray" meant to go without one's dinner. The Earl was buried in St Giles churchyard. Many of the inhabitants would have come from Ireland and the area became known as Little Dublin. The houses were old and insanitary. It was run on a system of subletting where the people who actually dwelt in the houses were royally screwed. A tiny group of people owned the area who would then let streets to speculative businessmen who would then in turn let out houses whose rooms would then be let out and so on and so on until some families were renting a corner of a cellar. These cellars often flooded and were filled with effluent. Under these circumstances you can see why people would turn to drink. As Peter Ackroyd put it in his *Biography of London*, "only sex and drink could make the situation bearable" and indeed the area was notorious for sexual licence and prostitution. The inhabitants of the slums had nothing to sell so they sold themselves. Ackroyd goes on to say that "by the 18th century drinking reached massive, even crisis, proportions". A canting (slang) song from the late 18th century gives a flavour of the place:

> "The first time I saw the flaming mot (girl or whore),
> Was at the sign of the Porter Pot.
> I called for some purl, and we had it hot
> With gin and bitters too!
> We threw off our slang at high and low,
> For we both got as drunk as Davy's sow... "

There were too many people crammed into too small a place. There was no peace and your senses would have been continually assaulted by vile smells, sounds, cold and damp. There's now very little left of the old slum area. It was cleared in the 19th century when New Oxford Street was built through the middle of it. One of the most notorious sites is now Google's London headquarters. Yet this area is still a congregation area for the destitute.[65] On a recent visit

---

65 It's also a centre for the occult. There are at least three alternative bookshops ie magic, conspiracy theories and general woo woo, within a mile of St Giles Church.

to St Giles Church there were tramps sleeping or trying to sleep on the hard wooden pews. St Martin's Church houses a centre for the homeless and the tower of Centre Point, which was in the heart of the old parish of St Giles, acts as a congregation point for down-and-outs. Hogarth would have recognised some aspects of the area even today.

The Gin Act of 1751 brought the business under some semblance of control. Distilling licences for £2 were issued, but what really did for the first gin craze was not legislation but a series of bad harvests that forced up the price of grain. Food as well as gin became more expensive and the poor couldn't afford to get drunk on such an epic scale. People were still looking for an escape from misery and poverty. If anything, by the early 19th century, when gin palaces started to appear, things were worse. London had expanded from a city of 750,000 in 1751 to 1.4 million by 1815 and by 1860 it was over 3 million. One of the downsides of industrialism was that previously skilled workers were pushed out of their trades as they became redundant. Livelihoods were lost and suddenly all workers could command were pittance wages in sweatshops. Conditions such as these persisted until the 20th century. William Blake referred to the British working class as "white negroes" who "seek salvation in gin and debauchery". There was also rural poverty especially in the south of the country where the population existed on the "verge of starvation" according to the social historian John Burnett. For many the only answer was prostitution. Visitors to London were often shocked by the scenes of degradation that they saw.

Dostoevsky, who must have been no stranger to poverty, on a visit to London in 1862 painted a heart-breaking image of a girl "not older than six, all in rags, dirty, barefoot and hollow cheeked; she had been severely beaten and her body, which showed through the rags, was covered in bruises ...

She kept on shaking her tousled head as if arguing about

something, gesticulated, and spread her little hands and then suddenly clasped them together and pressed them to her little bare breast."[66] No wonder that children were enthusiastic gin drinkers. Henry Mayhew wrote in the 1850s, "The girls, I am told, are generally fonder of gin than the boys." If you lived here you would need an escape of some sort. It seems that whenever gin was cheap enough, Londoners would drink themselves stupid. And gin was indeed very cheap. A quarter pint of gin in 1830 was around threepence-ha'penny compared with twopence for beer. Gin was even sold in prisons.

But it wasn't just the poor and the hopeless who were getting off their faces. Drink and drunkenness were institutionalised in the city. Many workers were paid in the pub, some as we have seen were even paid in drink. It seems there was something about London that encouraged the population to indulge in excess. Samuel Johnson knew well the perils of drink. He eventually gave it up as he knew that once he had had one drink he would then seek utter drunkenness. He wrote that "a man is never happy in the present unless he is drunk". If you could anaesthetise yourself with gin then you would. A true Londoner would seize on any opportunity to go on a spree. Historian M Dorothy George wrote: "temptation to drink and gamble were interwoven with the fabric of society to an astonishing extent, and they did undoubtedly combine with uncertainties of life and trade to produce that sense of instability, of liability to sudden ruin." I think this gets to the crux of London life. It was a gamble, the highs and lows were crammed in next to each other and no drink mirrors the rollercoaster ride of urban living more than gin. And things haven't changed these days. London is still driving

66 *Winter Notes and Summer Impressions.*

155

people mad whether through alcohol or drugs. In London you are never far from someone shouting like King Lear on a street corner. Londoners seem particularly prone to suicide, madness, drug addiction and gambling. It is as if there is something about London that can send you mad. It's a good time to quote Nathaniel Lane, the Restoration dramatist, who on being committed to Bedlam said: "They said I was mad: and I said they were mad: damn them, they outvoted me."

Yet against all the odds, gin started to become respectable. Gin palaces, despite their seedy image, were actually a sign of how gin was no longer made by backstreet distillers; a sign big money moving in. Gin, the drink of destitution and misery, was reinventing itself as a dry, subtly flavoured drink for the urban sophisticate. Acceptable gin is cheap to make. All you need is alcohol, which can be made from anything, and juniper. It's even easier to make an ersatz version. In Hogarth's day raw alcohol was flavoured with turpentine and sugar and passed off as gin. While during Prohibition so-called bathtub gin was made from acetone and sulphuric acid. The gin served in gin palaces would have been a fairly rough spirit sweetened with sugar. This sweetened style of gin is now known as Old Tom.

1832 saw the birth of something like modern gin. It was called London Dry and made possible by a new kind of still invented by an Irishman called Aeneas Coffey. The Coffey still enabled the gin to be manufactured continuously, rather than made in batches as with a traditional pot still. It produced something very close to pure ethanol, not a spirit with a lot of character but a blank canvas for flavour. Desmond Payne, the master distiller at Beefeater, told me: "Juniper and other botanicals were no longer there to hide taste of alcohol. Now they took centre stage." Odd as it may sound, making gin is a lot like making perfume. Both depend on capturing fragile natural aromas in alcohol and then blending them into a harmonious whole. Coffey's company became John Dore & Sons in 1872 after the foreman who took over the business. Now based near Guildford, they are still producing stills for the gin business. The stills themselves last indefinitely. All the stills at the Beefeater Distillery in London bear the legend "John Dore & Sons, Bow".

Beefeater was founded in 1863 by a chemist called James Burrough. He had worked as a chemist in Toronto and on his return to Britain bought a distillery in Chelsea. He made all kinds of spirits but came up with the recipe for Beefeater gin. Gin was changing from a drink flavoured solely by juniper to something more complicated. Beefeater still makes the gin according to Burrough's recipe by steeping the botanicals in neutral alcohol which is then redistilled to release the flavour into the gin. This new gin reflected how London was at the centre of world trade containing as it did: lemons and oranges from Spain, coriander from India, liquorice from China, angelica from Russia, and orris root and almonds from the Middle East. According to Desmond Payne, James Burrough would go into Covent Garden market and hunt for the right flavours for his gin.

Making gin was becoming a respectable business for a gentleman. Charles Tanqueray, who founded the eponymous distillers, came from a Huguenot family, and his father was a clergyman. William Nicholson, one of the biggest names in 19th century gin, is rumoured to have chosen the egg and bacon (pink and yellow to you and me) colours of the MCC. Horses belonging to his company pulled Wellington's funeral cortege in 1852. You don't get much more respectable than that. Mrs Beeton had gin recipes in her *Book of Household Management* which was first published in 1861. Many of the great names of modern gin have their roots in this period. Gilbey's, the wine merchant and Dickens's favourite brand, converted the former railway shed in Camden, the Roundhouse, into an enormous drink warehouse. Tanqueray was sold in ceramic crocks rather than in barrels as a way of establishing brand identity and ensuring that the gin was not adulterated. The move away from barrels meant that gin changed colour from yellow, caused by the wood of the barrel, to the colourless spirit we know today. This was aided by Gladstone's Single Bottle Act of 1860 which meant for the first time gin was sold in bottles. The big companies founded an elite club, the Worshipful Company of Distillers. This was almost a return to how things were pre-William III: a small group of powerful large-scale distillers controlling the market rather than the chaos of the gin craze.

In 1850 the gin distillers lobbied successfully to avoid paying duty on export spirits. This led to a boom in gin drinking amongst ex-pats. Gin became the drink of choice for world-weary Empire builders. It still is, even if there's no Empire left to build. Perhaps the best gin and tonic I've ever had was at a hotel in Malawi, made with plenty of ice, limes and the excellent local gin. I don't know why someone hasn't started importing it to Britain. The gin-soaked old colonial type became a cliché of literature. Flory, the hapless hero of George Orwell's novel *Burmese Days*, proclaims, "I can never get it into my servant's head that SOME people can exist without gin before breakfast." That drink would probably have been a pink gin, gin mixed with Angostura Bitters. It was the colonies that provided gin's definitive incarnation, the gin and tonic. Quinine, in the form of bark from the cinchona tree, was taken to alleviate the effects of malaria. It originally came only from the Spanish empire in South America. The British struggled without a regular supply. In one disastrous encounter during the Napoleonic wars known as Walcheren Expedition 106 British soldiers died in combat, but over 4,000 died from malaria. Eventually the Spanish hold on the trade was broken when the British successfully grew cinchona trees in India and Ceylon, and the Dutch in Java.

The next step was the invention of a solution to make the consumption of the quinine easier. At first they were sold as tonics (hence the name) but they proved so popular when mixed with gin to alleviate the taste of the quinine that they were soon marketed to consumers. Schweppes, founded in 1783 by a Swiss scientist, Johann Schweppe, launched their Indian Tonic Water in 1870.

Gin's success was down to the fact that it is the consummate mixer. All those subtle aromatic flavours mean that gin goes with a wide variety of flavours, making it the perfect base for cocktails. The taste in mixed drinks in the 19th century moved from punches, which broadly speaking were about disguising the taste of the alcohol, to cocktails, which were about accentuating them. This began to occur as purer spirits became available from the 1830s onwards. Cocktails came originally from America, but the taste for these drinks spread quickly. With steamships, railways, newspapers and telegrams, America and Britain were linked in a way that will seem very familiar today. The first cocktail book, the *Bartender's Guide* by Jerry Thomas from the Occidental Hotel in San Francisco, was published in 1863. Born in New York in 1830, Thomas was a celebrity barman able to command hundreds of dollars for appearances. He even toured Europe. The book included such gin-based classics as the gin fizz, the Martinez and the Tom Collins. *The Savoy Cocktail Book* of 1930 was written by another American, Harry Craddock, but named after the London hotel where he worked (at the American Bar). By this time gin was the dominant force in cocktails with the king of cocktails, the Martini, being gin-based. This is thought to have been an evolution of the Martinez which is mainly sweet vermouth and gin. The Martini took these two ingredients but in dry form. The magic is in the synergy between two quite similar drinks, gin, a flavoured spirit, and vermouth, a flavoured wine. The twist of lemon brings out the citric notes in both and the botanicals are allowed to sing unencumbered by any sugar. Gin had attained its ultimate form and the Martini signalled the arrival of the USA as the major influence on world drinks.

DRINKING THE EMPIRE

For most of the 20th century gin was king, but it went into a steep decline in the late 60s. Squalor and death could not dent gin's appeal, but its reputation was destroyed when it became associated with Margo and Jerry from *The Good Life*. From this suburban exile, two events signalled that gin might be becoming cool again. One was the launch of Bombay Sapphire in 1987 – the first new gin to be launched in years. The second was the 1994 debut single by Oasis which contained the line "I'm feeling supersonic, give me gin and tonic." There are now literally hundreds of so-called "boutique" gins, so different from when the choice was just between Gordons and Beefeater. I have no idea how many will be going by the time this book appears, so I'm going to recommend a few with some staying power:

Beefeater 24
The Rolls Royce of gins. Containing Japanese green tea, this is very smooth and harmonious with none of the botanicals shouting loudly. Much too good to mix with tonic, I'd drink it neat or with a little grapefruit juice.

Adnams Copper Still Gin
Made by the Southwold brewer, it's pretty, floral and feminine; would make a lovely martini with a twist of lemon or you could wear it as perfume.

Brighton Gin
Brighton with its tawdry glamour is uniquely suited to gin.

This is probably too good to use for recreating your favourite bits from the novels of Patrick Hamilton or Graham Greene.

Tanqueray Export
The big one. This has a huge hit of juniper for the ultimate G&T.

Tanqueray Old Tom
A recreation of the old sweet gin style, but this time the sugar isn't there to disguise the rough spirit. Excellent in a sweet cocktail such as a Martinez.

Xoriguer Mahon Gin
One of the world's finest gins is made on Menorca. It's made from brandy and matured in oak barrels. For much of the 18th century the island was occupied by the British. Gin is hugely popular on the mainland too. Larios, one of the world's bestselling gins, is Spanish. They take their gin and tonics very seriously, always using plenty of gin, plenty of ice, fresh limes and the minimum amount of tonic. If only the standard of the average British G&T was as high.

11

ICE

Visitors from America are often bemused by the lack of ice in the British hospitality trade. When one orders tap water in a restaurant it is, more often than not, warm and given begrudgingly. Most pubs still use a bucket full of partially melted ice for making gin and tonics. Americans are baffled by this. They have had a regular supply of ice since the 19th century. They would harvest ice in the winter and store it in specially designed ice boxes to keep it cold.

The Chinese, of course, were there first. In an essay called "Cathay to Caledonia", Elizabeth David writes about how early the Chinese were with "the harvesting and storing of ice", which "are recorded in a poem of circa 1100 BC in the *Shih Ching*, the famous collection of Food Canons". The Chinese pioneered the storing of fish in ice enabling the modern fishing industry; there were ice houses used for storing the winter's harvest all over the country. It's not known whether they applied their knowledge to the cooling of alcoholic drinks, but the British did. William Hickey, the diarist, noted a feast in 1769 he enjoyed in Canton where he drank "Claret, madeira and hock, all excellent and cold as ice".

19th century British visitors noted the American fondness for drinking nothing but iced water at meals. This continues to this day when in every cafe, diner or restaurant you will be given a glass of ice water which will be continually refilled. Ice boxes were common in America by the 1820s. In 1838, the *New York Mirror* wrote how an ice box "is now considered as much an article of necessity as a carpet or dining-table".

The Americans, however, didn't limit themselves to cold water. Ice was an essential ingredient in the first great American drink, the cocktail. Before there was the Martini there was the cobbler. This is simply sherry sweetened with sugar and served with crushed ice, orange slices and mint. These new-fangled drinks became popular in Europe. Charles Dickens was a great fan of sherry-based drinks. Martin Chuzzlewit, in the eponymous novel, refers to it as a "wonderful invention". By the late 19th century, steamship technology allowed ice to be harvested in vast blocks in America or Canada and sped across the Atlantic. American bars such as the one that opened in the Savoy in 1889 were so-named because they served iced drinks. Ice became madly fashionable in Victorian England for those who could afford it. According to George Saintsbury, a literary critic and pioneering wine writer, it was a "barbarous time", when people drank their claret chilled and put ice cubes in their champagne.

Despite this, ice was never much more than a fashion for the upper classes. Unlike in America it never became ubiquitous. It was different when abroad. The ultimate hymn to the joys of a cold beer, *Ice Cold in Alex*, is a British film. Thomas Hardy of the eponymous winery (not the writer) opened a wine bar in Adelaide selling tongue sandwiches and iced claret. The British in India took Arab techniques of using saltpetre (potassium nitrate) to cool things enough to make ice cream to chill their beer.

Back at home, though, native beers such as porter or pale ale were served at cellar temperature. The fact that Britain was slow to take to lager might have something to do with the lack of access to affordable ice. Lager beer relied on having large quantities of ice so that the beer could be stored (or lagered) near freezing. With the advent of railways this ice could easily be transported across the continent. Or it might be that the British simply prefer their beer cool rather than cold. Our summers don't tend to be very warm so for British people, ice is still not an essential. And it really annoys visitors.

12

COGNAC

Before the Second World War, the drink of the British upper classes was a brandy and soda. It was known by the Bright Young Things as a "b & s". The only person I knew who was partial to a "b & s" was my grandfather. It's hard to imagine him as a BYF though he did once win a Charleston competition. There's an exchange between Bertie Wooster and his butler Jeeves concerning this most English of drinks in P G Wodehouse's *The Inimitable Jeeves*:

> "'I say, Jeeves,' I said.
> 'Sir?'
> 'Mix me a stiffish brandy and soda.'
> 'Yes, sir.'
> 'Stiffish, Jeeves. Not too much soda, but splash the brandy about a bit.'
> 'Very good, sir.'"

The British have a long relationship with brandy. Originally it was brandy not rum that the Royal Navy turned to when the beer ran out. According to Boswell, Samuel Johnson once said, "Claret is the liquor for boys; port, for men; but he who aspires to be a hero (smiling) must drink brandy." Cognac would have been the brandy of choice. Its roots lie in the Dutch desire to make wine easier to transport by sea. The answer was distillation. The

Dutch encouraged the plantation of acidic white grapes that made indifferent wine but excellent brandy. Brandy from the vineyards around the town of Cognac was handy for shipping from Nantes or La Rochelle. Where the Dutch pioneered, the British followed. Thomas Hine was a 16-year-old lad from Devon who was sent to France in 1791 by his father to learn about the cognac business. Five years later he married a local girl, Elisabeth, daughter of a Cognac merchant. He developed links with Britain and proved such a good businessman that he took over his wife's family's firm which changed its name to Thomas Hine & Co. Of the big boys Hennessy, the largest producer, was founded by Richard Hennessy, an Irish aristocrat who fought in Louis XV's army. Jean Martell, founder of the eponymous firm, was from Jersey.

Crucial to the magic of cognac is the affinity between the distilled wine and the nearby Limousin oak. The climate around Cognac, though warmer than Ireland and Scotland, has a similar dampness. A huge amount of water is needed for distillation and a cool humid climate helps the spirit mature slowly. The slower the maturation, the finer the spirit. British connoisseurs noted that when the brandy was shipped young in cask and then matured in the colder English climate, it was even better. You can still buy a category called "early landed" which is one of the few drinks nowadays still shipped in cask and bottled in England.

As usual with drink for the British market, there was the pure product and then something doctored to British tastes. Additives such as sugar syrup, prune juice and a wood solution made from boiling oak were added to give the brandy an antique feel. This vulgar brandy feels the full force of Evelyn Waugh's disdain in one of the most famous scenes from *Brideshead Revisited* where Charles Ryder has dinner with Rex Mottram, an arriviste businessman, in Paris. Ryder orders a cognac but Mottram, who claims to be a bit of an expert on the subject, isn't impressed. He wants something ancient. So sheepishly the waiters produce a dusty old bottle kept for customers just like him. They pour out a sweet, syrupy concoction that leaves thick rings on the glass much to Mottram's delight and Ryder's contempt.

From the heyday of Waugh and Wodehouse, the brandy habit has declined amongst the British, but it's now massive amongst hip hop types in America. Courvoisier and Hennessy are the favoured brands. So successful has this unlikely collaboration been that Max Beaulieu, from cognac-expert.com, thinks there should be a statue of Busta Rhymes in Cognac. You should Google Beaulieu's interview with the writer Nicholas Faith just to hear Faith reciting rap lyrics in his patrician English accent. I was going to quote some but there is an awful lot of swearing.

It's a long way from Wodehouse.

DRINKING THE EMPIRE

Cognac is usually a blended spirit. The merchant houses generally buy in spirits from small producers and then age and blend them. You can also buy brandies directly from growers but these are rare.

The regions within champagne are, in decreasing order of excellence: Grande Champagne, Petite Champagne, Borderies, Fins Bois, Bons Bois and Bois Ordinaires. Unless otherwise stated, the cognac will be a blend of areas and ages. The age statements are:

VS – Very Special – minimum two years ageing

VSOP – Very Special Old Pale – minimum three years

XO – extra old – minimum six years

Hors d'âge – beyond age – also minimum six years but used to denote a high end product.

Here's an unusual one that I really like:

Hine Grande Champagne Cognac Bonneuil 2005
Nothing to do with sparkling champagne, but from the most prestigious area within Cognac famous for its limestone soil and fine brandies. This one is unusual in that not only does it come from one area, Grande Champagne, but from a single vineyard, Bonneuil, and vintage. It's very wine-like and the fruit has elegant notes of caramel and pepper. I think Evelyn Waugh would approve.

13

CLARET, ENGLAND'S WINE

The Médoc, the area that makes the most famous red wines in the world, is not a beautiful place. On an overcast day, taking a train north from the city of Bordeaux, the surrounding countryside reminded me of the bleakness of the Fens. The Fens link is an apt one as both regions were once marshes that were drained by Dutch engineers in the 17th century. The flat landscape with occasional slopes, you couldn't call them hills, is a far cry from the drama of the Douro or the rolling hills of the southern Rhône. Those famous names Lafite and Mouton mean nothing more than hills in the local dialect. They're the best land for growing wines on here because they're the nearest this flat area has to the slopes of textbook vine-growing areas.

Continuing the bleak theme is the town of Pauillac. Much of the 18th century town centre is boarded up and abandoned and most of the residents now live in Mr Bricolage[67] villas on the outskirts of town. Anthony Barton from Langoa-Barton told me that the town was more lively when the nearby Shell oil refinery was open, but now there aren't many job opportunities. But, as you leave town heading towards St-Julien-Beychevelle, you will see the tower of Château Latour, then Château Pichon-Longueville

---

67 Ubiquitous French DIY chain.

Comtesse de Lalande glaring across at the fairytale turrets of her rival Pichon-Longueville Baron. Over the border into St-Julien, a small stream divides the two communes, and the great names come thick and fast: Léoville-Poyferré, Leoville-Las-Cases, Langoa, Gloria and Beychevelle. St-Julien, in contrast to Pauillac, is a picture perfect yellow stone village built in a grand but tasteful 18th century style. To the outsider it seems bizarre that such a small village has so many ornate châteaux all with beautifully landscaped grounds. Clearly someone has money around here even if not much of it has reached the average Médocian. It's a sort of strange place, unpromising and desolate, but punctuated by these symbols of enormous wealth, so different to the ancient monastic landscape of Bordeaux's great rival, Burgundy.

You might think it odd to have got so far into this book and yet only just be mentioning the wine that more than any other is associated with the British. For the traditional British wine lover, claret is wine. If you ask me what was the greatest wine I've ever had, I'd probably say that it was a claret, Mouton-Rothschild 1996. It wasn't the rarest, the oldest or the most unusual or even the most beautiful, but it was the wine that came up to the standards I've been taught to appreciate in wine: power with elegance, fruit tempered by tannin and acidity. It *was* a beautiful wine no doubt, but it was also an intellectual treat. I didn't just sit back in rhapsody, I studied it in the glass and appreciated its exquisite balance. Fine wine until very recently was Bordeaux. Almost the only wine kept for investment was classed-growth claret. Most other fine wines, Napa Cabernets, Rioja, Chianti, Penfolds Grange, were originally made in the image of Bordeaux. The grapes of Bordeaux, Cabernet Sauvignon and Merlot (and indeed Malbec and Cabernet Franc) are planted around the world because people are always trying to make a local claret. Roger Scruton, the philosopher and wine lover, writes:

"After punishing body and soul with Australian
Shiraz, Argentine Tempranillo, Romanian
Cabernet Sauvignon and Greek Retsina,
we crawl home like a Prodigal Son and beg
forgiveness for our folly. Claret extends a warm
and indulgent embrace, renewing the ancient
bond between English thirst and Gascon
refreshment… "

It is indeed a profound bond. For a long time Bordeaux was part of England. It was acquired for the English Crown in 1152 when Eleanor of Aquitaine married Henry, Duke of Normandy, later Henry II of England. In what must be one of history's most impressive dowries, Eleanor brought with her Poitou, Gascony, Auvergne, Limousin and Périgord, areas that are famous for some of the best food and drink in France. The English kings already had Touraine, Anjou, Maine and, of course, Normandy. So the English now controlled a hefty chunk of western and northern France. Theoretically the English owed allegiance to the French Crown. The French king was the overlord but he would have had little control. Burgundy, too, was not ruled directly by France at the time. It only became part of France in 1477.

Inevitably the English came into conflict with their notional overlords. History, or at least the history I was taught, explains the resulting conflict, the Hundred Years War, as about the French trying to throw out an invading English army, but it was more complicated than that. Most of the Gascon nobility were loyal to England; in fact, they pursued their own battles with France without any encouragement from the English. Even referring to the English as the English is an anachronism as the English knights would have spoken Norman French. The English were in Gascony for a long time. It was home. Edward I spent much of his reign there. He built fortified towns or *bastides* to keep out the French. Fortified towns are a feature of modern day Gascony. To this day many French wines are called Le Bastide; literally the fort. The tower that features on the label of Latour would have guarded against the French. It was destroyed when the French drove out the English. The tower I saw from the road was built in the 17th century. The two territories, England and Gascony, were deeply intertwined. A 13th century Lord Mayor of Bordeaux, Henry le Waleys, was later mayor of London. The Gascons themselves were descendents of Basques and they would have spoken a dialect of Occitan[68] rather than French.

The merchants of Bordeaux enjoyed special privileges under English rule. That much-maligned King, John, who lost England's Normandy territory, as well as his crown jewels in the Wash, is actually remembered fondly by the Bordelais as he encouraged trade by exempting nobles and burghers in Bordeaux from all taxes on their wines. John himself, a notorious alcoholic, was one of Bordeaux's best customers. Other English kings spent equally freely on wine. Edward II ordered 1,000 *tonneaux* of wine to celebrate his marriage to Isabella of France in 1308. This is equivalent to roughly 1.2 million modern bottles.

The Hundred Years War was not just an English colonial war, but part of a struggle by Gascon nobles to preserve their ancient independence against a power-hungry French state. The English and Gascons were finally defeated in 1453 at the battle of Castillon. England lost all her territory in France except Calais which Queen Mary subsequently lost in 1558. The English nobles and soldiers were mostly allowed to leave and take their wine with them, but the Gascons were punished. They were not trusted by the

---

68 Occitan is the root of the word Languedoc – literally land of the Oc where people said Oc instead of Oui. Until the First World War many French people would not have spoken French as a first language.

French. The Bordelais, in particular, were considered suspect. Charles VII of France wrote in a letter to James II of Scotland that "everyone knows it has been English for 300 years, and the people of the district are at heart entirely inclined to the English party." He built a massive fortress, Château Trompette, to tower over the city and show the Bordelais who was boss. It was demolished in 1818 to make way for the Place Quinconces, the area that now marks the centre of the city.

Bordeaux has long enjoyed a closer relationship with London and indeed Bristol, King's Lynn, Leith, Hamburg and Amsterdam, than it has with Paris. Before railways it would have been extremely difficult and expensive to transport wine overland to Paris. Roads were in a terrible state and there was always the risk of being robbed. The English had something the Bordelaise wanted too, namely woollen cloth. It was the classic British story of wine for cloth. After the loss of Bordeaux, claret remained the English wine of choice. The connection was never completely broken, even when the countries were at war again. This wine would have been a pale, refreshing red, *clairet*, the root of the word claret, that would have been drunk as soon as possible after the vintage or it would turn sour. It would have been closer to a rosé than the modern dark wine.

Claret as we know it has its roots in the 17th century. The development of most wines in this book can't be credited to one person but, in this case, there was one man who created modern claret. Arnaud de Pontac was a lawyer and President of the Bordeaux Parliament. He had an estate just outside the city, Haut-Brion, in the region now known as Graves because of its gravelly soil, which was great for growing vines and not much else. We don't know exactly how this new kind of Bordeaux wine was made but it lasted longer and tasted quite different to the old claret. It must have been made from specially selected grapes and, most importantly, aged in new oak barrels which were kept full to avoid oxidation. It was the prototype of the wine we enjoy today.

But where Pontac was a true pioneer was in selling his product. Previously wine from Bordeaux would have been sold generically from the region, but Pontac built a name for his wine in London. There was very high duty on French wine, so it was only worth selling the expensive stuff in England. In 1666 Arnaud's son opened a tavern in the City called the "Sign of The Pontac's Head" where he sold Haut-Brion for seven shillings a bottle which was around four times the price of ordinary wine. It became the talk of the town. John Locke tried it. Pepys pronounced on its "peculiar taste"; he called it "Ho Bryan" and indeed down the years the British have had a lot of fun misspelling and mispronouncing the name of the wine. Like a game of Chinese whispers, John Hervey, Earl of Bristol, referred to it in 1705 as Obrian, Christie's the auction house called it Oberon, and the writer Maurice Healy referred to it as O'Brien. Haut-Brion saw the birth of wine as a brand. But it was something of an anomaly. It took a salesman of the genius of Pontac to sell this high status wine directly to its biggest market. Even today most of the châteaux in Bordeaux sell via intermediaries.

Where Pontac led, others followed but they planted not in Graves but in the newly drained Médoc. At the time the region was even more remote and forbidding than it is today. The marshland was drained in the 17th century by a team of Dutch engineers led by a man with a suspiciously English-sounding name of Humphrey Bradley (his family were English but he was born in the Netherlands). The land was bought speculatively by wealthy Bordelais, lawyers, merchants, members of Parliament and nobility. They were the kind of people who wanted serious returns on their investments. The land was cheap so these entrepreneurs could build up large estates which are still in existence today.

Compared with the holding of your average Burgundian grower, Bordeaux estates are vast. Even the finest claret today is made in large quantities. Wines such as Lafite are not expensive because they are scarce, but because of their reputation. In a flat region, it was the moderate hills that proved the best place for growing grapes and it was these relatively steep areas that soon gained a reputation for making top quality wine. The low-lying ground that didn't drain so well or catch the sunlight still makes more rustic wines. These cheaper wines were bought by the Scots, the Irish, the Germans and the famously parsimonious Dutch. This is Henry Vizetelly writing about Château Gruaud-Larose in St-Julien in 1873:

> "During the last century when the M. Gruaud, who has given his name to the vineyard, owned the property, it was his practice at the conclusion of each vintage to hoist above his chateau the flag of the particular nation which he thought his wine most likely to suit. Thus whenever it was thin and poor, and consequently cheap, he ran up the German colours; if full of flavour and body, and correspondingly dear, the British standard was unfurled; and on those occasions when it proved to be of an intermediate character, the Dutch flag floated over the square tower of the Château Gruaud."

From looking at a sale in 1705 and 1706 of "new French clarets" in London we can see that other wines apart from Haut-Brion are already selling on their reputation: Latour, Margaux and Lafite. The big four had been established.

It was difficult but highly lucrative doing business with Britain. France and England were often at war but somehow the wines always got through, though often at a price. At one time during the Seven Years War between England and France, which ran from 1754 until 1763, to get past the ban on French goods, English merchants would pretend that they had taken the wine as a prize in an act of piracy. For a brief period this fake piracy was rife in the English Channel. Things, however, became even more difficult in the early 19th century due to Napoleon's Continental System. When Napoleon was finally defeated it came as a great relief to the Bordelais. Continuing the tradition of Anglophilia, Jean-Baptiste Lynch,[69] the Mayor of Bordeaux, in 1814 welcomed the defeat of Napoleon so that he could continue selling wines to his best customers. He gladly surrendered the city to General Beresford at the head of a British army. The period directly after the Napoleonic Wars, though, was a difficult time for the Bordeaux wine trade as Britain was almost bankrupt, and suffered a depression and unemployment made worse by the vast numbers of demobbed soldiers and sailors who were unable to find work.

But soon Britain began to recover and 1830 to 1880 were Bordeaux's golden years. The best grape varieties were being identified for the production of long-lived wine: Cabernet Sauvignon and Franc, and Merlot, though Malbec was much more important than it is now, as was a variety that is almost extinct in Bordeaux, Carmenère. It's still grown widely in Chile where, for a long time, it was thought to be Merlot. In Bordeaux techniques were becoming more advanced. Winemakers knew that it was important to protect wine from oxygen. Sulphur dioxide, which had been used since Roman times, was now being used systematically to preserve wine. Burning a sulphur candle in a barrel kills microbes that can spoil wine and turn it to vinegar. Wine

---

69 He was a descendent of the Lynches from Galway who we read about in the port chapter.

would be decanted (racked) from barrel to barrel leaving behind the dead yeasts (lees) that could cause bacterial infection. The science was just beginning to be understood. Pasteur, in the 1860s, discovered that it was bacteria that turned wine into vinegar and that alcohol was produced by an interaction between yeasts and sugar.

Among General Beresford's army was a Colonel Charles Palmer. Palmer was the son of a West Country brewer. Despite his father's humble beginnings, Charles had been moulded into a proper English gentleman. British society was now an open aristocracy based on property and patronage. If you had the money, you could buy land and with it power and rank. His father had made a fortune running the first London to Bath mail coach. Charles Palmer was educated at Oxford and Eton and later became MP for Bath. With his father's wealth he bought a commission in the most fabulous regiment of the time, the Tenth Hussars. This was the Prince of Wales's regiment, based in Brighton and famous for their louche antics and extravagant uniforms. The Prince Regent, impressed by fancy French uniforms, had copied them for his regiment. So lavish was their kit, which soldiers had to buy themselves, that it precluded anyone except the very wealthy from joining the regiment. Fittingly for such a dandyish regiment, Beau Brummell was also a member though he didn't actually ever do any fighting.

After Napoleon's final defeat at Waterloo, Palmer was travelling by coach to Paris. In the carriage was a Marie Brunet de Ferrière. She was on the way to sell her family property in Bordeaux so that it could be divided up amongst her family as per the Napoleonic code. Some form of seduction took place on that long coach journey. He was a dashing playboy soldier, she was a beautiful widow who claimed her property made wine equal to Lafite. One thing soon led to another and, before he knew it, he had bought the property for considerably more than she could have sold it for in Paris. In some versions of the story, something sexual went on between them too. The stage coaches of France were notorious for brief encounters of such nature. There was something about the confined spaces, the rocking motion and there wasn't much else to do. What is certain is that Palmer paid 100,000 francs for the property, and you can see the original bill of sale at the château today.

Palmer expanded the estate and appointed a Mr Gray to look after the property. He then set about trying to do a Pontac, as it's known in Bordeaux,[70] and sell his wine directly to London. He changed the name to Château Palmer and aimed to make it the most fashionable wine in London. With his regimental connections, this should not have been a problem. For his wine's London debut, Palmer set up a tasting with the Prince Regent at the Carlton Club. All the demi-monde of London society were in attendance. The Prince tried the wine and, according to a bystander,[71] pronounced it "holy Palmer's kiss". All was going swimmingly until Lord Yarmouth, determined to take the arriviste Palmer down a peg or two, proposed a comparative tasting with another claret supplied by a London wine merchant, John Carbonell. Yarmouth was one of the Prince's cronies, famous for his debauchery and the model for the Marquis of Steyne in Thackeray's *Vanity Fair*. Palmer, the wine, was just as it is now, a graceful even delicate wine, perhaps one of the most Burgundian wines in Bordeaux. Carbonell's, in contrast, was a stout dark wine heavily laced with Hermitage. The Prince preferred the heavier wine which might have had something to do with the anchovy sandwiches that Yarmouth was serving alongside; not many

---

70 It's not really known as this.

71 Captain Gronow, a Welsh Grenadier Guardsman, who described the encounter in his memoirs *The Reminiscences of Captain Gronow*.

wines can stand up to those stinky little fish. The Prince was a man of notoriously vulgar tastes, but we shouldn't be too hard on him – nowadays at blind tastings most people almost always plump for the less subtle wine.

The contest was a disaster for Palmer. He had to suffer the indignity of being lectured by the Prince on the shortcomings of his wine. Nobody would now buy it now that it had met with the Prince's disapproval. The Royal disfavour had destroyed other men before. Beau Brummell was exiled to France after approaching the man next to the Prince of Wales at a ball and, looking in the Prince's direction, saying "who's your fat friend?" The Prince was particularly portly. Brummel died in syphilitic penury in Calais. In an attempt to save face Palmer challenged Yarmouth to a duel. Whether the duel actually happened and, if so, who won has not been recorded.

The Prince Regent by James Gillray

Palmer returned to Bordeaux and, thinking he had been doing it all wrong, pulled out all the vines, replanted them and generally ruined his estate at great expense in order to make something more like the vulgar wine supplied by Carbonell. Things went from bad to worse when it turned out that his estate manager, Mr Gray, was fleecing him. The Reform Act of 1832 meant that he lost his Bath seat, his wife left him and eventually he went bankrupt and the estate was sold to settle debts. He died penniless in 1845. The estate was sold to a wealthy family of bankers of Portuguese-Jewish descent (and rivals of the Rothschilds), the Pereires. They saved the estate and built the glorious château in 1853 that now adorns the label, but kept the name, Palmer.

It's a tragic tale and reads like a morality play: the social climbing man from the sticks destroyed by conniving aristocrats. Despite his failure, Palmer had originally had a good product and a good business plan. The way to make money from Bordeaux was to market the wine in London. Palmer learned how hard it was to sell wine directly, but also learned a bit about the English taste in claret. The Upper Classes wanted the best, but they weren't necessarily concerned with purity. The sort of claret popular in London at the time would not have been pure Bordeaux. It would have been mixed by merchants in the city of Bordeaux with heavier wines to make it more palatable to English tastes. The Victorian wine expert Cyrus Redding wrote, "it has been thought necessary to give pure Bordeaux growths a resemblance to the wines of Portugal ... Bordeaux wine in England and in Bordeaux scarcely resemble each other." T G Shaw, a wine merchant, writing in the 1860s thought that the English palate had been ruined by too much strong drink:

"as port, sherry and other kinds with between 30 and 40 percent proof spirit still constitute upward of 70 percent of total consumption,

> it cannot be fairly supposed that men who
> have little else in their mouths all day can have
> palates capable of appreciating the delicacy and
> bouquet of great growths."

This is reminiscent of how American tastes were viewed until recently by French wine producers and British merchants. It was believed that all those over-ripe Zinfandels, not to mention Coca-Cola, had ruined the American palate for the refined wines of Burgundy. And perhaps there is some truth in the generalisation? I remember having dinner with a friend of my wife's and her mother, a wealthy lady from Los Angeles. I ordered a decent bottle of Rhône thinking she would like it. She had a glass and said it wasn't bad for a light little wine and then pointed at the alcohol level on the bottle, 14.5 percent, saying that she liked something a little stronger.[72]

Bordeaux wine was sold through intermediaries. Brokers sourced the wine which was then sold to merchants based in the city of Bordeaux. These merchants were on the whole not French, they were English, German, Danish, Dutch or most prominently Irish. One such merchant was Tom Barton, born in Enniskillen in 1695. He was sent by his family to France to sell wool and ended up in Bordeaux in 1722. It is likely that he was a smuggler or "owler" as wool smugglers were known. Wool from Ireland had to be sold through England, and the English set the price to protect their own woollen industry. Exporting directly to France was illegal but lucrative. Tom Barton, later known as French Tom, would have bartered wool for wine and eventually went full time into the wine business in 1725. By 1743 he had made enough money to buy an estate in Bordeaux

---

72 Looking back, she may actually have been joking. Perhaps a deadpan commentary on the stereotype of the uncouth American.

as well as one in County Tipperary. He died in 1780 an extremely wealthy man.

The wealth set up the Barton family in Ireland and bought influence. His children became members of the gentry and one a Member of Parliament. Tom's grandson Hugh arrived in Bordeaux in 1766. During the Napoleonic Wars, Hugh Barton handed over the reins of the wine merchant business to Daniel Guestier. So successful was he that Barton offered him a partnership when the war ended, thus forming one of the great names in Bordeaux, Barton & Guestier. The Bartons bought Château Langoa in St-Julien in 1824 and it became Langoa-Barton. They were now wine producers as well as merchants. It's the château that has spent the longest time in the same hands. In true British fashion, the Bartons never became naturalised. They remained Anglo-Irish. During the Second World War, the Germans tried to confiscate Langoa-Barton but the cook came out and said that it was owned by an Irishman, Ronald Barton, and therefore belonged to a neutral country. The cook herself was Irish and waved her passport at the Germans and amazingly they went away. Ronald Barton actually had a British passport and was a liaison officer with the Free French at the time. His nephew, Anthony, and his daughter Lillian, who told me the story, are Irish citizens.

Another great Bordeaux name is Nathaniel Johnston et Fils founded by William Johnston also from Ireland but of Scottish descent. It's still going today and run by descendants of the founder with the decidedly unFrench name of Denis, Archibald & Ivanhoé Johnston. Their office and cellars are still situated on the Quai des Chartrons, outside the city wall of Bordeaux, where all the foreign merchants were based until the 1980s. Consequently these foreign merchants were known as the Chartronnais and later as Nobilité de Bouchon, the Aristocracy of the Cork. Though most weren't English, it was the English culture that dominated and many spoke French with an English accent. They lived a rarified existence playing cricket and tennis and always marrying into each other's families. Clubs in Bordeaux were modelled on the St James's model. Many merchants' sons were educated in England. Anthony Barton, the current owner of Château Langoa-Barton, is one of the few surviving relics of this breed, born in Ireland, educated in England and has lived in France since he was in his early 20s. Now in his 80s he, though he is an Irish citizen, comes across as every foreigner's idea of the perfect English gentleman. Despite the fact that most of the châteaux and the merchant houses are now owned by international companies, the British influence lives on in the dress, manners and perfect English of the Chartronnais.

Great wealth flowed into Bordeaux in the 19th century. The châteaux that dot the Médoc today are not old like the castles of the Loire, they were built with new money but designed to look venerable. They were a bit of instant history for a new region, constructed to help market the wines. This wealth was built on the London market. Just as with port, the best clarets improved with age and wine appreciation became fashionable. There was a distinct hierarchy of producers which was set in stone in the 1855 Classification under Napoleon III. This was a ranking of all the châteaux of the Médoc for the Paris Exhibition. The top wines known as First Growths[73] were as they are to this day, Lafite, Haut-Brion, Margaux and Latour. Yquem was also included at the top for its superlative sweet wines. Mouton was promoted to the top in 1973, the only change in 170 years. Palmer, whose reputation had dipped somewhat, was put in the third tier. At a more everyday level, Gladstone's

---

73 In French Premier Cru. Another great difference between Bordeaux and Burgundy, in Burgundy the classification is based on land, in Bordeaux it's based on the producer.

1860 act of Parliament lowering duty on French wine, ending nearly 200 years of punitive taxes, led to renewed enthusiasm for the wines of Bordeaux amongst the middle classes of Britain. Gilbey's wine merchants built a business empire based on selling claret to the bourgeoisie (as well as producing their famous gin).

The wines of Bordeaux now had an international reputation and yet, since the end of Pontac's time, the great châteaux had no way of selling their wines directly to their biggest market, London. Despite, or perhaps because of the lavish châteaux, some were chronically short of money, as usually one year in three would be a bad vintage and so many, including some of the First Growths, locked themselves into deals known as *abonnement* where the merchants would fix a price for future vintages which they would then be obliged to buy. This provided security for the château, but meant in excellent vintages that the merchants made a killing and the château nothing extra. Wine would leave the châteaux soon after vintage and be stored in wood by the merchants. Very little wine was bottled by the châteaux themselves. The ageing would have been done by the merchants and then sold to other merchants in London who would bottle it. Sometimes they didn't bottle it very well. When buying old claret one of the things to check is not only the vintage and how the wine has been stored, but who it was bottled by.

In other wine regions such as the Douro or Madeira, the growers simply sold grapes or bulk wine to merchants. It was the merchants who had control, made the serious money, and took the risks when they sold it on. In Bordeaux, however, things were different. Most of the growers in the Médoc were not peasants. They were upper- and middle-class businessmen not just looking to provide for their families, but to make some money. They were entrepreneurs.

The history of Bordeaux is about the tension between the merchants based in the city of Bordeaux who were largely British or at least Anglophone and the producers who were French. Sometimes these growers have tried to break out of this loveless marriage. Adulteration was a particular point of conflict. In 1764 growers tried to ban the Chartronnais from beefing up their wine with foreign products. The merchants of Bordeaux argued that firstly, in many years the wines needed it and secondly, if they didn't, then unscrupulous merchants in London would do it themselves and they would do it badly and ruin Bordeaux's reputation. Tom Barton led the protest against the new regulations, allied with many British, Dutch and indeed French merchants. The Chartronnais won this time. Looking at records of Barton & Guestier from around 1788–90, one can see that they were buying a lot of wine from outside Bordeaux including Hermitage. Nathaniel Johnston wrote of how he doctored the Lafite 1795: "made up with Hermitage (it) was the best liked of any of that year." If your Bordeaux was doctored with Hermitage, now one of the most expensive wines from the northern Rhône, you were probably buying the best from a good merchant. In his 1826 *Manuel du Sommelier*, A. Jullien wrote that "the wines of the first growths of Bordeaux in France do not resemble those sent to London, in which is put a certain quantity of Spanish and French midi wine… " However it was doctored, most Bordeaux sold in Britain would have contained at least two percent of other wines.

From our perspective this seems heretical but it was often necessary in order to make them palatable. Bordeaux is in many ways not a very good place to reliably ripen grapes. The weather is changeable. It often rains. Most growers couldn't take the risk to properly ripen the grapes, so they would harvest while the weather was good and trust the merchants to work their wines in their cellars. The wine would have been very tannic as whole bunches including stalks would have been fermented so many may well have needed something southern to soften them. They would have been stored, often for many years, in large Baltic oak barrels by the merchants until they were ready. The wine would not only be dosed with foreign wines, but would be decanted to fresh barrels occasionally leaving behind sediment. Keeping and nurturing and, yes, adulterating and blending the wines was a difficult and laborious process. Some merchants were better at it than others.

If you wanted pure Bordeaux, you had to buy direct. Thomas Jefferson wrote of how "genuine wine is to be got and not from any wine merchant whatever." Jefferson insisted that his wine came directly from the châteaux and wasn't tampered with or "improved" by merchants either in Bordeaux or in London. It's something that many visitors to London comment on. There is a still a snobbery about buying wine from a merchant, though not so much in Britain. In France a large proportion of wine sales are direct. People feel that they are getting better wine. What was important about Pontac and Haut-Brion in 17th century London and why they could charge such high prices is that it was guaranteed as being genuine and unadulterated by any merchant. It was imported directly from Bordeaux and sold by the property owners. You could not be so sure about most Bordeaux and, indeed, most wine sold in London taverns.

Other wines beloved of the British, port, champagne and sherry, are, to some extent, manufactured products. Wines were bought by merchant houses, blended and then fortified or refermented in bottle to create a consistent product which was then sold under a brand name. Bordeaux, in contrast, was meant to be a product of a particular estate and vintage. The merchants never, unlike in Oporto, became brands in their own right. Instead the names of the estates became famous. The best estates had brands, but they did not have the money or expertise[74] to capitalise on them; the merchants had the capital, but no brands. It was an odd state of affairs. It's interesting to compare Bordeaux with Rioja in Spain. Here the system worked more like in Oporto with big companies buying in grapes or wine and holding large stocks. Blending between vintages was common to create a consistent product. The best Rioja labels capture the Art Nouveau exuberance of this young industry and the wire mesh around the bottle to guarantee that it had not been tampered with was a marketing masterstroke. Even today Rioja as a region is much better than Bordeaux at marketing its wine and has a much stronger brand recognition.

Rioja as a quality wine region was developed by Bordeaux producers looking for good wine to sell because their own vineyards had been devastated by phylloxera. I've mentioned this little pest in passing before, but I think it's probably a good moment to examine it in a little more detail as it's vital to understanding wine in the late 19th and early 20th centuries. Phylloxera is a tiny louse native to the eastern seaboard of America. Native American vines had developed an immunity to it, but when these vines were brought over to Europe around 1858, it almost wiped out the European vine, Vitis vinifera. The louse's journey may have been helped by modern technology. In the age of sail the Atlantic crossing would have often been too long for it to survive. Sailing ships took three weeks whereas by 1860 steam ships had brought that down to twelve days. It's survival rate was enhanced further by the invention of the Wardian Case, a special box which enabled plants to be transported safely across oceans and which was named after its inventor, Dr Nathanial Ward. The boxes, of course, also enabled the pest itself to survive.

---

74 But they did have the money to build fairytale castles so perhaps it comes down to expertise and ambition rather than purely money.

Between 1858 and 1863 large quantities of American vines were imported into France. There was a fashion for exotic plants in Europe and there was no quarantine or controls. Vines began dying in the Languedoc in the 1860s. At first growers were baffled, but in 1868 Jules-Emile Planchon from the University of Montepellier discovered that the problem was an aphid almost invisible to the naked eye. He named it phylloxera vastatrix (the destroyer). At first many growers didn't believe Planchon or thought that this tiny creature couldn't cross mountains or rivers. But sometimes slowly and sometimes quickly it spread first across France and then across the world. It's a mysterious wee beastie, as some areas remain unaffected to this day. Bollinger own a small walled vineyard in Champagne that was never affected and Quinta do Noval's Nacional vineyard in the Douro also escaped unharmed. Both Bollinger and Quinta do Noval make fabulously expensive wines from their ungrafted vines. Vines planted in sandy soils tended to avoid the louse. South Australia remains free due to having some of the strictest quarantine controls in the world, as does Chile.

The louse feeds on the roots of vines and at first they struggle to produce ripe fruit and then die. In the 1860s viticulture had boomed in the south of France as the railways enabled cheap wine to be sent to big cities. Now one by one the vineyards succumbed to phylloxera. In 1878 it arrived in Bordeaux and by 1885 the harvest was less than a quarter of what it had been in the previous decade. The richer châteaux tried all sorts of elaborate and expensive techniques to hold off the louse such as injecting the roots with potassium sulpho-carbonate. This proved only temporarily successful. The only option left was to graft European vines onto resistant American rootstocks which slowly began to happen by the 1890s. In 1875 France was producing 84.5 hectolitres of wine, by 1889 this had collapsed to 23.4 million. For the first time in French history, sizeable quantities of wine were imported into the country mainly from Algeria and southern Europe. Much of this would be blended and relabelled as Bordeaux, Beaune etc. Whereas previously the genuine product would have been laced with foreign wine, now outright fakes were being concocted by unscrupulous merchants.

Phylloxera was a tragedy for France and for the growers of Bordeaux. Many vineyards were simply not replanted and those that were would not make fine wine for many years. Great wine needs established vines.[75] Furthermore farmers were overfertilising their new vines to produce large crops of tasteless grapes. In the early decades of the 20th century the wines made from the newly grafted vines weren't a patch on the pre-phylloxera vines. Phylloxera, however, wasn't the only biological problem in Bordeaux. At the same time phylloxera was killing vines they were also falling victim to downy mildew. This fungal infection worked in a more insidious way than phylloxera. With phylloxera the vines slowly died, but it did not greatly affect the taste of the grapes. Mildew seemed only to touch the leaves of the vine and the resulting wines often tasted fine just after fermentation, but then something awful would happen. W Beatty Kingston, an English journalist, wrote at the time:

> "Mildew told upon the grape juice after
> fermentation as well as upon the fruit before
> gathering. Wines that had apparently stood
> well for a couple of years in wood showing no
> symptoms of taint suddenly became affected
> at the expiration of that period, went thin and
> bitter and were practically unmarketable."

---

75 Nobody knows exactly why older vines tend to produce more flavourful grapes.

This was a disaster for the Bordelais. People would order Bordeaux at their favourite restaurant in London and on opening find that it had completely gone to pieces. They would send it back and next time think twice before ordering claret. The wine writer Nicholas Faith thinks that mildew was far worse for the reputation of Bordeaux's wines than phylloxera, and it was during this time that champagne capitalised on Bordeaux's failure to create a consistent product and marketed its way to success. The mildew was eventually cured by spraying the vines with copper sulphate powder, now known as Bordeaux mixture. To this day each row of vines in Bordeaux has a rose bush at the end which functions as an early warning system for the dreaded mildew.

The British middle classes began to turn their backs on Bordeaux and on table wines in general. They took to spirits and fortified wines which were so much more reliable. This was a trend across Europe; people were drinking branded drinks such as Campari, Pernod, Byrrh and Noilly Prat, as well as fortified wines such as sherry or Banyuls from the south of France. Bordeaux, which seemed to have the world at its feet in the 1860s, struggled into the 20th century. Economic and biological problems strengthened the role of the Chartronnais because the wines needed more work than ever in the cellars and the growers needed the financial muscle of the merchants. The industry was just getting over phylloxera when the First War World began; this was followed by the Depression and the Second World War. It was only in the 1960s that Bordeaux regained its place as the most sought-after wine in the world.

DRINKING THE EMPIRE

Claret is divided into two types, those made on the left bank of the Garonne river, Graves and the Médoc, which are mainly made from Cabernet Sauvignon, and those on the right made from Merlot in St-Emilion and Pomerol. All tend to be expensive. I'm going to concentrate on the Médoc because it makes the archetypal British claret. I won't be dwelling either on the excellent white wines of Graves or the superlative sweet wines from Sauternes and Barsac, only to say that the latter are underpriced and if you like sweet wines, which I do, you should buy them in quantity.

This is a hard section to write because claret is so vintage sensitive. I can't recommend consistent brands. Most of the big names in Bordeaux such as Haut-Brion, Mouton-Rothschild and Palmer are now ridiculously expensive. Though if you do have cash to splash, some vintages are underpriced such as 2004 and 2008.

Of the next tier down, still expensive, I am very partial to the wines of St-Julien such as Léoville-Barton, Gruaud-Larose and Beychevelle. All are expensive but not extortionate. At the time of writing you should be able to buy a bottle of Léoville-Barton 2004 for around £50.

Happily there are more affordable Bordeaux out there. Wines such Poujeaux and Potensac (needs lots of ageing) can offer a taste of Médoc grandeur for less money. And then moving into almost bargain territory, ie under £20 a bottle, are châteaux such as Sénéjac, Tour de By and Charmail.

If you go outside the Médoc, there are some areas that are actually cheap. Côtes de Castillon makes Merlot-heavy wine not dissimilar to its illustrious neighbour St-Emilion. They tend to be fleshy and enjoyable young. Three good names are: Château Roque Le Mayne, Château Puy Garance and Château Montlandrie.

Finally if you want to try something similar to pre-Pontac claret then you should look out for clairet which is a sort of dark rosé made in Bordeaux. Or perhaps something like a really light Cabernet Franc from the Loire might be the nearest thing.

14

ADULTERATION

We've seen how in Bordeaux wine would be beefed up with Spanish wine, how port was adulterated with elderberries and how sugar and brandy were part of the recipe for 19th century champagne. Though such practices sound pretty crude and possibly even fraudulent, many of the things done to wine were necessary to make them drinkable. In the days before refrigeration and before wine was shipped in sterile glass bottles, a barrel of wine might go through all kinds of trauma before it arrived at a merchant. Many of these dubious-sounding cellar practices were *de rigueur* to rescue wine that had suffered on the journey to Britain. Both Sir Kenelm Digby and Christopher Merret wrote of techniques for pepping up wine. If you found your wine only lightly doctored, you were doing well. At least what you were drinking was based on the wine you ordered. Some wines, however, were entirely spurious. In his book *A Tour to London: or, New Observations on England, and Its Inhabitants* the French writer Pierre-Jean Grosley remarked on the quality of wine available. He's worth quoting at length:

> "With regard to red wines I was informed
> by a vintner … that the country people
> gather in hedges around London the sloes
> and black-berries, which they publicly sell
> to the wine-merchants; that many of these

merchants have in the country brambles and wild shrubs, which bear fruits of this fort; and when they are ripe, the vintage commences in London: that is to say, the wines then begin to be brewed, the chief ingredient of which is the juice of turneps (sic) boiled to a total dissolution ... This juice, mixed with that of wild fruit, with beer, and litharge, after a slight fermentation, produces the Port wine, drunk in taverns and places of public diversion in and about London: it is an ingredient, which is blended, according to the rules of the vintner's art, in a greater or less quantity, with all their Bourdeaux (sic) wine, and even their Burgundy, which, as it comes out of the hands of many wine-merchants, often consists only of the poor dregs of Languedoc and Provence. I drank no pure unmixed wine, except in two houses... "

It wasn't just the poor who drank bad wine; it was everyone. The majority of wines in Britain in the early 18th century were adulterated, and many of them weren't even wine at all. Concoctions of raisins, sugar, rum, lemon juice and water would be passed off as madeira or port. These are the wines that Grosley is referring to when he talks about the fruit picked in the hedgerows. By the end of the 18th century it was estimated that half the port consumed in London was produced locally. Joseph Addison wrote in *Tatler* of the "fraternity of chymical operators ... who squeeze Bourdeaux out of a sloe and draw Champagne from an apple".

Because it was already to some extent a manufactured wine, port proved particularly susceptible to these "chymical operators". Much of it was sold on its alcoholic strength and colour rather than taste. John Croft, author of an early book about port, wrote of a recipe containing "Raisin wine ... generally made of the very worst sort of raisins that come from Smyrna compounded with British spirits, extracted from malt". Cyrus Redding's *A History and Description of Modern Wines* covers the matter of fake wines comprehensively. He notes a recipe for port consisting of Cape red, Spanish red, salt of tartar, brandy and gum dragon (a natural gum like gum arabic also known as tragacanth). The resulting "port" could be heated until it formed a crust so that it looked mature. These recipes appeared in books for publicans.

Champagne was also much imitated. All you needed were the bubbles and you could pass something off as the real thing. If you were lucky you'd get a sparkling wine from the Loire or the Jura, unlucky and you'd end up with something made from gooseberries. Fake madeiras were made from Vidonia (Canary wine), doctored with port, Cape wine, malaga, sugar, almonds and colouring. Common additives included gum benzoin added for a brown mature look, orris root (also used in production of gin and perfume), raspberry brandy, tartaric acid, citric, elderberries, logwood, alum, cider and cochineal (crushed beetles).

Not all of these additives were necessarily bad for you or harsh on the palate. Alum, or potassium aluminium sulphate, added acidity and is commonly found in pickles. In your average £5 supermarket wine today you might find tartaric acid, sugar, added tannin, added colour, enzymes, water, sulphur dioxide and yeast, plus fining agents such as fish scales and egg whites which remove particles to make the wine clear and then fall out of the wine, and oak chips to mimic barrels. Even some very expensive wines such as Penfolds Grange have tartaric acid added (and in some vintages tannin too). Almost all wine from France excluding the far south will have added sugar.

Other additives, however, could be dangerous. Oxalic acid was sometimes used to pep up a flabby wine just as tartaric acid is used today. It could lead to kidney problems. One of the additives mentioned by Pierre-Jean Grosley was litharge or lead oxide. It makes things taste sweet and is highly toxic. Cider-makers in the West Country used to hang lead bars in their cider to improve it and it has been used since Roman times to sweeten wines. There is a theory that one of the reasons the Roman Empire collapsed was because of lead poisoning, whether in their water pipes or in their wine.

In Britain in 1875 the British Food & Drug Act was passed which made it illegal to adulterate food, drink and drugs. It was designed to protect consumers from poisoning and fraud. The French response was rather different in that it was designed mainly to protect producers rather than consumers. After phylloxera had devastated vineyards, genuine wine was in short supply and adulteration was rampant. Large quantities of Algerian wine were shipped to France and blended into dubious "Beaune". Many couldn't afford this so drank *piquette*, from fermented sugar and grape skins. In the 1920s and 30s France began to codify its vineyards and working practices. It became known as the Appellation Contrôlée system. Originally it was just set up to protect producers against fakes masquerading under renowned names. The first appellation was set up by Baron Pierre le Roy de Boiseaumarié in Châteauneuf-du-Pape in 1926. It specified the vineyards entitled to the geographical name and the permitted grape varieties. This was over 150 years after similar measures were taken by Pombal in the Douro. Other regions in France followed and later Italy and Spain would have their own similar systems.

Despite such regulations, wine adulteration is a perennial problem. The Austrian wine industry was almost wiped out by a scandal that emerged in 1985 when it became apparent that antifreeze, diethylene glycol, had been added to some of their wines. This would have made the wines taste sweet. Just how the Germans, Austria's biggest export market, liked them. Antifreeze is actually harmless. In Italy a more serious problem arose when some people died after drinking wine adulterated with methanol. Oddly it didn't affect the industry like it did in Austria.

In the 1970s a scandal rocked Bordeaux to its core when the prestigious merchant house of Cruse were found to be selling cheap southern wines as AC Bordeaux. The head of the family, Herman Cruse, committed suicide though he wasn't involved in any of the dubious affairs. In the same decade there was a *Sunday Times* exposé of British wine merchants. They discovered that most of what was being sold as Grand Cru Burgundy was, in fact, what the French called "soup", ie a concoction that at best would be ordinary Burgundy beefed up with wines from the Rhône and Algeria and, at worse, wouldn't contain any Burgundy at all. Burgundy in Britain was usually closer to Châteauneuf-du-Pape than the delicate fragrant wine that we know today. These scandals broke the hold that the merchants had on the wine trade.

In the 1980s there was the case of a German collector, Hardy Rodenstock, who sold a bottle of Lafite 1787 at auction for $156,000 that he claimed had belonged to Thomas Jefferson. It was never proven conclusively, but this is now generally thought to have been a fake. Then there was the case recently of Rudy Kurniawan (real name Zhen Wang Huang) who fooled the American wine establishment by creating forgeries of famous wines. When police raided his home they found hundreds of old bottles, forged labels and recipes for creating famous wines. He'd buy worthless old bottles of Burgundy, doctor them with $100 Californian Pinot Noir and sell them as a Domaine de la Romanée-Conti, the most fabled estate in Burgundy. Much of the wine in collectors' cellars, particularly in China, is thought to be spurious.

Some wines that spuriously sported prestigious names, however, would go on to glory in their own right. Marsala wine was originally sold as Sicilian Madeira and, until recently, two of the greatest wines in Australia, both made by Penfolds, were sold under the names of French wines: Grange Hermitage and St Henri Claret. In fact, the Australian wine industry is built on wines that were originally labelled Chablis, Hock, Port, Sherry and Tokay.

15

CHAMPAGNE AND RESTAURANTS

There's a wonderful book, *Dinner and Diners*, by Lieutenant-Colonel Newnham-Davis, a former Indian army officer, that captures the mood of the late Victorian and early Edwardian period. He was restaurant critic for *Pall Mall Gazette* and he was always taking other people's wives out to restaurants with no hint of impropriety. It's a curiously timeless book. His review for Simpson's in the Strand, founded in 1850 and still serving much the same sort of food today, comments on how old-fashioned the place is. Simpson's aside, under the influence of Escoffier the food in late 19th century London was becoming increasingly elaborate. Menus were always in French and groaning with truffles, butter, sole, lamb and caviar. The wine Newnham-Davis drinks more than any other is champagne. He wrote: "In Paris, no man dreams of drinking champagne, and nothing but champagne, for dinner, but in London ... ladies as a rule will consider a dinner incomplete without champagne. Ninety-nine out of a hundred Englishmen, in ordering a little dinner for two, turn instinctively to the champagne page of the wine-card... " In London champagne had become as much part of the uniform of eating out as white tie and tails. It was a way of showing your taste and superiority. Not everyone approved. H L Feuerheerd in his 1902 book, *Gentleman's Cellar and Butler's Guide*, complains about being served "nothing but champagne during the whole dinner ... I thank my stars if after the cheese I can get a glass of port."

Until the middle years of the 19th century, sparkling champagne had been a very hit or miss affair despite the best efforts of the Royal Society. Bubbles were still very erratic; one might end up with a few big bubbles described in French as *yeux de crapauds* or toad's eyes, no bubbles at all or just a slimy mess. The wine would have fermented only once. Stronger glass and corks had helped make it a viable industry rather than a freakish curiosity, but the majority of the production of the Champagne region was a still red wine. During Napoleon's reign only a third of production was sparkling. French wine connoisseurs thought the fizzy stuff rather vulgar. Bertin du Rocheret, a wine merchant, compared the sparkling product disparagingly to "beer, chocolate and whipped cream". Production was a haphazard affair and up to 40 percent of bottles exploded. Cellarmen in Champagne would wear iron masks to protect them from exploding bottles and were paid danger money.

The transformation from a vulgar curiosity to consistent product was down to the work of some top French scientists and one remarkable widow. Louis Pasteur's work on yeasts and microorganisms meant that the process of fermentation was beginning to be understood. The role of added sugar to fuel a second fermentation was studied by Antoine-Augustin Parmentier and Jean-Antoine Chaptal. Chaptal's scheme during the Napoleonic Wars to plant sugar beet throughout France to thwart the Royal Navy blockade meant that for the first time cheap sugar was available, essential for creating sparkling champagne. To this day, the lands around Champagne which aren't qualified to grow grapes for the famous wine grow sugar beet to create bubbles. In 1836 André François invented the *gleuco-oenometre* so now the amount of sugar in the wine could be measured. Previously too much was often added, leading to breakages. By the

1840s improvements in glass production too meant that the bottles were now more reliable.

Despite all these innovations, wines might still be cloudy due to spent yeasts (known as lees) in the bottle. Decanting off the lees to a clean bottle would help clear the wine, but would lose some of that precious fizz. Barbe-Nicole Clicquot took over her husband's firm when he died in 1805 and set about solving this problem. Around 1811 she invented the process known as *remuage*[76] where the bottles are turned upside down so that the yeasts congregate around the cork. She discovered that this worked best if the bottles were at a 45 degree angle pointing down and gently turned every so often. The spent yeasts would then be ejected by the pressure of the wine when the cork was removed in a process known as *dégorgement*. The bottle would then be topped up with some sweet wine and brandy and then quickly recorked. Madame Clicquot's cellar techniques for creating a clear wine meant that a bright consistently sparkling wine could now be produced in quantity. Thomas George Shaw wrote in his 1863 book *Wine, the Vine, and the Cellar* how champagne was becoming more reliable: "Champagnes formerly became often 'scuddy' which means they lost their limpidity and brilliancy; but this is rarely now the case."

The French may have had the technical expertise but, as usual, it was outsiders who proved most adept at selling the product. Though in this case they weren't British, they were German. Their legacy can be seen in the names of some of the great champagne houses: Bollinger, Heidsieck (all the different Heidsiecks), Roederer, Deutz, Mumm, Taittinger and Krug were all created by German entrepreneurs. Max Sutaine, a contemporary champagne merchant, thought the preponderance of Germans was because many were

---

76 Sir Kenelm Digby wrote about a similar technique of inverting bottles of sparkling cider.

originally employed by French firms for their language skills. The French at the time, like the English today, spoke no language except their own. Having learnt about the wine and the trade, the clerks, as in Jerez or Porto, went into business on their own account using the contacts from their previous employers. Unlike the British, though, most became naturalised Frenchmen apart from the Mumms who had their assets confiscated on the eve of the First World War.

Initially the biggest market for sparkling champagne was Russia. Legend has it that the Russian soldiers stationed in France after the defeat of Napoleon picked up a taste for champagne and brought it back home. Veuve Clicquot and Roederer were the two dominant houses in the Russian market. The Russians liked their wine very sweet. In the 1850s most champagne drunk was sweet. Cyrus Redding writes that many of these wines were "of a very inferior quality, and being sweetened and seasoned with sugar and spirit could only answer for instant consumption". Mid-19th century champagne would not only have been sweet, it would have been a rich yellow wine fortified with brandy, like a sort of sparkling sweet sherry. Some destined for the Russian market were even fortified with yellow Chartreuse[77] to make them stronger still. The most prized wines from Champagne for connoisseurs were still the red table wines but, thanks to railways, these were increasingly coming into competition from reds from other parts of France that could be made cheaper and more reliably. The 1840s saw a decline in production of still wines as the champenois began to focus on the wine that made them unique.

Demand for sparkling champagne from Industrial Revolution Britain began to increase. From 1844 to 1870 exports of champagne rose from around 4 million bottles

---

77 A herb-infused spirit made by Carthusian monks near Grenoble. There are yellow and green versions.

to nearly 14 million chiefly to Britain and America. The Civil War temporarily knocked America out as a serious champagne consumer and Britain became the main market. Something odd now happened here: initially the British liked their champagne as sweet as most of their drinks. Thomas Shaw writes of how British "palates have been so long habituated to strong, dark, brandied wines, that we prefer this inferior champagne". But this began to change. Slowly a taste for dry champagne took hold in Britain. Why did the English switch to dry champagne when all their previous tastes were towards sweet unsubtle drinks? Champagne was generally drunk as dessert wine on the Continent, but the British already had strong sweet wines, port or madeira, so they wanted something to drink before or with the meal. According to André Simon, the dry wine pioneer was an English importer called Mr Brune who tasted some of the 1846 vintage in Epernay unsweetened and loved it. He imported some but it didn't go down well with his customers. By 1857, however, a swing towards drier vintages had begun. Because they were not hidden under lashings of sugar and brandy, these wines required riper grapes. This trend for drier drinks was mirrored in sherry and gin.

There were improvements in viticulture including a mapping of the Champagne region for the location of the best places to grow grapes suitable for sparkling wine production. The best grapes were being isolated, Pinot Noir, Pinot Meunier and Chardonnay, but also ones that now rarely feature in champagne such as Pinot Blanc, Arbane and Petit Meslier. Producers were helped in the drive for quality by abundant quality vintages in the 1860s. The 1865 was the first vintage where most wines were shipped to Britain dry. Before wines were about 15 percent liqueur, made up of sugar and brandy, afterwards it was about two percent. The vintage began to assume a great importance. The 1874, a very ripe vintage, Pommery became something of a cult wine in London. The switch from sweet to dry was slow and incomplete. In London they liked their wine very dry, but in the provinces the taste for sweet wines persisted longer. At the Paris Exhibition in 1900 most of the champagne served would have been sweet. It was only in Britain and to a lesser extent America where brut (bone dry) was the norm. Much of what was sold as dry wouldn't have seemed dry at all for modern palates. Champagne still has illogical sweetness gradations: extra-dry is actually quite sweet and demi-sec is very sweet. Even the brut ones drunk by Lieutenant-Colonel Newnham-Davis would have still been very different to modern champagnes which are dominated by Chardonnay. They would have contained many more black grapes, Pinots Noir and Meunier, and so would have been heavier wines perfectly suited for drinking with the lavish food of Escoffier. The Savoy wine menu from 1901 lists not only a selection of champagne vintages, but tells you how sweet each one was so you could select the exact wine to suit your palate.

These dry wines would have needed long ageing which meant champagne firms had to tie up large amounts of capital in maturing wine. Improvements in champagne technology meant that the wines were now suitable for something like mass production. Champagne like port, sherry[78] and madeira is a capitalist product. In champagne the smaller houses lost out to the bigger producers who had huge economies of scale. Moët et Chandon in the 1890s employed 1,500 people, held stocks of 10 million bottles, owned 20,000 casks and their cellars were lit with thirty tonnes of candles per year. Champagne had picked its moment perfectly. Bordeaux had been hit hard by the phylloxera and two fungal infections, powdery mildew and

---

78 Champagne and sherry are in some ways sister products. Both are made on chalky soils, both are generally a blend of vintages and both undergo a chemical process called autolysis which gives them a nutty, bready sort of taste.

oidium. Phylloxera was devastating Bordeaux in the 1870s, but it did not arrive in Champagne until 1890. Old bottles of Bordeaux which had been fine when young would become undrinkable after a few years, a relic of oidium (a fungus that affects grapes). Champagne, however, was reliable. It could be blended and it filled the space left by claret and cognac – whose production had also plummeted due to the vine diseases. The other great beneficiary was whisky.

Whereas Bordeaux required an arcane knowledge of châteaux, champagne was branded. Everyone would have heard of Pommery or Perrier-Jouët. In the early days of the 19th century many champagnes were sold like their still cousins by the names of vineyards, but increasingly the names of merchants came to predominate.[79] These brands were disseminated by mass advertising and by agents around the world such as Charles "Champagne Charlie" Heidsieck who was particularly successful selling his wines in America. Champagne was one of the first drinks to have mass advertising. It was ahead of its time. Bass beer also went in for international advertising but, in general, mass advertising for wines didn't take off until the 1920s or 30s. The most recognisable name in port, the Sandeman Don, didn't appear until the late 1920s. Advertising was an expensive process but it paid dividends. Nowadays, British drinkers who would never spend £30 on a bottle of wine might spend that without thinking on champagne.

Much of the advertising featured images that would have appealed more to women depicting elegant ladies in fashionable Edwardian attire looking like Julie Christie in *The Go-Between*. (For men there were saucy showgirls and naughty 90s gents.) For the first time women's spending power was a factor. Restaurants such as those written up

---

79   However, this is now beginning to be eroded (see end of chapter).

by Newnham-Davis were designed to appeal to women. Pubs by mid-Victorian times were no longer visited by respectable people, especially not by women. They had become places just to drink; they didn't offer table service and didn't offer food. The invention of the bar at which drinkers were served, as opposed to a hatch from where drinks were distributed, meant that people could be served quicker with less staff. It was mass production for alcohol distribution. Children had also been excluded meaning there was less of a curb on drunkenness. Pubs were becoming places for working-class men to escape from their families. Restaurants offered something new. Sir Coutts Lindsay, a restaurant owner, wrote of "a want which has long been felt to exist in the West End, namely a place conducted on such principles and in such a manner as allows of its being visited for the purposes of refreshment by clergymen, ladies and others ... "

New-fangled restaurants opened in the West End. The Criterion opened in 1878 followed by the Trocadero and the Gaiety. The Savoy was opened in 1889 by Richard D'Oyly Carte, the theatre impresario behind Gilbert and Sullivan; the head chef was Auguste Escoffier and it was managed by César Ritz. Ritz's wife Marie-Louise wrote: "Women were beginning in the Eighties to demand equal rights with men – even in such matters as food! When Ritz decorated and furnished his hotels he always considered *first* the requirements and taste of ladies... "

Despite its immense prestige, there is something curiously egalitarian about champagne. The branding system undermined the power of merchants and waiters in restaurants. In 1882 Gilbey's wine merchants were forced to stock brands of champagne rather than their own labels due to customer demand. People felt confident ordering brands knowing they were getting reliable quality. Gladstone's Single Bottle Act of 1860 meant that for the first time

Art nouveau Pommery poster from 1902

people could buy wine by the bottle, rather than having to visit wine merchants and buy a case. Champagne became available everywhere, not only in restaurants, but grocers' shops and department stores.

Railway hotels and railways were great purchasers of champagne. People could pop out for a bottle of champagne. In *Diary of a Nobody* by George and Weedon Grossmith, the hero of the book is an everyman who lives in suburban Holloway and works as a clerk in the City and is constantly sending out for a bottle of "Jackson Frères".[80] Lots of people were doing very well out of the Industrial Revolution. If people were celebrating, they would order champagne. There was status, but no snobbery attached to it. Even

---

80 I wonder if this was a made-up grocer's brand or perhaps Jacquesson, one of the oldest and grandest champagne houses. Probably the former.

relatively poor people would splash out on champagne, as they do today. The statistics tell the story: in the 1860s 3 million bottles per year were sold in Britain; by 1880 it was 9 million. Britain was by far the biggest export market for champagne as it is to this day.

DRINKING THE EMPIRE

If you want to try something like the still champagnes that would have been fashionable in England and France, you should try wines from the village of Bouzy (pronounced boozy). They make wines like very light burgundies from Pinot Noir. Try from a producer such as Barnaut in a hot year such as 2009.

Veuve Clicquot do a Rich Reserve which, if not as sweet as the stuff drunk by the Czars, will give you some idea of how good a sweeter champagne can be.

Of the big champagne brands my favourite is probably Pol Roger, especially for their vintage wines. Other ones I like include Louis Roederer, Bollinger, Charles Heidsieck and Billecart-Salmon.

If you want to try something like a Victorian London champagne look for a Blanc de Noirs (white made from black grapes). Also note that Pol Roger vintage wines tend to be made from a large percentage of Pinots Noir and Meunier. These go really well with heavier foods and even red meat.

Very slowly the might of the monolithic champagne brands is being weakened. They buy their grapes from or grow them all over the champagne region and blend them into a consistent branded product which, in my opinion, has been the key to champagne's success. Now we are beginning to see single-vineyard champagnes from small growers. Some good names to look out for include Larmandier-

Bernier, Pierre Gimonnet and Fleury Père & Fils. If you want something to sip with your Escoffier-style meal at the Savoy the rich Fleur de L'Europe from Fleury Père & Fils is hard to beat.

16

WHISKY, THE SPIRIT OF THE EMPIRE

Whisky runs in my family's blood. Well, that's a bit of an exaggeration, but I do have an uncle who is a big cheese in the whisky business. He has worked for such famous names as Talisker and Cardhu. He was until recently retired, but, like an ageing safe cracker, he has been lured out for one last job managing a new distillery at Ballindalloch in the heart of Speyside. It was a treat to be shown around Ballindalloch by the master distiller, or Uncle Charles as I call him, but one element was missing at the end of the tour, the whisky. This new distillery has only been distilling for three years and it will be some time before the spirit can be called whisky and even longer before it will have matured sufficiently to sell. The week before I visited, Charles and Camilla officially opened the distillery. By all accounts it was a fairly low-key visit. The royals are regular visitors to the region – their residence at Balmoral is just down the road. In true British tabloid style, the papers were full of stories about them enjoying a dram afterwards even though there was no whisky available. Whisky, though, hasn't always been so respectable. At one time it would rarely have left the Highlands and it wouldn't have been aged. The idea of the Royal Family coming to try it would have been outlandish.

Whisky has been made in Scotland for a long time. The word is a corruption of the Gaelic for Water of Life, *Uisge Beatha*. One theory is that it was introduced to Scotland by Irish monks in the 12th century. It is made by producing a kind of ale from cereal, usually malted barley, which would then be heated in a pot still and the resulting alcohol condensed in water-cooled pipes known as a worm tub. The basic apparatus of distillation hasn't changed in 800 years. Similar drinks would have been made all over the world, but in the Highlands of Scotland distillation was elevated into an art form and the resulting spirit was highly prized. In the late 18th and early 19th centuries the best whisky was illicit.

The number of laws passed to regulate and tax whisky production and sales can be overwhelming. They seem specifically designed to discourage legal distilling and keep smugglers in business. In the early days, though, limits on distillation had a very practical purpose. Scotland struggled to feed its population. Plentiful arable land is confined to the Lowland regions. Life in the Highlands was at subsistence level much of the time. It was fine or even essential for families to distill whatever excess they had to earn a little cash, but as soon as distilling started up on a larger scale there was always the risk that it would lead to a shortage of grain. This is partly the rationale behind the draconian whisky policies of the 18th and early 19th century. Terrible harvests culminated in 1757 when all distilling was banned throughout the British Isles until 1760. Large-scale legal distilling could only take place thanks to the revolution in agriculture that took place in the 19th century that increased yields dramatically, and later the importation of grain from America and Canada. Much Scotch today is made from imported grain.

The duty on distilling was designed to raise money for the Government, but it was so ineptly designed that it hampered the legitimate industry while encouraging criminal activity. Just as the country was divided culturally and linguistically, excise regulations divided Scotland into Highland and Lowland parts. This division was known as the Highland Line: a line on the map from Greenock just north of Glasgow on the Firth of Forth to Dundee on the Firth of Tay cut Scotland in two. North of the line, Highland whisky was made only from malted barley like a single malt today. It was distilled in small copper pots as it had been for generations. South of the line, Lowland whisky was made from other grains with some malted barley. Malt and grain, Highland and Lowland, evolved separately. Grain spirit in the south became an industrial product. The two biggest distilleries were Kilbagie and Kennetpans. They were mammoth operations: Kilbagie had 850 acres of produce to turn into whisky and in 1779 produced 3,000 tons of spirit. This whisky was not a high-class dram. Much of it would be redistilled to make gin for sale in England or mixed to make toddies. Malt from the Highlands, in contrast, became a much-sought-after drink in its own right. Highland distilling was often in the hands of illiterate farmers who would pool a still and most was sold locally. For much of the 18th and 19th century distillers in the Highlands could sell their whisky within the Highland region, but were not allowed to export to the Lowlands let alone to England. As their whisky was more highly prized than the Lowland version, it led to a boom in smuggling.

Walter Scott wrote that "smuggling was almost universal during the reigns of George I and II; for the people unaccustomed to imposts (sic) and regarding them as unjust aggression upon their ancient liberties made no scruple to elude them wherever it was possible to do so." In 1778 smuggling was so out of control that private distillation was outlawed completely. Excise officers were licensed to confiscate stills or destroy them. A philanthropist and leader of the Free Church of Scotland, Thomas Guthrie wrote in his autobiography: "Everybody with a few exceptions, drank what was in reality illicit whisky – far superior to that made under the eye of the Excise – lords and lairds, members of Parliament and ministers of the Gospel, and everybody else." Guthrie was born in 1803 and is remembering the Highlands of his boyhood. Often only through sale of whisky could rents be paid, so landlords turned a blind eye to illicit distilling on their land.

A contemporary, Eliza Fletcher, wrote in her autobiography: "The men of the place resorted to the woods or to the sequestered glens among the Campsie Hills, and there distilled whisky… "

As one drives around Speyside today, it's easy to understand why illegal distilling and smuggling was so prolific in this area. The terrain is hilly with lots of woodland. The ground is covered in thick gorse and heather. There are plenty of places to hide stills and at the time roads, where they existed, would have been mere tracks. It's a place that still feels wild and beyond the reaches of the government. London and indeed Edinburgh seem very far away. It has another essential for making good whisky, lots of fresh water. It's one of the rainiest places in Britain and the lack of both heavy industry and large-scale farming means that the water was and still is beautifully pure. Water is needed to make the whisky, but it's also needed to cool the spirit. Distilleries get through a lot of it. At Glenfarclas, not far from Uncle Charles's distillery, they use between 200,000 and 1 million litres per day. I tried the water from the lake next to their distillery. It comes from melted snow filtered through peat and heather. It tastes glorious. They should bottle it to sell alongside their whisky. The abundant water would later prove useful to drive water wheels as distilleries became industrialised.

One 17th century whisky wasn't subject to tax and briefly became a brand known throughout Scotland – Ferintosh. It became the first commercial distillery in the country. It was founded by Duncan Forbes, a supporter of William III whose castle at Culloden on the Black Isle near Inverness was sacked by Jacobites in 1688. For his loyalty he was granted the privilege in perpetuity of distilling duty free any surplus grain from his estate. His whisky became famous throughout Scotland, prized by Walter Scott and most famously Robert Burns. Burns was a Lowlander, but not keen on the local whisky. The privilege granted by the King was eventually revoked in 1784 and the Forbes family stopped distilling. Burns mourned: "Ferintosh! O sadly lost! Scotland lament frae coast to coast!"

In 1816 the Highland Line was finally abolished, duty reduced by a third and smaller pot sizes were also allowed which made small-scale legal distilling possible again. This led to an immediate boom in Highland whisky. It was the beginning of commercial licensed distilleries and would become an important source of revenue for the Government. One of the most vociferous proponents of the new legislation was the Duke of Gordon. In 1820 Alexander Gordon, Duke of Gordon, stood in the House of Lords and defended Highland whisky as something intrinsic to the area. It could not be stopped, nor was it a good idea to try. He argued for legislation to allow and encourage whisky so that illicit stills would become redundant. Gordon's enthusiasm for legalised distilling may have had something to do with the fact that one of his tenants was a certain George Smith of Glenlivet, whose illicit whisky was highly prized.

The Government wanted to change whisky production from a private affair to something public and commercial so that it could be taxed and controlled. Britain was losing the last vestiges of feudalism and becoming a capitalist society. Landowners in Scotland who may have once had Jacobite sympathies were brought into the British fold because they could make money from their land. Legal distilling was a good way of doing this.

1823 saw the passing of the Excise Act which further liberalised distilling, but also provided more resources and power to excise officers. Their job was helped by the invention of the Spirit Safe by Septimus Smith which allowed distillers to analyse the spirit, but without being able to syphon any off. These marvellous contraptions are still used in distilleries to this day made from polished brass with glass panels so that the spirit can be analysed, and enormous padlocks which until the 1980s only the exciseman would have the key for. In fact, there are locks all over distilleries, even on the stills themselves, to prevent contraband and pilfering. Landowners were encouraged to suppress illegal stills and encourage legal ones. There were penalties for having illicit stills on your land. The carrot and stick approach worked wonders. The statistics tell the story: 14,000 illicit distilling activities were uncovered in 1823, but by 1834 it was down to 692. Illicit distillation never became a major problem again.

To take advantage of the new climate, Smith built a new distillery at Glenlivet. It was the first new distillery to be licensed under the new act. In just two years after the act the number of licensed distilleries doubled and legal whisky production rose from 2 million to 6 million gallons a year. Glenlivet was so prestigious that it gave its name to the whole region, now known as Speyside. Other distilleries added Glenlivet to their names, just as in Burgundy where villages amend the name of their nearest famous vineyard to the village name: for example, Puligny with the vineyard of Montrachet to make Puligny-Montrachet. So in Scotland you had names such as Glenfarclas-Glenlivet which sounds like a play by David Mamet. Glenlivet eventually bought the rights to the word and are now rather grandly known as "The Glenlivet". They style themselves as "the single malt that started it all".

Lowland whisky was something quite different to fine spirits such as Glenlivet. Robert Burns described it thus: "the whisky of this country (ie the Lowlands) is a most rascally liqueur." It was made from other grains apart from malted barley including oats, maize and wheat. Until 1826 it would have been made in a similar way to Highland malt ie in a pot still, though on a much bigger scale. But in 1826 Robert Stein of the Stein distilling family who owned Kilbagie invented the continuous still. This meant rather than having to distill a batch, clean out the still and replenish it, distilling could take place constantly. In 1830 the new still produced about 150,000 gallons of whisky in a year which is roughly thirty times what a Highland still could produce. The new spirit was smooth, high in alcohol and of good quality, though it didn't have much flavour. At around the same time a former excise man, Aeneas Coffey, was perfecting his continuous still in Dublin which worked on similar principles. Coffey's still eventually won out over Stein's as it was easier to manufacture and worked more efficiently. By 1836 30 percent of Lowland whiskies were made in Coffey stills.

Both Highland and Lowland whisky in the early 19th century would have been a mystery to the majority of Englishmen. In the literature of the Georgian and early Victorian period, it's apparent that drinking whisky while in Scotland was the modern day equivalent of licking hallucinogenic toads while in the Amazon or eating rancid whale in Iceland. Samuel Johnson treats whisky as a local curiosity in his *Journey to the Outer Hebrides* published in 1775: "A man of the Hebrides ... as soon as he appears in the morning, swallows a glass of whisky. Yet they are not a drunken race, at least I never was present at much intemperance... " It became a custom for travellers to the Highlands to comment on how frequently whisky was drunk and in such quantities. This is from *Letters from a Gentleman in the North of Scotland to His Friend in London* by Captain Edward Burt, published in 1754:

> "Some of the Highland Gentlemen are
> immoderate Drinkers of Usky, even three

or four quarts at a Sitting; and in general,
The People that can Pay the Purchase, drink
it without moderation. Not long ago, Four
English Officers took a fancy to try their
strength in this Bow of Ulysses, against a
like Number of Country Champions, but the
Enemy came off victorious; and one of the
Officers was thrown into a Fit of the Gout,
without Hopes; another had a most dangerous
Fever, a third lost his Skin and Hair by the
Surfeit, and the last confessed to me, that when
Drunkenness and Debate ran high, he took
several opportunities to sham it." (I assume this
means that he poured his away.)

As excise laws changed and legal Highland whisky took off, canny Scots set about exploiting the lucrative market to the south. In order to do this, they needed two things: a consistent product to market and then the right way of marketing it. The consistent product came in the form of blended whisky. The French had been blending old and new brandies for years to create a consistent commercial product. Sherry and other fortified wines were usually blended products and, indeed, many wines were also blended, though this was usually done illicitly so that the customers didn't know. Perhaps the first blend marketed in England was Usher's OVG – which stood for Old Vatted Glenlivet – a blend of whiskies from the Glenlivet region. They took advantage of a change in the law in 1853 which allowed a distiller to store whisky under bond (ie without paying any duty on it), which brought down costs considerably. This brand was still going strong in the 1970s. It was a premium brand as it was entirely made from malted Highland whisky.

The big change, however, was when it was discovered that you could blend flavourful, but expensive Highland malts with the much cheaper, blander Lowland whiskies made in Coffey stills. You would have some of the flavour of Highland whiskies, but without the expense. It was general merchants rather than the distilleries themselves that were at the forefront of blending and exporting this new type of whisky. One such shop was Chivas Brothers in Aberdeen. Like Fortnum & Mason today they sold luxury foodstuffs, as well as wine and spirits. Their blends, forerunners of today's Chivas Regal, were heavy with Speyside whiskies. Whisky was generally aged by merchants, rather than by the distilleries themselves, and from the 1850s merchants began to market their own blends. They would buy whiskies from around Scotland and blend them to a house style. Big brands such as Teachers, the Famous Grouse, Ballantines and Johnnie Walker have their origins in this period. These blends were made up of whiskies from many different distilleries both malt and grain – whiskies of different ages, different intensities and different flavours. Scotland's astonishing variety of distilleries is down to the success of blends. Single malts did not become big business until after the 1960s.

In the early 19th century most whisky would have been sold straight out of the still and drunk within a year. It would have been clear like vodka. It's interesting trying new make whisky (spirit that has been recently distilled). I was lucky enough to sample some at Glenfarclas. It's really nothing like vodka, being packed with fruity notes and a distinct malty cereal richness. It already has such complexity and smoothness even before the long ageing process in sherry barrels. It's how much whisky would have tasted. If you wanted to mature it, you had to do it yourself. The merchants changed this. They would buy the spirit from the distillery and then store it in barrels that had previously held sherry, claret, madeira, rum or port. The Scots drank these in quantity so there were plenty available. So whisky is perhaps the ultimate Empire of Booze drink in that it incorporates flavours from all the other great "British" drinks.

Barrels that had held sherry were the most prized means of storing the whisky as they gave the maturing spirit a smooth fruity taste. You can still taste this in some particularly sherried Speyside whiskies such as Glenfarclas who only use sherry casks (normally oloroso) for maturing their whisky. In 1864 William Sanderson, creator of the VAT 69 blend – the whisky that Shackleton took on his 1915 expedition to the South Pole – wrote "it is well-known that whisky stored in sherry casks soon acquires a mellow softness which it does not get when put into new casks; in fact the latter if not well seasoned, will impart a *woodiness* much condemned by the practiced palate. In sherry casks the spirit likewise acquires a pleasing tinge of colour which is much sought after."

As with port, madeira and sherry, the whisky merchants responded to the needs of their customers. Different blends were designed for different markets, so a London blend would be different from a Glasgow one. From the early days the success of Scotch whisky owed as much to the imagination and energy of the marketing as the quality of the spirit. The growth of Scotch coincided with the birth of Highlandism. This was a peculiar phenomenon where Lowland Scotland, a predominantly settled mercantile society, took on the trappings of the Highlander as a way of differentiating themselves from Englishmen who they were now yoked to in the Union. It has roots in the Napoleonic Wars. Scotland became a popular holiday destination for the English when the Continent was cut off. When the war was won, the Highland regiments dazzled the French when the allied armies marched into Paris. Waterloo was a great symbol of the strength of the Union. This is embodied in Lady Butler's painting *Scotland Forever!* showing the Scots

Greys' charge at Waterloo which can be seen at Leeds Art Gallery. The painting became enormously popular. There was a print of it at George Orwell's boarding school which he describes in *Such, Such were the Joys*:

> "In the big schoolroom there was a steel engraving of the charge of the Scots Grey at Waterloo, all looking as though they enjoyed every moment of it. The school was pervaded by a curious cult of Scotland ... Our picture of Scotland was made up of burns, braes, kilts, sporrans, claymores, bagpipes and the like, all somehow mixed up with the invigorating effects of porridge, protestantism and a cold climate."

This might almost be from a research paper on how to best market Scotch. There was even a brand called Thin Red Line in reference to the red tunics worn by the British at the battle. It was novelist Walter Scott who we can most thank for this invented image of Scotland. Scott stage-managed the visit of King George IV to Scotland in December 1822. Everything, right down to what the King wore, was under Scott's aegis. He used it as a celebration of Scottishness. There's even a story that the King asked to try the then-illegal Glenlivet. George IV was the first Hanoverian King and, indeed, the first monarch to visit this part of his realm since Charles I. George IV was the Prince Regent while his father George III was losing his mind and is one of the most ridiculed monarchs in British history. Our image of him is coloured by contemporary cartoons such as Gillray's image of a bloated Prince Regent picking his teeth with a fork (see page 181) or more recently by Hugh Laurie saying "trousers" in *Blackadder III*. Sir John Plumb, a historian writing in the 20th century, captured the ridiculousness of George's visit to Scotland, but he also captures its significance:

> "He paraded Edinburgh in the kilt, resplendent in the Royal Stuart tartan and flesh-coloured tights, and yet managed to keep his dignity. The Scots loved it. Quaintly enough George IV had struck the future note of the monarchy ... be-kilted, be-sporraned, be-tartaned, riding up Princes Street ... to the roaring cheers of loyal Scots, he was showing the way that the monarchy would have to go if it were to survive an industrial and democratic society."

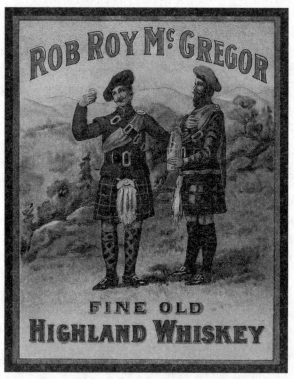

Art nouveau Pommery poster from 1902

It's the model for the Royal Family today who never look happier than when pretending to be Scottish. George's visit not only helped strengthen the union between two countries, England and Scotland, a union that would go on to create the Empire, export industrialism globally, fight two world wars and endure, if now in much diminished form, up to the present day. It also symbolised the union between the two parts of Scotland, the Lowlands and the Highlands. The differences between these two regions of Scotland were perhaps even more pronounced than those between England and Scotland. The Lowlanders spoke Scots, a Germanic tongue like English, the Highlanders spoke Gaelic, the Lowlanders were Presbyterian whereas the Highlanders were mainly Catholic. The Lowlanders were mercantile, industrious and practical, whereas the Highlanders were wild and romantic. These are of course stereotypes, but they speak a truth. Robert Louis Stevenson wrote: "the division[81] of races is more sharply marked within the borders of Scotland itself than between the countries... "

Whisky showed how the two Scotlands could unite to sell themselves to the world using a sort of invented Scottishness. "Brand Scotland" as it's perhaps now known has been astonishingly effective. The historian Tom Devine wrote: "Highlandism answered the emotional need for a distinctive Scottish identity without in any way compromising the Union." This constructed Scotland was then used to sell whisky. Sales promotions played on romantic Highland imagery – stags, tartan, claymores,

---

81 This division has a long history. John of Fordoun wrote in 1380: "the manners and customs of the Scots vary with the diversity of their speech. For two languages are spoken among them, the Scottish (Gaelic) and the Teutonic (Scots): the latter which is the language of those who occupy the seaboard and the plains, whilst the race of Scottish speech inhabits the Highlands and outlying islands. The people of the coast are of domestic and civilised habits ... The Highlanders and people of the islands on the other hand are a savage and untamed nation ..."

roaring fires in windswept castles etc. This was the template for nearly all advertising of Scotch whisky from the Victorian era right up until the present day. David Daiches, academic and whisky enthusiast: "I cannot help admiring the gaiety, the debonair quality, the splendid dash and vigour of much of that pioneering advertising." Only in the early 21st century did whisky marketers start to tire of it. In 2008 CEO of Diageo Paul Walsh referred dismissively to Scotch being marketed through "bagpipes, heather and tartan".

George IV's visit was the beginnings of a love affair between the Royal Family and Scotland. John Begg built Lochnagar which Queen Victoria visited in 1848 and henceforth it became Royal Lochnagar. Queen Victoria built Balmoral on Deeside in the early 1850s. In 1843 Chivas Bros were given a royal warrant by Queen Victoria to supply whisky. Scotland in the 19th century was developing as a playground for the British aristocracy. The twin sports of shooting and golf became a vital part of the Highland economy. Whisky marketing capitalised on their aristocratic associations with brands that celebrated country pursuits, such as The Famous Grouse created by Matthew Gloag & Sons of Perth.

All this colourful marketing disguised the fact that whisky was made using the latest technology. Distilleries pioneered electric light, telephones and later computers. Grain distilleries especially became mechanised. Scotch was as much part of Scotland's transformation into one of the world's foremost industrial powers as shipbuilding or steel. Whisky played a part in turning Scotland from a poverty-stricken backwater to an industrial giant. Distilleries were first powered by water and then by coal. The success of the Campbeltown distilleries owed much to a local supply of coal. Later the emergence of Speyside as the powerhouse for Scotch was largely due to the railway linking the region with Aberdeen.

Scotch whisky's path to global whisky hegemony was not without rivals. Even by the late 19th century the Scottish whisky industry was a small player, both at home and globally, compared with the Irish. In 1875 Gilbey's, the wine and spirit merchants, sold 83,000 cases of Irish whisky to only 38,000 cases of Scotch. Two crises both beginning with P would enable Scotch to take over the world, phylloxera and much later Prohibition. Around 1875 the first outbreak of phylloxera occurred in the Cognac region. By the 1880s vineyards of Grande Champagne in Cognac were affected. By the 1890s there was a crisis in gentlemen's clubs of Britain as they had run out of brandy.

Whisky stepped into the breach and has never looked back. Conspiracy theorists might like to note that there is a school of thought that the louse may have come from Britain. There were outbreaks in Hammersmith and Cheshire in the 1860s. Phylloxera was noted in a vineyard in Ireland in 1867 in County Wicklow on Lord Powerscourt's estate. Furthermore, British inventions such as the steamship, the Wardian case for carrying plants and the railway enabled its rapid spread and in the end it was a British produced drink, whisky, that gained the most from the epidemic.

Light and delicate blended whisky was developed specifically for the English brandy palate. Whisky distillers borrowed from cognac producers the technique of blending heavier and lighter spirits together to create a consistent product. Even the French turned to whisky; Williams and Sons of Aberdeen won a diploma in Paris for their blend in 1878. Today the French drink more Scotch than brandy. In fact, France is and has been for a long time the single biggest export market for Scotch after America. By the 1890s whisky was also the most popular spirit in British Isles. The whisky magnates then set their sights on the rest of the world. John Walker & Sons opened a branch in Sydney in 1887. Andrew Usher sold in Japan. Scots spread across the

Empire; they were disproportionately represented amongst soldiers, colonial administrators and engineers, and with them spread the taste for whisky.

The new blended whisky was created by entrepreneurs, people who were in it to make money rather than from a distilling background. The Dewar brothers, John and Thomas Dewar, the sons of John Dewar, exemplified the breed. Their grandfather had been a farmer in Perth. In 1846 he set up a spirit business. His son John Alexander expanded the business and the two boys took it global. John was the businessman and Tommy, as he was known, was the showman. He was fond of pulling creative marketing stunts, such as in 1886 when he paid a bagpiper to play at the Brewers Show in London to drown out everyone else. It certainly got people's attention. He travelled around the world beating the drum for Dewar's whisky. In true British fashion, John and Tommy were soon absorbed into the British Establishment. Tommy got a knighthood in 1901 and John a Baronetcy in 1907. Tommy was made Baron Dewar of Homestall, Sussex, and evolved into an echt English country gentleman known for breeding racehorses. Following the tradition of British self-made families, it was the third generation that became upper class. In 1911 the London offices on the South Bank, Dewar's Wharf, had an enormous electric sign installed of a Highlander in a tam o' shanter raising a glass of Dewar's White Label and when he drank his beard and kilt swayed. Above the Highlander was the legend: DEWAR. Before the First World War Dewar's had a cart pulled by Shetland ponies and driven by a man in Highland regalia through streets of Berlin. They were innovative too: Tommy Dewar commissioned the world's first cinema advert for their whisky in 1898.

The Haig company had a yacht advertising their whisky that sailed up and down the south coast of England tempting holidaymakers no doubt from their deckchairs.

An early Haig slogan was: "d'ye Ken John Haig?" Their whisky was driven around London by magnificent horses and uniformed drivers. My favourite example of the sheer persistence of whisky marketing is from John Begg, a blended whisky containing Royal Lochnagar. Their slogan was "take a peg of John Begg". Glasgow had a significant and expanding Jewish population so this was even translated into Yiddish for a Glasgow Jewish paper as "Nem a schmeck dun Dzon Beck."

Even more ingenious were Pattison's who trained hundreds of grey parrots to say, "Drink Pattison's Whisky." Pattison's later collapsed in a financial scandal that rocked the whisky world to its foundations. The whisky writer Ian Buxton compares it with the Enron scandal. The Pattisons had been inflating their profits through dodgy accounting practices. They had also been passing off cheap ordinary whisky as superior Highland malt. The Pattisons were found guilty of fraud. William Ross of the Distillers Company was damning in his criticisms of their business practices although he had helped fuel the bubble by supplying them with whisky on very generous credit terms. The Pattison scandal could have happened to a number of other firms who were living beyond their means. Some whisky magnates had more in common with American robber barons such as Carnegie than traditional staid Scottish businessmen.

Ten other firms were brought down by with the Pattisons. There was a major bust across the industry following the scandal and many distilleries either closed or were bought by the Distillers Company (DCL) who went on to dominate the whisky business for much of the 20th century.

The Pattison scandal also exposed a tension at the heart of the blended whisky business. Whisky was sold on the reputation and the image of Highland malt whisky, but most brands were predominantly made up of Lowland grain whiskies. To this day the big brands don't declare the make-up of their whiskies. The malt distillers didn't like their good name being used to sell an inferior product. In fact, they didn't want the word whisky to be used to describe grain spirits. This tension came to a head in 1905 in Islington in London of all places. The council successfully prosecuted two publicans under the 1875 Food and Drugs Act for serving whisky that was 90 percent grain spirit. This struck at the heart of the big blenders' business. A Royal Commission was set up to investigate the thorny question of what was whisky. In 1909 it delivered the verdict that grain spirit could be classed as whisky, but also mandated a minimum maturation period of three years. It was a victory for the blenders, but also probably a victory for Scotch whisky overall. Would it have become so successful if only the pure, pungent and expensive malt spirits were allowed to be called whisky? William Ross of the Distillers Company wrote: "but for blending the trade in pure Scotch malt whisky would not have been as large as it is today... " Highland and Lowland needed each other.

Scots drank whisky in epic quantities. At times Glasgow has suffered something akin to London's gin craze, but with whisky instead. In 1789 there was a ban on spirit being exported to England to turn into gin that led to a surplus of cheap whisky and public drunkenness etc. It was said that about three hundred weavers and their families who lived at Govan near Glasgow between them drank over 6,000 gallons of whisky a year. Drink was traditionally the biggest expense at weddings and funerals. On the Isle of Lewis 120 families drank yearly 4,000 gallons of whisky. It wasn't just the adults putting it away. Children were at it too. Here's Elizabeth Grant of Rothiemurchus:

> "Aunt Mary had a story that one day a woman
> with a child in her arms, and another bit thing
> at her knee, came up among them; the horn

cup was duly handed to her, she took a 'gey
guid drap' herself, and then gave a little to each
of the babies. 'My goodness, child,' said my
mother to the wee thing that was trotting by
her mother's side, 'doesn't it *bite* you?' 'Ay, but I
like the bite,' replied the creature."

Though this was nothing compared with the thirst of the
Americans. In his book *The Alcoholic Republic* the historian
W J Rorabaugh estimates that the average American in
the early 19th century drank a pint of spirits per day! The
understandable reaction to such excess was the temperance
movement which flourished on both sides of the Atlantic.
Initially this just meant temperance, moderation, but it soon
moved to prohibit alcohol entirely. It became influential
both in Parliament and at a grassroots level when combined
with evangelical Christianity. Much of the energy behind
temperance came from Abolitionists looking for a new
cause. They'd freed the black man from slavery, now they
turned their attention to the working class at home who
they saw as enslaved by alcohol. Many of the techniques of
the anti-slavery movement were used: religiously infused
public meetings, mass petitions, articles placed in the press
and striking prints depicting the misery of alcohol. One
such was *The Bottle* by the caricaturist George Cruikshank
showing the alcoholic decline of a family over eight prints.
It became hugely popular, not least, oddly, amongst
publicans. There's a print in the lavatory of one of my local
pubs from my boyhood, The Plough at Hyde Heath in
Buckinghamshire.

The movement had great successes in Britain. Pub
licensing laws were introduced which for the first time
proscribed opening hours. One of the first of these laws was
the 1854 Sale of Liquors on Sunday Act, which meant that
on Sundays pubs were only open from 1 to 2pm and then

6 to 9pm. You could only get a drink outside these hours if you were a traveller. The absurdity of this is immortalised in George and Weedon Grossmith's *Diary of a Nobody* when Charles Pooter is denied entry to a pub on Hampstead Heath because he's from Holloway, but his friends are let in, claiming to be "bona-fide travelers" from far-off Blackheath. Worse was to come during the First World War. Some pubs were nationalised! The evening closing hour was changed from 12.30am to 11pm and pubs were shut in the afternoon between 3 and 6pm.

As Chancellor of the Exchequer, before he became Prime Minister in 1916, David Lloyd George, a Methodist teetotaller, was keen to impose outright prohibition. The 1909 budget, which became known as Lloyd George's People's Budget, increased the distiller's licence fee. This was ostensibly to raise money, but it led to less distilling taking place and therefore decreased the revenue overall for the exchequer. This didn't bother Lloyd George who saw temperance as a moral crusade. As with much alcohol legislation, it was an unholy marriage of the greed of the government dressed up in concern for the nation's health. Peter Mackie (of Mackie & Co) wrote:

> "The whole framing of the Budget is that of
> a faddist and a crank and not a statesman.
> But what can one expect of a Welsh country
> solicitor being placed, without any commercial
> training, as Chancellor of the Exchequer in a
> large country like this?"

Lloyd George was never able to have alcohol banned entirely though. In American, however, the temperance movement succeeded in its ultimate aim. Congress passed the 18th Amendment in 1919 prohibiting alcohol. Americans awoke to perhaps the bleakest day in their history. Of course people were still going to want to drink and at a stroke America's alcohol supplies moved into the hands of criminals. At one point it was estimated that there were over 32,000 illegal drinking dens known as speakeasies in New York City alone.

For most drink companies this would have been a disaster and, indeed, it did prove disastrous for the Irish whiskey producers who refused to deal with bootleggers across the Atlantic. They further suffered after independence when they lost their old Empire markets. Not so for the Scots. They had no qualms about selling boatloads of their product to third parties off the coast of America. Exports to Canada, Cuba, Bermuda and in particular the Bahamas boomed. From these points whisky was smuggled into American waters on speedboats. Scotch whisky was also sold legitimately as medicine.

No whisky took advantage of Prohibition quite like the Cutty Sark brand. Cutty Sark was created especially for the American market on the 23rd March 1923 by the wine merchants Berry Bros & Rudd, ie after Prohibition had begun. In Cutty Sark's official history they say it's because nobody thought that Prohibition would last that long. Or it may be that they simply saw an opportunity with the Americans out of the whisky business. The name is apt as a symbol of 19th century globalisation and Anglo-American connectivity, the tea clipper. The whisky became synonymous with Captain Bill "The Real" McCoy, the American whisky smuggler extraordinaire of the period who, like many good smugglers, didn't touch his own contraband; he was teetotal. Despite that there's a somewhat unlikely story that McCoy had a hand in the blend of Cutty Sark, recommending a paler blend for the American market. Also unlikely is that the expression "the Real McCoy" was originally about him, as sadly it has been dated back to 19th century Scotland. The alliance of this American criminal with the venerable St James's wine merchants of Berry

Bros & Rudd seems unlikely too, but it would prove to be very lucrative for both parties. McCoy was born in 1877 in Florida. He began smuggling in 1920 with his boat the *Tomoka*. He became famous for his sheer audacity: at one point he chased a US customs boarding party off his boat at machine gun point. To keep things as much above board as possible for Berry Bros, the whisky was first shipped to the agents Bethell Robertson & Co based in Nassau, Bahamas, before it was then smuggled by McCoy into the States. For all his legendary status, McCoy's smuggling career was brief. He was arrested on 24th November 1923 and served nine months in prison which seems like a light sentence. He never returned to smuggling.

Men like McCoy provided a much-needed service for Americans by smuggling good quality booze like Cutty Sark instead of the ersatz whisky made from caramel, ethanol and water, or bathtub gin made from sulphuric acid that as supplies ran short in the US, or prices became too high, many had to turn to. Worse still than these concoctions was a drink called Jamaican ginger or "Jake" for short. This contained triorthocresyl phosphate which would either kill you or leave you crippled. Partial paralysis led to people walking strangely – the Jake[82] walk as it was known. It's no wonder someone like McCoy was seen as a hero. Brands such as Cutty Sark provided security and reassurance, at a price.

When Prohibition was lifted in 1933, exports of Scotch whisky to the States really took off. The Scottish product had the reputation and the brand recognition. It wasn't just Cutty Sark, all the big brands had been smuggled into the US. By 1939 4.8 million gallons were shipped to the

---

82 There's a sub-genre of songs about Jake including Jake Leg Blues – worth looking up on Youtube: "I can't eat/ I can't talk/ been drinkin' mean Jake/ Lord, now I can't walk."

US. During Prohibition, the Irish whiskey business had collapsed and the Americans had effectively destroyed their own distilling industry. Who knows, but if it wasn't for Prohibition, Bourbon not Scotch could have been the most popular whisky in the world. After the Second World War, the Scottish were in an even stronger position. Many American servicemen had picked up a taste for Scotch whilst in Britain. Other special light whiskies such as J & B were developed for the US market, the whiskies that feature so heavily in the TV series *Mad Men*, based on the exploits of Madison Avenue advertising executives in the 1950s. Scotland was undisputed champion of whisky, a position that it still holds to this day, despite the challenges of a resurgent Ireland, America and, most notably, Japan.

But despite this position of global strength, business had not been consistently lucrative. As we have seen, whisky is prone to cycles of boom and bust. The problem with whisky then as now is that it takes time to mature, so owners cannot always react quickly to demand from their customers. This is a problem whisky shares with sherry and madeira. Creating good blended Scotch depends on access to large supplies of different whiskies. Therefore when times were good, distillers would open new distilleries and lay down large stocks of spirit for maturing. Often by the time the whisky was mature the demand would have evaporated. Scotland is full of ghost distilleries, relics of long ago booms. Campbeltown, for example, was once home to thirty-four distilleries, and now only three remain. Whisky from these extinct distilleries is highly prized. The most recent bust was in the 1980s which was a boon for consumers as it meant that good whisky was available cheaply, frequently in the form of supermarket own label brands. These were often whiskies from highly regarded distilleries sold generically. We are currently going through a boom period which is why so much Scotch is now sold without age statements. At the moment there simply isn't enough old whisky to go around.

DRINKING THE EMPIRE

In terms of its whisky production Scotland is divided up into five regions: Highland (including Islands), Lowland, Speyside, Campbeltown and Islay (which is sometimes grouped with Islands). Each has its own distinct style of whisky. For example, Islays are famously pungent and smoky because the malt used is dried using peat smoke. Speyside whiskies tend to have a lot of sherry influence. These characteristics have more to do with tradition, the size of the stills and the role of the distiller than anything intrinsic to the place where they are distilled. Most malts today are aged in used bourbon and sherry barrels, though other barrels are used. These are all malt whiskies. There are also grain whiskies which you sometimes find as single grain bottlings. These are very rare as generally grains are blended.

Here are a few whiskies, both blends and single malts, to try:

Glenfarclas 15 Years Old
Perhaps the quintessence of the Speyside style with its gentlemen's club aromas of sherry and tobacco mingled with walnuts and molasses. It's big and a little sweet and I love it.

Ardbeg uigeadail (no age statement)
I sometimes find Islay malts too smoky, but this one has a power that is deliciously tempered with a sweetness that comes from old sherry and bourbon barrels.

Highland Park 12 year old
A superbly balanced whisky from Orkney. There's a great combination of pepper, fruit, honey and a floral quality here too. This is what I buy for people whose tastes I don't know. All whisky lovers love this whisky.

Springbank 12 year old cask strength (55.3 percent)
One of only three surviving distilleries in Campbeltown out of an original thirty-four. This shows big smoky, dark chocolate flavours. You can see why Campbeltown malts were highly prized by blenders.

Glenkinchie 12 year old
Light, floral and fruity, this Lowland distillery is another that my Uncle Charles used to work at.

Blended whisky
The best-known whiskies, however, are blends of single malts with grain whiskies. There's a certain amount of snobbery about blends, but this is misplaced. Many famous distilleries were founded specifically to provide whisky for blends. Nowadays most distilleries are owned by drinks giants in order to provide a consistent supply of whisky for their blends ie Strathisla is owned by Chivas Regal and provides the backbone to their whiskies. So without the blends most single malts would not exist. The best blends contain a high percentage of quality malts. Big brands do not mean bad whisky. The good ones are of astonishingly high quality containing some old rare malts. Marrying whiskies as disparate as Macallan and Highland Park into a harmonious blend is a difficult business. That is exactly what the master blender does at Famous Grouse, Scotland's bestselling whisky. The best analogy for blended whiskies would be a Grand Marque champagne such as Bollinger non-vintage. At Bollinger they have to blend wines from

different years, different grapes and different vineyards into an unchanging product. They are not going for big strange flavours, but something elegant, luxurious and distinctly Bollinger. The house style is all and it's just the same with Scotch.

Famous Grouse
This was my grandmother's favourite whisky. You can really taste the sherried Macallan whisky in the blend. They also do a very nice Black Grouse which has a higher proportion of Islay malts for a smoky taste.

Cutty Sark
Mad Men Scotch: sweet, fruity and very smooth. This one is great in a whisky and soda.

Johnnie Walker Black Label
My go-to blend. A big measure of this luxurious blend in a cut crystal glass always makes me feel incredibly successful. It's good with a little ice in too.

Johnnie Walker Green Label 15 year old
A blend of four malt whiskies with no grain. This is what was known until quite recently as a vatted malt. On the nose there's a rum-like quality combined with raisins; in the mouth, though, it's fiery, smoky and a little floral, then a sweet toffee note builds and builds. Incredibly harmonious. Give this to people who say they think blends are inferior.

17

THE DECLINE OF IRISH WHISKEY

Ireland more than Scotland can lay claim to being the birthplace of whiskey. Note the spelling with an "e". The Americans also spell their whiskey with an "e", except Maker's Mark, for some reason. The secret of distillation probably came to Scotland from Ireland. There's a story about Elizabeth I of England being sent a cask of Irish whiskey in the 16th century. Bushmills in Northern Ireland date their foundation to the licensing of a distillery on their premises in 1608. Much later Samuel Johnson favoured Irish whiskey over Scotch, writing that "the Irish sort is particularly distinguished for its pleasant and mild flavour."

As in Scotland most early distillation would have been small-scale and out of reach of the taxman, but with the beginning of Free Trade with Britain in 1780, the Irish whiskey business began to take off. By the early 19th century the big four Dublin distilleries were firmly established. They were: John Powers at John's Lane, John Jameson of Bow St (both still big brands now), William Jameson and George Roe.

Irish whiskey in these giant distilleries was made in pot stills similar to those used in the Highlands, but on a much bigger scale. They didn't just use malted barley, other grains were used, and the product was triple distilled which made it smoother than the Scottish product of the time. Large-scale legal distillation didn't take off in the Highlands until the 1820s, so the Irish had a 40 year jump on the Scots. The Irish business dwarfed its rivals over the sea. Such was Irish whiskey's reputation that unscrupulous distillers would ship Scotch to Ireland to mature briefly, from where it became Irish and could be sold for more money.

In 1887 between them the big four put out around 11 million litres of whiskey. From this peak, gradually at first and then all of a sudden, the industry began to decline. Some of that can be put down to the sheer energy of the Scots charge. The ingenuity they put into marketing and selling their product left the Irish standing. The Coffey still that could produce a pure spirit quickly and cheaply was an Irish invention, yet it was initially shunned by the Irish distillers. They carried on producing whiskey in their pot stills whilst the Scots were winning over new drinkers with their lighter blended whiskies.

But what really destroyed the Irish industry in the 20th century was Prohibition in the United States and independence at home. Irish whiskey relied heavily on the US market. At one point before the First World War there were over 400 different Irish whiskey brands on sale in America. Prohibition cut this market off at a stroke and, unlike the Scots, the Irish refused to have anything to do with the illicit trade.

In 1922 The Irish Free State was born. The Valera government came to power in 1932 and pursued a policy of autarky. A row over money owed to Britain resulted in a trade war between 1932 and 1938 which proved disastrous for export-led industries such as whiskey. Guinness managed to get around this by moving their headquarters to London and eventually opening an enormous brewery in Park Royal. Britain could do without Irish goods, but Ireland would struggle without her biggest market. Then as now the Irish and British economies were deeply intertwined. It was a colossal act of misjudgement[83] by Eamon de Valera as many Irish industries suffered hugely.

More distilleries closed after the Second World War and the industry consolidated until, in 1975, the remaining Irish brands, including Jameson and Powers, all moved to a new distillery in Cork, the New Midleton. With Bushmills in Northern Ireland there were now only two distilleries left on the island and none in Dublin, once the world's whiskey capital.

DRINKING THE EMPIRE

The Irish whiskey renaissance began with the opening of the Cooley Distillery in 1987 which revived one of the great brands, Tyrconnell. In 2014 another grand old name, Tullamore Dew, opened a new distillery at its original home of Tullamore, County Offaly. There are now twelve distilleries in Ireland including Bushmills in the North. Many of them are so new that they have not started producing whiskey yet, so most Irish whiskies come from Cork. It's amazing the variety that comes out of that one distillery. It might not have the romance of all those rainswept distilleries in Scotland, but even in the doldrums, the Irish were producing some fine whiskies.

Tullamore Dew Trilogy 15 year old
As the new distillery opened only last year, Trilogy is blended from whiskies produced at that unlovely Cork facility. This is a beautifully balanced luxury blend, sweetly fruity with notes of pepper and vanilla. It's the sort of thing

---

83 Though not as great as his misjudgement of 1945 when, on learning of Hitler's death, he went to the German Embassy in Dublin and signed the condolences book.

I'd get out if I was entertaining some high-powered Indian businessmen.

Bushmills Black Bush
One of the bestselling Irish blends. It contains a high proportion of malt from Bushmills blended with grain from the New Midleton distillery. It's smooth, rich and mellow with a taste of chocolate and raisins.

18

DID BRITAIN RUIN AUSTRALIAN WINE?

In Britain we have this image of Australian wine that dates back to the 1980s when Australia began exporting large quantities of wine to these shores. It's inextricably linked in my imagination with Oz Clarke and Jilly Goolden camping it up on the *Food Program* on BBC2. So, for many, it's colourful waistcoats and fruity fun-filled wines. Australia as a country sells itself on its youthfulness, its modernity and its difference from stuffy Old Europe (especially stuffy old Britain) and its wines reflect this. However, there is another story of Australian wine. Some of the oldest Syrah (or Shiraz) vines are not in the Rhône valley in France where the grape originated, but in the Victoria, an hour's drive from Melbourne at Tahbilk. Here they produce tiny quantities of a very pure intense wine called "1860 Vines" Shiraz made from pre-phylloxera vines planted when Queen Victoria was in her prime. This vineyard was recently chosen by an American publication, *Wines & Spirits Magazine*, as one of the 25 Great Vineyards of the World alongside Château Lafite in Bordeaux, Krug's Clos du Mesnil in Champagne and Hermitage La Chapelle in the northern Rhône. "1860 Vines" Shiraz is a living link to a lost golden age of Australian wines in the 19th century when they were winning prizes in Europe, exporting to Britain and competing with the best from France and Germany.

One of the first thing British settlers to Australia did was to plant grapes and make wine, although often very badly. The wine writer Patrick Matthews writes that "The first wave of Europeans to settle Australia were English and Scots who energetically set about putting vines in unsuitable places." In 1803 the *Sydney Gazette and New South Wales Almanac* printed guidelines on when to prune vines. The instructions were translated from French and didn't take into account that they were in the southern hemisphere, so the article suggested pruning in January or February just before the Australian harvest took place around March. Viticulture in Australia involved a lot of trial and error. They certainly weren't alone in this as the Dutch were just as clueless in South Africa. When the governor Jan van Riebeeck founded an estate near Cape Town he sent out men on horses to bring back soil samples from the surrounding area. As a Dutch farmer used to growing crops, the earth he picked was the richest and most fertile, ie the worst for growing vines. It was a similar story at the estate just outside Sydney, Camden Park, founded by Captain Arthur, commander of the fleet that brought the first settlers to Australia in 1788. The estate is still there, but the sub-tropical climate and fertile soils around Sydney proved completely inappropriate for planting vines. Vines need poor soil to grow good grapes. In fertile soil they produce too much foliage and too many grapes with not enough flavour.

The first person to do things properly was Dr James Busby, the first in a long line of Australian wine doctors. John Beeston in his book on Australian wine calls Busby "the apostle of the vine", although in many ways Busby was more like a prophet crying in the wilderness. He doesn't sound like the easiest of people to get on with. The *Australian Dictionary of Biography* describes him as a "tiresome conversationalist, a lone hand, crotchety, oversensitive, and embittered". It sounds like some winemakers I've met. There's nothing like working with something as unpredictable as wine, though, to make people turn a little peculiar. Busby was born near Edinburgh in 1801. He arrived in Sydney in 1824 and bought an estate which he called Kirkton after his hometown in Scotland. Unlike his predecessors he really knew his stuff and wrote manuals on vine growing and winemaking such as *The Treatise on the Culture of the Vine* which borrowed heavily from the French scientist Chaptal. In 1831 Busby wrote a second book called *A Manual of Plain Directions for Planting and Cultivating Vineyards and for Making Wine in New South Wales.*

Busby had studied viticulture and winemaking in Europe. He brought vine cuttings acquired on his travels and founded a nursery that would go on to be the basis of the Australian wine industry. The cuttings included Grenache, Carignan and Mataro (aka Mourvedre). Whilst in the Rhône valley Busby discovered the prototype for that Australian classic the Cabernet-Shiraz blend. He wrote that, "The finest clarets of Bordeaux are mixed with a portion of the finest red wine of Hermitage." In Jerez he noted how amontillado sherry was blended in a solera. In Portugal he wrote of how brandy added to port "of which the chief fault is that of being too strong already" made it "fit for hogs only". Which is interesting as it suggests that much port was then unfortified. Nothing escaped his attention and it seems that he got a welcoming reception on his viticultural travels.[84]

Busby's farm was in the Hunter Valley, still an important

---

84 The French and Spanish winemakers Busby encountered were so open with him that it reminds me a little of the British motorcycle industry in the 1960s. The big Japanese companies such as Honda and Suzuki wrote to Triumph and asked if they could have a look around. Britain had the biggest motorcycle industry in the world at the time. Triumph said yes, the Japanese learnt a lot and had the brainwave of making similar bikes, but that didn't leak oil, and by the 1970s they had the biggest motorcycle industry in the world. Perhaps I'm pushing the analogy too far, but when French winemakers in the Languedoc etc. go out of business, they often blame Australian wines for taking away their old markets, especially in Britain. I wonder if they curse their ancestors for being so open with Busby. The Australians made wines that were reliably ripe, just as the Japanese made reliable bikes.

grape growing region in Australia. It's particularly famed for its whites, Chardonnay and a local speciality, Hunter Semillon. But it's not an ideal place to grow grapes. It has a peculiar climate: humid with lots of rain, hail and cloud so, despite the heat, the grapes never ripen too fast. In fact, quite the opposite. They often don't ripen at all. It owes its success to its location as the best place or perhaps the least worst place to grow grapes in a 150-mile radius of Sydney. Busby's 1830 vintage was sent to London in February 1831. It was appreciated if not loved. One person who tried it compared it to an unfortified port which is still a good description of the burlier sort of Australian wines.

In 1833 Busby then went to New Zealand where it is rumoured he made the first wine there. He seems, though, to have become an unhappy and embittered man. Perhaps the problem was that his wines weren't appreciated wherever he travelled. Most Australians at the time, like most British people too, preferred other drinks such as rum or beer, and this would prove a perennial problem in the development of Australian wine.

Busby, like many Victorian vine evangelists, saw wine as morally improving. He would have agreed with Thomas Jefferson: "No nation is drunken where wine is cheap, and none sober where the dearness of wine substitutes ardent spirits as the common beverage." Busby, like many early Australians, had high hopes for his nascent country. Though it was founded as a penal colony, Australia was not a gulag. Prisoners once released were given land to farm and often prospered. It was hoped that they would help build a new civilisation.

One way to make this new Eden was through wine. The French writer and scientist Dr Jules Guyot argued that the best way to lift peasantry out of penury was not through the production of staples such as wheat and milk, but through cash crops, specifically grapes. He argued that it was far better and more lucrative to plant vines, and then make money to buy staple goods. This is a quote from a translation of his work: "in the present circumstances the vine employs and gives food to from three to eight times the number of persons and affords, besides, net profits in the same proportion... " Guyot's work was highly influential particularly in Australia. New arrivals took to planting grapes with gusto. Nowhere more so than in the new colony of Victoria. Originally part of New South Wales, Victoria seceded in 1851 to form a separate state. It says something about the nature of Australia that states could secede from states without any bloodshed. They toasted the separation with a wine made on the estate of a Charles La Trobe near Melbourne. Victoria was a much better place to grow vines than New South Wales. The climate in Victoria especially around Melbourne is particularly suitable for producing high quality table wines. *Illustrated Australian News* wrote in April 1866:

> "The Southern half of the continent of
> Australia would appear to be peculiarly
> adapted for the vine ... but in Victoria, more
> especially, the whole country seems adapted
> for growing the vine to perfection ... the vine
> thrives and produces wine of the most delicate
> quality, for which at some future date when we
> produce them in excess of our own wants, a
> demand will doubtless arise in Great Britain."

Gold, discovered in the 1850s, transformed Melbourne into a wealthy and sophisticated city, far more sophisticated and wealthy than Sydney, as it is to this day. I'm joking, of course, but it's in this period that the great rivalry between the two cities developed. Melbourne thought their rivals coarse and Sydney thought that Melbourne was snobby. Many of those who made money from the gold rush then invested their money following Guyot's advice in vineyards, rather as they did in Sonoma near San Francisco. The gold rush led to a vine rush. It seemed a good way of investing capital and there was plenty of that in 1850s Victoria. The newly rich of the city were thirsty for wine.

The Yarra Valley, about forty miles from Melbourne, quickly became noted for its table wines. The quality of the wines produced was helped by the fact that many of the immigrants came from wine-growing parts of Switzerland such as Paul De Castella who bought the Yarra Yering estate and planted Cabernet Sauvignon cuttings taken from Lafite in Bordeaux. He noted how the climate was perfect for making light red wines. As he put it, a "lightness so peculiar to the Yarra wines". The 1861 wine won first prize of a gold cup offered by the Melbourne *Argus*. Another Yarra estate, still in family hands, was Yeringsberg founded in 1863 by another Swiss, Frédéric Guillaume de Pury. Mark Twain in his 1897 travel book, *Following the Equator*, wrote of how good the Victorian wines were:

> "The Stawell region is not productive of gold
> only; it has great vineyards, and produces
> exceptionally fine wines. One of these
> vineyards – the Great Western, owned by
> Mr. Irving (sic) – is regarded as a model.
> Its product has reputation abroad. It yields
> a choice champagne and a fine claret, and
> its hock took a prize in France two or three
> years ago. The champagne is kept in a maze
> of passages underground, cut in the rock,
> to secure it an even temperature during the
> three-year term required to perfect it. In those
> vaults I saw 120,000 bottles of champagne.
> The colony of Victoria has a population of

1,000,000, and those people are said to drink
25,000,000 bottles of champagne per year."

Melbourne was booming. This "champagne" was made by
Hans Irvine at Great Western who still make some of the
best sparkling wine in Australia. He employed former gold
miners to dig caves so that he would have a cool place to
mature all that sparkling wine and he imported strong glass
from France so that his bottles would not explode. The
winemaker, too, was imported, a Charles Pierlot, formerly of
Pommery Champagne. Twain wasn't the only famous author
with a taste for Victorian wines. Anthony Trollope visited
in 1870 and was very positive about their wines which he
deemed "certainly superior both in flavour and body to
the ordinary wine drunk by Parisians … It is wholesome
and nutritious and is the pure juice of the grape." This was
something you couldn't say about much of the cheap wine
sold in Paris or, indeed, in London at that time.

Trollope went on to say that the best "vin ordinaire" he'd
ever had came from Yering in the Yarra Valley. The 1860s
was the beginning of the first golden age of Australian wine.
Even the vine-eating louse, phylloxera, as it spread across
Europe initially proved a bonus for Australian wine as, not
only did it open up the export trade, but the governments in
Melbourne and Adelaide actively sought out ruined grape
growers in France and Italy to come to Australia and build
a new life.

South Australia was founded as a separate colony in 1836;
it would go on to be the powerhouse of Australian wine. A
pioneer of South Australian viticulture was a Dr Christopher
Penfold. Originally from West Sussex, he arrived in Australia
in 1841. He had brought with him cuttings of Grenache
from France. He bought an estate at Magill in what is now
the suburbs of Adelaide and made a fortified port-style wine.
He was a physician and gave his wine to his patients who

were suffering from malnutrition after the gruelling voyage to Australia. Many influential Australian winemakers were doctors: Dr Penfold; Dr Alexander Kelly; Dr Lindeman; Dr Cullen; Dr Max Lake, founder of Lake's Folly; Dr Otto Wein-Smith of Stanley Wine Company, creators of Leasingham brand. These doctors were some of the few professional, educated people in the country. They were doctors, but many were also scientists, explorers, farmers and chemists. These men read French writers on wine such as Chaptal and Guyot and interpreted them for Australia. They also saw their mission as concerning health and morality. Like Busby and Thomas Jefferson, many saw wine as a moral antidote and superior to rum. Dr Henry Lindeman, a surgeon and founder of Lindeman's wine, fought against rum interest in New South Wales and even accused the Parliament of being in the pay of big rum companies.

The other great force in Australian wine were Germans. In the mid-19th century a wave of German immigrants came from Silesia in what is now Poland to South Australia. Most of them settled near Adelaide in the Barossa Valley. Though they did not come from vine-growing parts of Germany, they quickly became extremely accomplished growers and winemakers. They were Lutherans who had been discriminated against by the Calvinist Prussian King, Friedrich Wilhelm IV. South Australia would become a "Paradise of Dissent" according to Douglas Pike, the editor of the first *Australian Dictionary of Biography*. At least that's the story. The historian Giles MacDonagh thinks it's more likely that they were Luddites who had been expelled from Prussia for their part in the Weavers' Riots. Whatever the reason, they left Prussia and came to South Australia in significant numbers. Even today the Barossa Valley has a very German feel with its Lutheran chapels, bakers and sausage makers, and it's still reflected in the names of families: Seppelt, Henschke, Gramp etc.

South Australia was at the forefront of wine technology. Its winemakers pioneered some of the first cooling techniques to stop fermentation temperatures getting too high. They needed it, as the climate around harvest time was extremely hot. At the Stanley winery in the Clare Valley, they had refrigeration fitted in the 1890s by an engineer called Alfred Basedow: "I can now cool 1000 gallons of wine 10 degrees (F) in a little over an hour." The Seppeltsfield winery founded by Ernst Seppelt from Silesia became a model of a modern 19th century operation. They made sparkling wines by the champagne method. It was an enormous operation and almost completely self-sufficient. It had capacity to mature over 5 million litres of wine. He fed his pigs on grape skins (apparently the resulting bacon was delicious). South Australia's dynamism was in contrast to stuffy old Victoria. Canadian engineers George and William Chaffey who had pioneered irrigation in California were invited to Victoria to build a similar scheme there. They kept on being thwarted by the Victorian bureaucracy, so took their scheme across the border into South Australia. It led to the creation of irrigated farming in Renmark and later in Mildura. Schemes such as these became the foundation of Australian bulk wine production and made possible the 1980s export drive to Britain.[85]

One of the early evangelists of South Australian wines was Ebenezer Ward. Born in Essex in 1837, he emigrated to Australia in 1859. He had a colourful career as a journalist and politician. A contemporary of Ward's, the editor of the *Port Adelaide News*, Edwin Derrington described him as a "deceiver, a sot, and a debauchee". Ward sued for libel and lost. As well as being a libertine, Ward wrote extensively on wine. He thought that "South Australia will without doubt

---

85 Nowadays, however, these regions are running into difficulties through lack of water and problems of soil salinity.

become one of the most important wine countries in the world." He paid great attention to how wine was made. This is Ward on a winemaker called Carl August Sobel, another German: "the chief characteristics appear to be care and cleanliness ... the addition of brandy, colouring matter or flavourings of any kind he regards as unnecessary except in wet or unfavourable vintages." He was fan of Gilbert's Pewsey Vale cellars and said that their Riesling was "the best wine of its class ever imported to this colony" and compared it favourably with Hock. Pewsey Vale is today famed for its Rieslings. He was the author of a book: *Notes from Vineyards and Orchards of South Australia*. Ward wrote that "there are only forty known varieties worth cultivating, but these are called by no less than 300 names." This has been an ongoing problem in Australian viticulture. Wines labelled Riesling would often be made from Semillon, Chablis would be made from Marsanne. People often didn't know what they were cultivating. There was a controversy recently when some vineyards had been marketing wines as the grape variety Fiano, a newly fashionable type from near Naples that, on closer inspection, turned out to be Savagnin (not to be confused with Sauvignon), a relative of Gewurztraminer.

From the 1860s wine production took off in Australia in a big way. This led to a spate of speculative vineyard planting, just as in the planting of the Médoc in the 18th century. One such speculator was Richard Horne who was Australian correspondent for Dickens's *The London Magazine*. He founded a public company to plant vines in Victoria. The consortium bought a property on Tabilk Run (sic) on the Goulburn river about eighty miles north of Melbourne. The name comes from the local aboriginal word: tablik-tablik meaning "place of many waterholes". In true Australian fashion they planted a full complement of grape varieties including: Shiraz, Riesling, Verdelho, Pedro

Ximinéz, Muscat, and Cabernet Sauvignon. One of the drivers behind the project was John Pinney Bear who later bought the winery outright. They hired a vineyard manager from Burgundy called François Coueslant. He designed the distinctive pagoda-shaped winery tower that is now a landmark of Australian wine and wrote extensively on viticulture. It was also his idea in 1877 to change the name of the property to Chateau Tahbilk (note the added H). The winery is still going, though they dropped the "Chateau" in 2000, and still produce a Shiraz from vines planted in the 1860s which managed to avoid phylloxera.

Coueslant clearly had an eye on the export market by adding Chateau to Tahbilk to make it sound more French. Others had the same idea: there is a Chateau Reynella in McLaren Vale and a Chateau Tanunda[86] in the Barossa Valley, both in South Australia and still standing. Australian wine was gaining some measure of acceptance abroad. Gladstone's budget of 1860 not only meant that for the first time wine could be sold by the bottle, but it also ended the preferential rate of duty on Cape wines and table wines now paid less duty than fortified. This opened the door to Australian wines. The period 1860 to 1880 was a good time for Australian table wine in Britain. Between 1854 and 1864 only 20,000 cases were exported to the UK. In 1885 and 1886 it was 87,000. Ten years later 300,000[87] cases a year or roughly one fifth of total production was going to Great Britain. Emu was the main label for Australian wines in London. They were mainly sold as claret or burgundy, but occasionally "Carbinet (sic) Sauvignon". In 1874 an article in the *Morning Post* stated confidently that "Australia

---

86 Perhaps an inspiration for Monty Python's Chateau Chunder, "a fine wine which really opens up the sluices at both ends".

87 This sounds like a lot of wine. But, to put this in perspective, France in the 1860s was producing about 80 million cases a year. Australian wine production was tiny.

promises ere long to become as celebrated for its wines as it already is for its wool and gold." In 1892 a quote from the Central Agricultural Bureau caught the optimistic air: "The future was bright before them and they need not hesitate in planting vines." The South Australians were particularly confident. Carl August Sobels wrote, "any person holding land in a winegrowing district should pay his attention to vine cultivation, as there is a good market for the product."

The wines were winning awards too. In 1899 Chateau Tahbilk won a Diploma of Honour at the Greater London Exhibition. At the Vienna Exhibition of 1873, there were twelve awards for Australian wine. At the 1882 Bordeaux Exhibition Australia won sixteen golds and twenty-seven silvers. The 1886 Colonial and Indian Exhibition in London was another great success for Australian wines. A contemporary source wrote: "the absolute purity of the wine was established ... every sample came out exactly what it professed to be – the pure juice of the grape. The general testimony was that Australian wines compared favourably with the best German hocks and the best French sauternes and claret." This was at a period when adulteration and contamination of wine was frequently in the news, so this was a ringing endorsement.

Australia was finding its own fine regions. Coonawarra in South Australia was founded by John Riddoch who made his money selling supplies to gold miners: always the best way to make money out of a gold rush. By 1881 he was wealthy and respectable enough to entertain George and Albert, the grandsons of Queen Victoria, when they visited Australia. He planted vines, mainly Cabernet Sauvignon and Malbec with a little Pinot Noir. He said, "my belief is that the future of Coonawarra depends on wine..." The region had cool nights and, for Australia, a plentiful supply of water, both necessary for growing healthy grapes. "Coonawarra claret promises to have a very high and wide reputation – indeed, there is no doubt but that it will be a beautiful wine of good body, fine colour, delicate bouquet, and low alcoholic strength." He was clearly a man of vision, as this is just how you would describe a good Coonawarra wine today. Right from the start he knew that he'd found a great place to grow Cabernet and, indeed, Coonawarra, along with the Médoc and Napa Valley, has proved one of the world's best places to grow this grape.

In 1882 the specialist trade publication *Wine & Spirit News* wrote: "Australian wine is year after year increasing in quantity and improving in quality", the wines of Victoria "of excellent quality, although perhaps wanting in the delicacy and finesse of the genuine Burgundy or Bordeaux wines". From quotes like this one would think that the Australian wine industry had the world or at least the Empire at its feet. But, within twenty years, the market for table wines had collapsed and Australia would be reduced to making colonial ports.

Phylloxera was first spotted in Victoria in 1877. The Victorian government's response was incompetent. Vine removal was subsidised, but with no incentive to replant with resistant rootstocks. There wasn't much incentive to replant because, following the 1893 property crash, the lucrative Melbourne market evaporated. Despite the energy being put into it, wine was still a minority interest except amongst the middles classes in Melbourne. The few Australian wine enthusiasts still left drank imported wine from Europe. Smart restaurants in Sydney didn't sell wine from the nearby Hunter Valley vineyards, let alone from South Australia or Victoria.[88] It wasn't easy to trade wine between states. Australia pre-Federation was an astonishingly dysfunctional group of colonies. They had different railway gauges, different tariffs and different measurements. To this day they

---

88   Just as in 1960s New York where nobody would be seen dead drinking domestic i.e. Californian wine.

have quarantine restrictions between states and different measurements for serving beer. The states of Australia were like warring aunts, always looking to snub each other. In 1878 New South Wales considered changing its name to simply Australia. Not surprisingly Victoria objected. The Victorian premier Graham Berry, a Londoner who never lost his London accent, was asked whether in retaliation he should change the name of their state to Australasia; he replied, "no because then New South Wales might well call itself the Southern Hemisphere." In 1888, South Australia refused to join in the celebration of the centenary of New South Wales. Why should we celebrate the establishment of "distant penal settlements", they asked? Even on Federation in 1901 the states kept their regional parliaments.

Federation in 1901 left the Victorian market open to the big South Australian producers and the home producers withered or died. The great Chateau Tahbilk was bought by the Purbrick family, who own it to this day, and they were reduced to selling their wines out of the back of a truck for 2.6 cents per litre. Following phylloxera there was no demand for the delicate wines of Geelong or Yarra that had built up such a reputation. The vineyards were pulled up and the land turned into dairy pasture.

Victoria's incompetent response to phylloxera was in contrast to meticulous response of the South Australians, who have managed to this day to effectively quarantine their entire state. The Hunter Valley in New South Wales is also free of the louse. As Victoria waned, South Australia waxed. The big wine companies had lobbied hard for Federation and took full advantage of it. The government of South Australia was aware of how important wine was for its wealth. Vine growing survived in some parts of Victoria such as Rutherglen and Milawa because they produced the sort of strong sweet wines that the home market was then demanding. South Australia had a natural advantage in that regions such as the Barossa Valley were much better placed to make the sort of wines that people wanted, fortified. Free trade throughout Australia led to domination by the big South Australian producers.

It wasn't only the home market that was turning away from table wines, the British were too. After a brief flowering of claret and claret substitute following Gladstone's Single Bottle Act of 1860, the great British public went firmly back to beer, spirits and fortified wine. Table wines were the preserve of the rich. Both countries would remain non-table wine drinking nations until after the Second World War. Even in 1975, 70 percent of wine consumed in Australia was still fortified. Alexander Kelly, another Scot and a doctor, wrote: "although the native wines are getting into more general use, it cannot be denied that, generally speaking, they have been decidedly unpopular."

François Coueslant from Chateau Tahbilk said, "English people accustomed to port and sherry like strong wine." Though this might be the other way round. Port and sherry became strong due to English tastes, rather than the other way round. Australian tastes may have been even sweeter than the British. A traveller for Guinness in the 1890s, J C Haines, whose job it was to sample Guinness around the world and check its availability and quality, commented how beer brewed in Australia was sweeter than the imported stuff.

Australian wine had quality problems too. Many of the vines planted in the boom years had been in regions too hot to produce good wine. There was a glut of low quality grapes from these regions and the quality of most of the wines exported wasn't good. Many of the wines suffered from bacterial infections. This was disastrous for the reputation of Australian wines. In *Casanova's Chinese Restaurant* the fifth part of *A Dance to the Music of Time*, Anthony Powell gives us a memorable encounter with an Australian "Tawny Wine

(Port Flavour) which even Moreland had been unwilling to drink ... Following a preliminary tasting we poured the residue of the bottle down the lavatory."

Table wines were often strange versions of European originals. Oliver Mayo, author and winemaker, wrote: "Britons brought to Australia odd views about what the wines of France were like. 'Claret' described wines which were almost undrinkable when young, on account of their acid and tannin content, and 'burgundy' described wines that were softer, richer in flavour, lower in acid and much higher in alcohol... " Australian wines were based on the adulterated French wines available in Britain at the time. Claret had a good dose of Hermitage (Syrah/Shiraz) in it. Burgundy was blended with wines of the Midi or the southern Rhône. Rather as some parts of America have preserved old English accents, Australians have preserved English-style claret and burgundy. It's common for modern writers to laugh at Australian burgundies made from Grenache and clarets made from Shiraz, but perhaps these wines weren't so different to the burgundies and clarets drunk in 19th century London.

"The Australians had British tastes not European", Robert Hill-Smith, who runs Yalumba, told me recently. Their winery in the Barossa Valley was founded by Robert Hill-Smith's ancestor, Samuel Smith, a brewer from Dorset (no relation to the Yorkshire brewer of the same name). He made some money in Victorian gold mines and bought the estate which is still in family hands. He named it Yalumba after the Aboriginal word meaning "all the country around". He built a marble winery that looks like a fort. It is still standing, a reminder of the venerability of Australian wine. There are magnificent old buildings all over the wine-producing areas such as Chateau Tanunda in the Barossa, Seppeltsfield and Wynn's in Coonawarra. Yalumba were a massive operation with their own distillery and cooperage.

It became known as the "Oporto of Australia". The marketing traded heavily on Empire motifs. There's a particularly good one of British soldiers in pith helmets fighting in the Indian North West Frontier War with the legend: "Yalumba Wines to the Front." Companies such as Yalumba were giving the British market what it wanted.

The other great export success were so-called sherries. These would generally have been made in imitation of the cream sherry style that was so popular in Britain and in Australia itself until quite recently. They may have been made from Palomino and Pedro Ximénez like

Image courtesy of Yalumba Wines. The company outlook is decidedly less imperialist these days.

proper sherry, though cheaper ones might be Muscat-based. Ingenious Australian winemakers even managed to produce a *flor* in order to produce their own versions of finos and amontillados. Cheaper bulk sweet wines for the British market were more profitable than good quality ones from the old areas. At the outbreak of the Second World War port (from Portugal) had 33 percent of the British market, with Australia second at 22 percent. France had only 6 percent.

Quality table wines were a tough sell until very recently. They rely on a steady demand from an appreciative and affluent home market. This demand was too erratic in 19th century Australia and, therefore, the ambitious table wines of the Yarra and elsewhere were doomed to failure. Australia, partly due to the arrival of wine-drinking immigrants from Italy, Greece, Croatia and Lebanon, is now a wine-drinking nation with demand for both everyday and fine wines. The other change needed was technological: reliable, affordable refrigeration would enable fresh, fruity wines to be made consistently and filters could remove yeasts and bacteria to keep them stable. Until these arrived the only wines that could be made in large quantities in a hot climate were based on other hot climate wines, port and sherry. At roughly the same time, wine, after many false starts, became genuinely popular in Britain. All the ingredients were in place for the Australian invasion that took place in the 1980s. This was spearheaded by Chardonnay, a recent arrival to Australia, but all those years of port production had left Australia with what Robert Hill-Smith calls "viticultural jewels in our backyard", namely acres and acres of old vine Grenache, Shiraz and Mataro. These were originally planted for "high sugar accumulation", but are now producing wines of tremendous concentration that Hill-Smith calls "rustic exotics". We have the crude tastes of the British to thank for some of Australia's great modern wines.

DRINKING THE EMPIRE

I'll recommend some specific non-vintage wines as there is a good chance you will still be able to buy them in a couple of years. Of the table wines, there's not much point giving specific recommendations as vintages vary, but I've listed some good producers.

Fortified wines

Australia makes some of the best and longest-lived sweet wines in the world. Rutherglen in northern Victoria is home to a few producers who make these originals in the traditional style. They are made from raisined overripe grapes fortified with brandy. One kind is made from Muscat and known as Liqueur Muscat, the other is made from Muscadelle and, until recently, was known as Liqueur Tokay, the Australian word for Muscadelle due to the usual Australian grape confusion. Because of trade agreements with the EU these can't be called Tokays, a prestigious Hungarian wine so, instead, the Australians have come up with the word Topaque to describe them which sounds like a shade of emulsion. No matter. The wines from companies such as Stanton & Killeen, Morris or Campbells are superb. They are aged using the solera system in hot sheds and have something of the madeira about them. Producers who have been making these wines since the late 19th century hold stocks of truly ancient wines that they use in minute quantities to add complexity to the finished wines. Like PX sherry or madeira, these are some of the longest-lived wines in the world. When young they are floral and gradually get closer to something like molasses as they age. There is a slightly unhelpful system for grading the ages of the wines released. I don't know why they don't just give them average ages like they do with port:

No statement: 3–5 years average age

Classic: 6–10 years
Grand: 11–19
Rare: minimum age 20 years

Stanton & Killeen Classic Rutherglen Topaque
This is an exemplary example of the Topaque style.
The marmalade on the nose is typical combined with
butterscotch. There's an intense sweetness balanced by
good acidity. Long nutty finish.

The other great Australian sweet wines are their tawnies.
These port-style wines are usually made from Grenache and
Shiraz in the Barossa Valley in South Australia. They are
sweeter than port, but should have plenty of acidity. I love
them. Sadly Yalumba, once "the Oporto of Australia", has
stopped producing new wine, but still has old stocks which
they release under the Museum Reserve label. Other names
to look out for include De Bortoli, D'Arenberg and Penfolds.

Yalumba Museum Reserve 21-year-old tawny
Smells of walnuts with a little furniture polish (in a good
way!). Extremely sweet, but not cloying. Lots and lots of
nuts and a beautiful finish. I could still taste this hours
later.

The Australian "sherry" business really is on its last legs.
Seppeltsfield in South Australia, however, still produces
flor-aged wines produced from Palomino. They are highly
regarded but sadly not exported.

Table wines
South Australia
Those looking for "rustic exotics" should look for old vine
Shiraz from the Barossa. The *ne plus ultra* of this style is
Penfolds Grange which is still superb, but now horrendously
expensive. You can get some of the magic from the St Henri

Shiraz (formerly known as St Henri claret) or even more affordable is the usually excellent Bin 28 Kalimna Shiraz.

None is more rustic or exotic than sparkling Shiraz especially from a producer such as Rockford. Seppelt also produces a sparkling Shiraz as well as some good fizz from champagne varieties.

Those looking for South Australian Hock should try Pewsey Vale Riesling beloved of top scallywag Ebenezer Ward. This is another Australian white that ages remarkably well. They sometimes release old vintages which are worth buying.

New South Wales

The first successful Australian wine region was the Hunter Valley. Its speciality is Semillon. From producers such as Tyrrell's, Brokenwood or Mount Pleasant, it's a true Australian original. The grapes are picked slightly underripe and initially the wine tastes vaguely grassy and of not much else. In fact, young Hunter Semillon is one of the hardest wines to spot in a blind-tasting. After about five years in bottle it starts to take on amazing flavours of toast and limes. It becomes so toasty that you'd swear it was oaked, but it is not.

Victoria

Victoria has recently become *the* place for Australian wine producers looking to produce fresher wines. There are now floral Syrahs that owe more to Crozes-Hermitage than Barossa Shiraz. Mornington Peninsula just south of Melbourne has become an epicentre for pricey, cool climate Pinot Noir.

If you want to taste what the elite of Gold Rush Melbourne would have been drinking look for Cabernet and Shiraz blends from the Yarra Valley near Melbourne. They are, especially in the Yarra, a world away from the Australian red stereotype. The Yarra also makes superb

Pinot Noir. Producers to look out for include Yarra Station for some good affordable Pinots and Yarra Yering, founded by another doctor, Bailey Carrodus, for expensive Bordeaux blends, Pinot Noir and an unusual wine made from Portuguese varieties. Also in Victoria Mount Langi Ghiran makes excellent Shiraz with real perfume.

Not dissimilar to Hunter Semillon is the Marsanne made at Chateau Tahbilk, and Mitchelton. After about three years it starts to taste of honeysuckle and becomes progressively richer as it ages. Tahbilk also does some extremely good Cabernet Sauvignons, as well as that legendary Shiraz, the "1860 Vines".

AFTERWORD

Though written as a spoof, as a guide to actual history *1066 and All That* by W C Sellars and J R Yeatman is without peer. Its history of Britain begins with the arrival of Julius Caesar and comes to an abrupt halt after the First World War:

> "America was thus clearly Top Nation, and history came to a ... "

The age of a global economy dominated by Britain came to an end with the First World War. The world market took a further battering with the Depression and the Second World War. Many countries put up trade barriers during the interwar period. Most of the drinks in this book such as claret, porter, madeira and table wines from Australia went into a steep decline from their 19th century heydays. The drinks that thrived did so because of the American market and American tastes. There's Coca-Cola, of course, but also drinks such as gin, vodka and light whisky became fashionable because of cocktails. It's easy to see the American influence as solely about homogenisation. When we think of Americanisation it's Budweiser that springs to mind, drinks made simpler, blander for the big broad American palate. Yet the American influence is far more complex than that.

American wine hit the headlines in 1976 for the first time with the so-called Judgement of Paris. This was arranged by English wine merchant Steven Spurrier. He pitted the best of Bordeaux and Burgundy against the best Cabernets and Chardonnays from California. The wines were tasted blind by a mainly French judging panel. The winners were both Californian: a Stag's Leap Cabernet Sauvignon and a Chateau Montelena Chardonnay. The outcry was immediate. Many of the judges thought they had been somehow duped. It is the tasting that inspired a thousand articles and put Californian wine on the map as well as making Spurrier's career.

Perhaps even more influential was the American wine critic Robert Parker. He was a lawyer from Maryland who started a newsletter called the *Wine Advocate*. He made his reputation by praising the 1982 Bordeaux vintage which many critics wrote off. Parker deliberately styled himself as the anti-British critic, not that he was anti-British – well, maybe a little – but that he was the antithesis of the clubbable British wine critic. Parker saw this type as being far too close to the trade to give an objective assessment of the wines. He had in his sights someone like Hugh Johnson, the world's bestselling wine writer, who, as well as producing innumerable books, is also the chairman of the Sunday Times Wine Club, makes his own wine and used to own a shop on St James's selling wine paraphernalia. Parker saw some critics as downright corrupt. He saw himself as the champion of the consumer. His newsletter (now a subscription website) takes no advertising and he doesn't accept hospitality from producers or merchants. He instituted a system for scoring wines out of 100 (well, out of 50 really as the score starts at 50). Wines that scored more than 90 sold out quickly. New estates around the world were catapulted to fame overnight thanks to a favourable Parker score.

Parker championed wines made by growers. All over the world, but in France especially, growers were bypassing the power of merchants and bottling their own wine. The adulteration scandals in Bordeaux and Burgundy made wine lovers think that the only way to guarantee quality was to go directly to the grower. Wines were increasingly bottled at the châteaux, rather than in London. Whereas previously most Rhône and burgundy would have been sold under the name of a *négociant* (merchant house who buy in wine), now it was the producer. Parker and other American wine critics enabled customers to cut out the middlemen and some of these growers became very wealthy indeed.

You can see Parker as he sees himself as a true American maverick who shook up the wine trade, but I see continuity in his approach. The wines that he was most confident with were ones that would have been familiar to a Victorian drinker: claret and claret-style wines (Napa Cabernets), port, and wines from the northern Rhône. Like port shippers and British wine writers before him, he was simplifying wine for English-speaking people who didn't know that much about it. His scoring system was a master stroke. Now there was a seemingly objective way of measuring how good a wine was. "I don't like this wine. Parker gave it 93. I'll take two cases!" Most controversially, Parker actually changed how wine was made. It was noted that he often gave the highest scores to the biggest, most alcoholic and oaky wines and some producers began to make wines in this style. They cut yields drastically, left grapes to ripen longer, extracted heavily and then lavishly matured it all in new oak. Whether this was a deliberate attempt to curry his favour or just the way that fashions in wine were going anyway isn't always easy to judge, but wines did get bigger when Parker was in his pomp. We can criticise these wines, but this is how the new wine drinkers of America and the world liked them. The analogy is with the change of port from a dry to sweet wine or the sort of burly adulterated clarets sold in London. It was a very British attitude to wine: we won't learn to appreciate the difficult wine, make it bigger, sweeter, stronger and more oaky to suit us. Many British wine writers held their noses, preferring a more classic style of wine, not realising that Parker was merely following in the footsteps of the British market. Parker, and he would probably hate me for saying this, has very British tastes.

The Judgement of Paris, too, was more evolutionary than revolutionary. You can see this as a victory for California and evidence of the decline of France, but you can also see this as a continuation and affirmation of British tastes. The Californians were comparing their wines with those created for the British market. They won because their wines tasted like claret and white burgundy. Both Parker and Spurrier played a part in the revival of Bordeaux which had been in the doldrums since the late 19th century. The 1980s, 90s and 2000s were a period of astonishing prosperity for the top châteaux.

Driven partly by consumer champions such as Parker and by advances in technology, wine at all levels is now of a quality that would amaze the 19th century British drinker. It is very rare to have a bad bottle these days (though quite easy to have a dull one). Much wine is now sold by big brands such as Penfolds in Australia or Casillero del Diablo in Chile. In 2004 a film was released called *Mondovino* about the globalisation of wine. It claimed that producers all over the world were creating wine in an international style. There was even a word for this, "Parkerization" – wines made to appeal to Parker's palate. The film was a cri de coeur arguing that if we didn't act soon then the local, unusual or difficult styles would disappear under a wave of oaky Cabernet. It never happened. At my local Marks and Spencer's supermarket in far from fashionable Lewisham, south-east London, I can now buy Greek, Croatian, Turkish and Georgian wines made from indigenous grape varieties. In the 1990s southern Europe was alive with the sound of chainsaws grafting Chardonnay, Cabernet and Merlot onto rootstocks; now there is interest in previously neglected grapes such as Cinsault, Fiano and Xinomavro.

Now no one country, style or man can be said to dominate. Parker has been unseated or rather stepped down: he sold his website in 2012 and is now in semi-retirement, and his place taken by a thousand bloggers, writers, sommeliers, importers, winemakers and enthusiasts. The trend now is for lighter wines. The most extreme has been in the form of so-called "natural wines". These are wines made, in theory, without any additives except perhaps a little sulphur dioxide as a preservative added at bottling. They disdain the big Parker-style wines. The philosophy behind them is based on the myth that there was some prelapsarian golden age of wine before it was ruined by technology. Without technology, wine would have been sour and would not have lasted long after the vintage (like many natural wines, in fact). But, more than just what's in the bottle, the "natural wine" movement is a reaction to the Anglo-American wine establishment. You rarely see natural wines from the Douro or Bordeaux. Their spiritual heartlands are the places with the least British influences: Burgundy, Beaujolais, the Languedoc and the Loire. This is reflected in the wines, but also in how the producers dress. At a recent tasting I went to, the producers weren't polished, immaculately dressed scions of old families that you get in Jerez, Bordeaux and Oporto. They looked like the real France: boozy, a bit smelly, sunburnt, uncompromising. Natural wine is wine to be drunk, often to excess, not to be scored out of 100. It's a celebration of *terroir*, of peasants with gnarled hands, of things that smell a bit pooey.

To complicate matters (things in wine are always complicated), this celebration of authentic Frenchness is aided and abetted by a network of American writers, sommeliers, bloggers and importers. Drinks that I used to drink precisely because they were unfashionable, such as sherry, Beaujolais and Mosel Riesling, have become the in-thing.

The craft beer movement that began in America in the late 1970s shares similarities with "natural wine". Both are reactions against homogenisation. American beer lovers were faced with the problem of there being very little good beer about so, if they wanted something with character, they had to make it themselves. From tiny acorns grow ... Hundreds of new breweries were founded and, on the whole, they took their inspiration from the 19th century heyday of British brewing. They created Imperial Russian Stouts, pale ales, Scotch ales and London porters, but most of all they loved IPA: turbocharged, hyper-hopped, high alcohol IPA.

These styles were then exported back to Britain and spread around the world, which is why I found myself sipping English IPA with a bunch of trendy Parisians last year. This interest in archaic styles has its parallel in spirits. The rebirth of small-scale distilling was pioneered in America. The American influence is now more about attitude than taste. People see Americans starting breweries, wineries and distilleries and think, I can do that. All the time the emphasis is on "authenticity". This may be a newly created authenticity, but when such a delicious diversity of drinks is now widely available it seems churlish to complain about over-imaginative marketing. If there's anything I've learned in researching this book, it's that official histories are usually invented.

The world now doesn't take its lead from Britain or America when it comes to drink. Instead it comes from rediscovering and reinventing old styles. But these paradigms of excellence are usually to some extent British creations. Those 18th and 19th century British merchants, inventors, charlatans, writers, scientists, doctors, entrepreneurs and farmers are still shaping what we drink today. The Empire of Booze is over. Long live the World of Booze.[89]

89 Starts working on sequel.

Embryonic versions of some of the chapters appeared in the following publications: chapter 1, *Spectator*; chapter 5, Timatkin.com; chapter 6, *Guardian*; chapter 8, *Guardian*; chapter 9, *Guardian*; chapter 11, *Guardian*; chapter 12, *Guardian*; chapter 16, *Guardian*. These chapters have been much-expanded and in most cases are completely unrecognisable from the original articles.

ACKNOWLEDGEMENTS

First of all I'd like to thank the Society of Authors for their generous grant which meant I could take time off work to finish the book. Also financially extremely generous were Miles Morland and my brother George Jeffreys. Thanks should also go to Michael Troy and all at Matthew Clark. For their help in shaping the book or reading early versions I'd like to thank Mike Jones, Lucy Bridgers, Philip Gwyn-Jones and Matthew Hamilton. Thank you to everyone at Unbound especially Isobel Frankish, Caitlin Harvey and Justin Pollard for having faith in *Empire of Booze* even when I didn't. For help and encouragement with my writing I'd like to thank Mary Wakefield and Freddy Gray at the *Spectator*, Mina Holland and Paul Laity at the *Guardian*, Rachel Johnson, Toby Clements, Tim Atkin, Elif Batuman, Seb Emina, Andrew Nixon and Craig Brown.

Finally the following people for their help with research: Jonathan Beckman, James Lane, Henry Chevallier-Guild, Julian Temperley, Mafalda Guendes and everyone at Sogrape, Louise Hill, Sue Glasgow, George Sandeman, John Dickie, Giacomo Ansaldi, Sebastiano de Bartoli, Joy Spence, Martin Skelton and all at González-Byass, Chris Blandy, Desmond Payne, Rod Jones, Henry Kirk, Patricia Parnell, Anthony Barton, Lilian Barton-Sartorius, Ian Buxton, Uncle Charles Smith, Myriam Mackenzie, Robert Hill-Smith, Freya Miller and all at Pol Roger.

I'd like to thank my parents who have always been there with support, encouragement and occasionally baffled smiles. Last of all thank you to my magical wife Misti without whom this book would never have left my head.

BIBLIOGRAPHY

Ackroyd, Peter; *London: The Biography*; London: Chatto & Windus; 2000

Adkins, Roy and Lesley; *Jack Tar: Life in Nelson's Navy*; London: Little, Brown; 2008

Baiocchi, Talia; *Sherry*; London: Jacqui Small; 2015

Barnett, Richard; *The Dedalus Book of Gin*; London: Dedalus; 2011

Barr, Andrew; *Drink: A Social History*; London: Bantam; 1997

Beeston, Richard; *A Concise History of Australian Wine*; Sydney: Allen & Unwin; 2000

Belfrage, Nicholas; *Brunello to Zibibbo: The Wines of Tuscany, Central and Southern Italy*, London: Mitchell Beazley; 2006

Bond, Ruskin; *Strange Men, Strange Places*; Calcutta: Rupa & Co; 1992

Boswell, James; *Life of Johnson*; London: Penguin Classics; 1791

Bradford, Sarah; *Englishman's Wine: Story of Port*; London: Macmillan; 1969

Brook, Stephen; *Complete Bordeaux*; London: Mitchell Beazley; 2012

Broom, David; *Whisky: The Manual*; London: Mitchell Beazley; 2014

Broom, David; *World Atlas of Whisky*; London: Mitchell Beazley; 2010

Brown, Pete; *Hops and Glory: One man's Search for the Beer that Built the British Empire*; London: Macmillan; 2009

Brown, Peter, and Bill Bradshaw; *World's Best Cider*; London: Jacqui Small; 2014

Bruning, Ted; *Golden Fire*; London: New Generation Publishing; 2012

Buxton, Ian; *Cutty Sark: The Making of a Whisky Brand*; Edinburgh: Birlinn; 2011

Buxton, Ian and Paul Hughes; *The Science and Commerce of Whisky*; London: Royal Society of Chemistry; 2013

Caillard, Andrew; *Penfold's, Rewards of Patience*; Sydney: Allen & Unwin; 2013

Campbell, Christy; *Phylloxera: How Wine was Saved for the World*; London: Harper Perennial; 2009

Canuto, Robert Louis; *Palmento: A Sicilian Wine Odyssey*; Nebraska: University of Nebraska Press; 2010

Coates, Clive; *Claret*; London: Century; 1982

Cornell, Martin; *Amber, Gold and Black: The History of Britain's Great Beers*; London: The History Press; 2010

Cornell, Martin; *Beer: The Story of the Pint*; London: Headline; 2003

Cossart, Noel; *Madeira: the Island Vineyard*; London: Christie's; 1984

Crowden, James; *Ciderland*; Edinburgh: Birlinn; 2008

Daiches, David; *Whisky: Its Past and Present*; London: Fontana; 1977

Dalrymple, William; *White Mughals*; London: Harper Collins; 2003

David, Elizabeth; *South Wind Through the Kitchen*; London: Penguin; 1998

Devine, Tom; *The Scottish Nation: A Modern History*; London: Penguin; 2011

Dickens, Charles; *Sketches by Boz*; London: Penguin Classics; 1836

Dickie, John; *Cosa Nostra: A History of the Sicilian Mafia*; London: Hodder & Stoughton; 2003

Digby, Kenelm; *The Closet of Sir Kenelm Digby Knight* opened with introduction by Anne MacDonell; London: Philip Lee Warner; 1910

Digby, Kenelm; *Private Memoirs of Sir Kenelm Digby*; London: Saunder & Otley; 1827

Evelyn, John; *Pomona*; London: Royal Society; 1664

Faith, Nicholas; 2015 *Guide to Cognac*; London: Infinite Ideas; 2015

Faith, Nicholas; *Australia's Liquid Gold*; London: Mitchell Beazley; 2003

Faith, Nicholas; *The Story of Champagne*; London: Hamish Hamilton; 1988

Faith, Nicholas; *Winemasters of Bordeaux*; London: Carlton; 2005

Ferguson, Niall; *Empire*; London: Penguin; 2003

Fischer, David Hackett; *Albion's Seed: Four British Folkways in America*; New York: OUP USA; 1992

Foss, Richard; *Rum: A Global History*; London: Reaktion; 2012

French, Roger; *The History and Virtues of Cyder*; London: Robert Hale; 1982

Gonzales-Gordon, M. M.; *Sherry, the Noble Wine*; London: Quiller: 1972

Grandin, Greg; *Empire of Necessity*; London: Oneworld; 2014

Green, Jonathan; *Green's Dictionary of Slang*; London: Chambers; 2010

Gronow, Rees Howell; *Reminiscences of Captain Gronow*; London: Dodo Editions; 1862

Grossmith, George and Weedon; *The Diary of a Nobody*; London: J. W. Arrowsmith; 1892

Hague, William; *William Wilberforce: The Life of the Great Anti-Slave Trade Campaigner*; London: HarperCollins; 2007

Halley, Ned; *Sandeman: Two Hundred Years of Port and Sherry*; London: Granta Editions; 1990

Hancock, David; *Oceans of Wine: Madeira and the Emergence of American Trade and Taste*; New York: Yale; 2009

Hannah, Daniel; *How We Invented Freedom and Why It Matters*; London: Head of Zeus; 2013

Herman, Arthur; *To Rule the Waves: How the British Navy Shaped the Modern World*; London: Hodder & Stoughton; 2004

Hymas, Edward; *Dionysus: A Social History of the Wine Vine*; London: Macmillan; 1965

Jeffs, Julian; *Sherry*; London: Faber; 1982

Johnson, Hugh; *The Story of Wine*; London: Mitchell Beazley; 1991

Keay, John; *The Honourable Company: History of the English East India Company*; London: HarperCollins; 2009

Kelly, Ian; *Beau Brummell: The Ultimate Brandy*; London: Hodder & Stoughton; 2006

Keneally, Tom; *Commonwealth of Thieves*; London: Random House; 2006

Kladstrup, Don and Petie; *Champagne: How the World's Most Glamorous Wine Triumphed Over War and Hard Times*; New York: Harper Press; 2005

Knightley, Phillip; *Australia: A Biography of a Nation*; London: Vintage; 2001

Labruyeye, Aurelie; *Chateau Palmer*; Bordeaux: Mollat; 2008

Di Lampedusa, Giuseppe Tomasi; *The Leopard* (translated by Archibald Colquhoun); London: Vintage Classics; 2007

Liddell, Alex; *Madeira: The Mid-Atlantic Wine*; London: Hurst Publishers; 2014

Ligon, Richard; *A True and Exact History of the Island of Barbados*; New York: EEBO Editions; 1657

Livermore, Harold; *Portugal: A Traveller's History*; London: Boydell Press; 2004

Livermore, Harold; *A New History of Portugal*; Cambridge: Cambridge University Press; 1969

Lukacs, Paul; *Inventing Wine*; New York: Norton; 2013

Macauley, Rose; *They Went to Portugal*; London: Jonathan Cape; 1945

Mack Smith, Denis; *Italy: A Modern History*; Ann Arbor; University of Michigan Press; 1959

Mack Smith; Denis; *A History of Sicily: Modern Sicily After 1713*; London: Chatto & Windus; 1968

Mansfield, Stephen; *The Search for God and Guinness*; New York: Harper; 2013

Massie, Allan; *The Thistle and the Rose*; London: John Murray; 2006

Matthews, Patrick; *Real Wine: The Rediscovery of Natural Winemaking*; London: Mitchell Beazley; 2000

Matthews, Patrick; *The Wild Bunch*; London: Faber; 1997

Mayo, Oliver; *Wines of Australia*; London: Faber; 1986

Mayson, Richard; *Port and the Douro*; Oxford: Infinite Ideas; 2012

McKay, Derek, and H. M. Scott; *The Rise of the Great Powers 1648–1815*; London: Routledge; 1983

Moss, Michael, and John Hume; *The Making of Scotch Whisky*; Edinburgh: James & James; 1981

Neri, Antonio; *The Art of Glass* (trans. Christopher Merret); Sheffield: Society of Glass Technology; 1611

Nesto, Bill and Frances Savino; *The World of Sicilian Wine*; Oakland: University of California Press; 2013

Newnham-Davis, Nathaniel; *Dinners and Diners: Where and How to Dine in London*: London: Dodo Press; 1899

Norwich, John Julius; *Sicily: A Short History*; London: John Murray; 2015

Pattinson, Ron; *Porter!*; Amsterdam: Kilderkin; 2012

Penning-Rowsell, Edmund; *The Wines of Bordeaux*; London: Viking; 1979

Perkin, Harold; *The Origins of Modern English Society 1780–1880*; London: Routledge; 1969

Porter, Roy; *Enlightenment: Britain and the Creation of the Modern World*; London: Allen Lane; 2000

Protz, Roger; *Classic Stout and Porter*; London: Prion Books; 1997

Rappaport, Erika; *Shopping for Pleasure*; Princeton: Princeton University Press; 2000

Redding, Cyrus; *A History and Description of Modern Wines*; London: Hardpress; 1860

Robb, Graham; *The Discovery of France*; London: Macmillan; 2006

Robin, Paul; *Culture Wars and Moral Panic: The Story of Alcohol and Society*; Cambridge: CPL; 2014

Robinson, Jancis; *The Oxford Companion to Wine*; Oxford: OUP; 2006

Roraburgh, W.J.; *The Alcoholic Republic*; London: OUP; 1980

de Rothschild, Philippe; *Milady Vine*; London: Jonathan Cape; 1984

Scruton, Roger; *I Drink, Therefore I Am*; London: Continuum; 2009

Sellers, Charles; *Oporto, Old and New*; London: British Library; 2012

Simon, Andre; *History of Champagne*; London: Ebury; 1962

Simon, Andre; *History of the Champagne Trade in England*; London: Wyman & Sons; 1905

Simon, Andre; *History of the Wine Trade*; London: The Holland Press; 1964

Simon, Andre; *Port*; London: Constable; 1934

Simon, Andre; *Bottlescrew Days*; London: Duckworth; 1926

Smith, Adam; *An Inquiry into the Nature and Causes of the Wealth of Nations*; London: W. Strahan and T. Cadell; 1776

Spence, Godfrey; *The Port Companion: A Connoisseur's Guide*; London: Apple; 1997

Spencer, Edward; *Cake and Ale*; London: Stanley Paul; 1913

Standage, Tom; *A History of the World in Six Glasses*; London: Atlantic; 2006

Stevenson, Robert Louis; *Treasure Island*; London: Kindle Editions; 1883

Stevenson, Tom; *Champagne*; London: Paul Wilson; 1987

Sugden, John; *Sir Francis Drake*; London: Pimlico; 2005

Sutcliffe, Serena; *A Celebration of Champagne*; London: Mitchell Beazley; 1988

Sweet, Matthew; *Inventing the Victorians*; London: Faber; 2001

Tames, Richard; *The Victorian Public House*; Oxford: Shire; 2003

Taylor, Alan; *Colonial America: A Very Short Introduction*; New York: OUP USA; 2012

Trevelyan, Raleigh; *Princes Under the Volcano*; London: Orion; 2002

Uden, Grant; *Drake at Cadiz*; London: Macdonald & Co; 1969

Vizetelly, Henry; *Facts about Port and Madeira*; London: Ward, Lock & Co; 1880

Vizetelly, Henry; *Facts about Sherry*; London: Ward, Lock & Co; 1876

Vizetelly, Henry; *Report on the Wines tasted at the Vienna Universal Exhibition of 1873*; London: Ward, Lock & Co; 1874

Voss, Roger; *Guide to Port and Sherry*; London: Mitchell Beazley; 1993

Walvin, James; *A Short History of Slavery*; London: Penguin; 2007

Wildman, Frederick; *Wine Tour of France*; New York: William Morrow; 1972

Williams, Ian; *Rum: A Social and Sociable History*; New York: Nation Books; 2006

Williams, Olivia; *Gin, Glorious Gin*; London: Headline; 2014

Wilson, A.N.; *The Victorians*; London: Hutchinson; 2002

Work, Henry H.; Wood, *Whiskey and Wine*; London: Reaktion; 2014

Yenne, Bill; *Guinness: the 250 Year Quest for the Perfect Pint*; New York: John Wiley & Sons; 2007

Useful websites:

Hogshead, wine blog with an emphasis on history, https://hogsheadwine.wordpress.com/

It's About Time, blog of historian Barbara Wells Sarudy, http://bjws.blogspot.com/

Ossett History, Yorkshire local history site, http://www.ossett.net/

Ron Pattinson's beer blog, http://barclayperkins.blogspot.com/

Jancis Robinson, wine website, http://www.jancisrobinson.com/

Martin Cornell's beer website,
  http://zythophile.co.uk/
Sherry blog,
  http://jerez-xeres-sherry.blogspot.com/
Rum Howler blog,
  http://therumhowlerblog.com/
Cognac Expert blog,
  https://blog.cognac-expert.com/

INDEX

SUPPORTERS

Unbound is a new kind of publishing house. Our books are funded directly by readers. This was a very popular idea during the late eighteenth and early nineteenth centuries. Now we have revived it for the internet age. It allows authors to write the books they really want to write and readers to support the writing they would most like to see published.

The names listed below are of readers who have pledged their support and made this book happen. If you'd like to join them, visit: www.unbound.co.uk.

Philippa A
Billy Abbott
Bruce Alcorn
Igor Andronov
Andy Annett
Stuart Archer
Helen Armfield
Kirsty Armstrong
David Ashcroft
Jeremy Baker
Paul Baldwin
Jason Ballinger
Craig Barrett
Alison Barrow
Adam Baylis-West
Rachael Beale
Clive Beautyman
Jonathan Beckman
David A Bell
Jon Bennett
Karen Bennett
Nicky & Dan Bentham

Lucy Beresford
Frode Bergh
Terry Bergin
Steve Berryman
Donald W. Birrell
Sally Bishop
Andrew Blain
Graham Blenkin
Sediment Blog
Douglas Blyde
Charles Boot
Charlotte Booth
Lorraine Bow
Bruce Bowie
Jaime Martínez
    Bowness
Robert Bramhill
Richard W H Bray
Rose Bretécher
Stroud Brewery
Lucy Bridgers
Nicholas Brilleaux

Roger Brissenden
Chantal Bristow
The British Bottle
    Company
Paul Brookes
Graeme Broom
Margaret JC Brown
Pete Brown
Sam Brown
Luke Bryant
Gareth Buchaillard-
    Davies
Rod Buckle
Kate Bussmann
Ian Buxton
John Byrom
David Callier
Charlie Campbell
Andrew Campling
Omar Nacho Campos
Xander Cansell
Tony Cantafio

David Cantrell
Emily Carding
Tom Carding
Roger Cavanagh
David Chalmers
Adrian Champion
Philippa Chandler
Paul Charlton
Helen Chesshire
Thomas Chubb
Richard Clarke
Malcolm Coghill
Robert Cole
Regina Connell
Jeremy Corbyn
Charles Corn
Phil Coultard
Helen Coyle
John Crawford
Helen Cullen
Tom Curtis
Geraldine D'Amico
Felix Dańczak
Nik Darlington
Jo Davies
Matt & Owen Davies
Nick Davies
Charlie Dawson
Peter Day
Steve Day
Luca De Carli
Sjoerd de Haan-
   Kramer
Steve De Long
Tom Dean

All at *Delayed*
   Gratification
   magazine
Maya Dharwarkar
John Dickie
Michelle & Stephen
   Dizard
Roger Down
Lawrence T Doyle
Rebecca Doyle
Vikki Drummond
Paul Duckett
John Durnian
Dom Dwight
Tim Ecott
Kathryn Edwards
Lauren Elkin
Tom Elliot
Scott Elliott-Brand
Hattie Ellis
Lamorna Elmer
Seb Emina
Timothy Entwisle
Mark Evans
Stuart Evers
Luke Falkner
Ian Fielder
Alison Finch
Richard Fitch
Trevor FitzJohn
Dennis Edward Patrick
   Flannery
Ben Fletcher
Clementine Fletcher
Aldo Framingo

Isobel Frankish
Max Fraser
Ron Fraser
Lynda Freeman
Timothy Frost
Adrian Gahan
Mark Gamble
William Garrood
Jorge Garzon
Bob Gentles
Liam Gibson
Gary Gillman
Nicholas Gledhill
Nick Glydon
Michael & Mirka
   Glyn-Jones
Richard Glyn-Jones
Andrew Goddard
Tariq Goddard
Emma Godden
Salena Godden
Richard Godwin
Bob Gordon
Pete Gordon
Niven Govinden
Richard Grahn
Mark Gray
Mike Griffiths
John A Groat
Marek Gumienny
Sam Hailstone
Graham Hales
Bob Hamilton
Matthew Hamilton
Stephen Hampshire

Claire R E Harris
Matt Harris
Alex Harrison
Joe Harrod
Jacqueline Hartnett
Caitlin Harvey
Henry Helliwell
Fiona Helyer
Richard Hemming
Zandy Hemsley
Mark Henderson
James Heron
David Herr
Jonathan Hesford
Lisa Highton
Colin Hill
Elisabeth Hill
Will Hill
Simon Hogg
Richard Holmes
Kerry Hood
David Hughes
Charlie Humphries
David Hutchinson
Harry Hyman
Aita Ighodaro
Lee Immins
Mags Irwin
Majeed Jabbar
Carolyn Jack
Benjamin Jackson
Daniel Jackson
Bonnie James
David Jeffery
George Jeffreys

Gordon Jeffreys
Steve Johnson
Charlotte Jones
Francis Jones
Howard Jones
Matthew Jones
Philip Gwyn Jones
Michael Kaltenhauser
Peter Kavanagh
Ros Kennedy
Dan Kieran
Doron Klemer
Pavel Kremer
laurie lane
Sid Launchbury
Dafydd Launder
Peter Lawrence
Lea & Sandeman Wine
Patricia Leckie
Jonathan Lemkin
Geoff Levett
Beth Lewis
Martin Lewis
Peter Lewis
LFM
Candace Lilyquist
Tamasin Little
Peter Littlechild
Sue Llewellyn
Stanislav Lobanov
Sarah Lockwood
Wink Lorch
Heidi Lotenschtein
Debora Lustgarten
Alisdair Robertson

Lynch
Cara Macdonald
Machine House
  Restaurant, Rossett.
  Please read, enjoy
  and return...
Stuart Mackay-
  Thomas
Chris Madel
Andrew Mangles
Chris Marks
Rupert Marks
Eddie Marshall
Andrew Martin
Phil Mason, Esq.
Patrick Matthews
Roger & Ann
  Matthews
Sophie McAllister
Claire McClean
Andy McCormick
Fred McElwaine
Mo McFarland
Dan McGing
Helen McGinn
Robert McIntosh
Paul Merrony
Deborah Metters
Colin Midson
Peter Milburn
Matthew E H Miller
Ed Mills
John Mitchinson
John Molyneux
Miles Morland

Doreen Morrrisey
Keith Moss
Wendy Narby
Kevin Narey
Ed Nattrass
Carlo Navato
Robin Navrozov
David Neill
Kristin Sutton
   Nelthorpe
Tom Nelthorpe
Anthony Newell
David Newman
Jay Newman
David Newsome
Jürgen Nickelsen
Gary Nicol
Lenny Nigro
Alisdair Nimmo
Andrew Nixon
Jonathan Northey
Reka O'Connell
Tania O'Donnell
Vicky O'Hare
Matt O'Kane
Neil Oatley
Tony Odam
Ryan Opaz
Sarah Chalmers Page
Wayne A. Palmer
Yianni Papas
Sarah Patmore
Shane Pederson
Dan Peters
Barnaby Phillips

James Phillpotts
Andrew Pickford
Justin Pollard
Finnegan Pope-Carter
Matthew Porter
Andy Portlock
Robert Print
Sally Prosser
Averil Provan
Gavin Quinney
Derek Randall
Soren Bonde
   Rasmussen
Alan James (Grandad)
   Rayner
Dominic Regester
Val Reid
Nicolas Rezzouk
Anne Richardson
Wyn Roberts
Imogen Robertson
Miriam Robinson
Kenn W Roessler
Steve Ronksley
Anya Rosenberg
Sarah Rosenbloom
Steve Rudland
Tristan Rutherford
Edward George
   Rutson
Christoph Sander
Richard Sandford
Ted Sandling
Bruce Schnitzer
Amanda & Louis Scott

Dr David A Seager
Will Sefton
Sam Sharp
Ohr Shottan
Aurelie Sicard
Matt Silver
Andy Smith
Willie Smyth
David Solomons
James Spackman
Nick Speller
Joe Staines
Jason B. Standing Esq.
Nick Stanton
Daneet Steffens
David Stelling
Katherine Stephen
Jason Stevens
Jim Stevens
Will Stirling
Gareth Stocks
Mark Stone
Claire Straw
Mark Sundaram
Jenny Svanberg
James Symon
Michael Thibouville
Greg Thompson
Nicholas Thompson
Ian Thompson-Corr
Marianne Thompson-
   Hill
Mike and Lesley
   Thurman
Paola Tich

Misti Traya
Trevor & Jason @
   Digby Fine English
Tjarda Tromp
Michael Troy
David G Tubby
Simon Tyldesley
Deirdre Tynan
James Urquhart
Lasse Vildrik

Jose Vizcaino
Tim Walker
Dave Walsha
Sarah Wasley
All at Weavers of
   Nottingham
Robert Wells
Paul Whelan
Andrew Wiggins
Thomas Wigley

Patrick Wilcox
Cary Wilkins
Ian Wilkinson
Gareth Williams
Robert Wilton
Ian Wolf
Simon Woods
Steve Woodward
Rachel Wright
Jason Yee